If They Come in the Morning

VOICES OF RESISTANCE

Angela Y. Davis

Ruchell Magee, the Soledad Brothers
And Other Political Prisoners

Foreword by Julian Bond

The Third Press

Joseph Okpaku Publishing Company, Inc.
444 Central Park West, New York, N.Y. 10025

A JOSEPH OKPAKU BOOK

ACKNOWLEDGMENTS

For permission to reprint the following, the publishers gratefully make acknowledgment:

An Open Letter to Angela Davis (James Baldwin) *The New York Review of Books*

The Soledad Brothers: How a Prison Picks Its Victims (Eve Pell) *Ramparts Magazine*

The Soledad Brothers: An Appeal (Angela Davis) *Black Scholar* and *People's World*

A Political Biography of Angela Davis, *National United Committee to Free Angela Davis*

Angela Davis Speaks From Prison, *Muhammed Speaks, The Guardian*

Angela Davis: Black Soldier (Robert Chrisman) *The Black Scholar*

FIRST PRINTING

Library of Congress Catalogue Card Number:
71–169154
SBN 89388–022–1

Printed in the U.S.A.

Designed by Barbara Kohn Isaac

To all who have fallen in the liberation struggle——
Jonathan Jackson, William Christmas, James McClain, Jon
Huggins, Bunchy Carter, lil' Bobby Hutton, Fred Hampton,
Mark Clark, Sam Napier . . . They must live again
through us and our struggles. Through our children and
our unborn, they must enjoy the rewards of victory——a
victory towards which they have already made infinite
contributions.

Now also for George, who fiercely resisted to the very
end. Under a hail of enemy fire, he fell August 21, 1971
at San Quentin prison. His love for his oppressed kin was
unbound, his revolutionary dedication unconditional, and
his contributions to our struggle incalculable. Though his
keepers sought to destroy him, George lives on, an example
and inspiration for us all.

August, 1971
Angela Y. Davis

Some of us, white and black, know how great a price has already been paid to bring into existence a new consciousness, a new people, an unprecedented nation. If we know, and do nothing, we are worse than the murderers hired in our name.

If we know, then we must fight for your life as though it were our own—which it is—and render impassable with our bodies the corridor to the gas chamber. For, if they take you in the morning, they will be coming for us that night.

JAMES BALDWIN

from *An Open Letter to My Sister, Angela Davis*

This book was prepared for publication by Angela Y. Davis, Bettina Aptheker and other members of the National United Committee to Free Angela Davis and All Political Prisoners.

Contents

Foreword

Writing of another political trial, his own, in 1951, Dr. W. E. B. DuBois said:

"What turns me cold in all this experience is the certainty that thousands of innocent victims are in jail today because they had neither money, experience nor friends to help them. The eyes of the world were on our trial despite the desperate effort of the press and radio to suppress the facts and cloud the real issues; the courage and money of friends and of strangers who dared stand for a principle free me; but God only knows how many who were as innocent as I and my colleagues are today in hell. They daily stagger out of prison doors embittered, vengeful, hopeless, ruined. And of this army of the wronged, the proportion of Negroes is frightful. We protect and defend sensational cases where Negroes are involved. But the great mass of arrested or accused black folk have no defense. There is desperate need . . . to oppose this national racket of railroading to jails and chain gangs the poor, friendless and black." *

Dr. DuBois' 1951 observations are twice as true twenty years later; the practice of charging and imprisoning the helpless and the friendless goes on. The "army of the wronged" has increased its ranks; Angela Davis, Ruchell Magee and the Soledad Brothers are presently its most notable legionnaires.

If They Come in the Morning reiterates Dr. DuBois' point that the celebrated and famous receive our attention; the nonentities and the nameless pass on by.

This collection of essays, letters, poetry and articles firmly roots Angela Davis, Ruchell Magee and the three Soledad Brothers

* *The Autobiography of W. E. B. DuBois,* International Publishers.

1

(they have become two through George Jackson's murder as I write) in the progressive forces of our time. There is a link from DuBois to her; a chain exists between Magee, Drumgo and Cluchette and the dark "army of the wronged" that has marched from the loins of Black America for the past 352 years.

But these names—so familiar to us all—are but the tip of an iceberg, a crag of black blue-hard coldness so massive it could sink America.

It will not suffice to have this collection read and approved. It will not suffice even to mouth slogan and rhetoric. Even Richard Nixon now says "Power to the People."

What is wanted for the subjects of this book, and for the "army of the wronged" not mentioned in these pages, is concerted and organized action.

They come from a proud people whose history of struggle against domestic colonialism here is well known. Our dangers lie in our unwillingness to close ranks around the known and the unknown, and our dangerous tendencies to forget when single battles are won.

Where is the defense committee for Donald Stone? For young Ben Chaney? For Roosevelt Jackson Jones? Where are the millions to march for freedom for those who may never march—except in lockstep—again.

They could come from the readers of this book.

Read it, and remember, and learn, and act!

JULIAN BOND

September, 1971

Preface

Political repression in the United States has reached monstrous proportions. Black and Brown peoples especially, victims of the most vicious and calculated forms of class, national and racial oppression, bear the brunt of this repression. Literally tens of thousands of innocent men and women, the overwhelming majority of them poor, fill the jails and prisons; hundreds of thousands more, including the most presumably respectable groups and individuals, are subject to police, FBI and military intelligence surveillance. The Nixon administration most recently responded to the massive protests against the war in Indochina by arresting more than 13,000 people and placing them in stadiums converted into detention centers.

It seems to us that the most important fact to be considered in the midst of this repression is that together with its attendant paraphernalia for coercion, manipulation and control, reflects serious infirmities in the present social order. That is, while we do not underestimate the coercive resources available to the state, especially the police and military forces for the suppression of all forms of opposition (and the centralization of control over those forces), we think that the necessity to resort to such repression is reflective of profound social crisis, of systemic disintegration. A central conclusion we have reached in preparing this book, in fact, is that the entire apparatus of the *bourgeois democratic* state, especially its judicial system and its prisons, is disintegrating. The judicial and prison systems are to be increasingly defined as instruments for unbridled repression, institutions which may be successfully resisted but which are more and more impervious to meaningful reform. They must be transformed in the revolutionary sense.

3

Repression is the response of an increasingly desperate imperialist ruling clique to contain an otherwise uncontrollable and growing popular disaffection leading ultimately, we think, to the revolutionary transformation of society.

At such a moment, when the ruling circles must rely consistently on coercion rather than on a popularly established legitimacy to govern, it is of paramount importance that the revolutionary and radical-democratic movements maintain an offensive posture, and assume the dimensions of a mass movement whose growth is geometric. It is precisely because of its offensive thrust that the struggle to free political prisoners assumes such a particular significance. For it further impugns the legitimacy of the state at a critical juncture, and simultaneously can return scores of brothers and sisters to their communities and the ongoing struggle. Coupled with an exposure of the prison system as an appendage of the capitalist state—as an instrument for class, racial and national oppression—and the demand for the abolition of that system in its present form, the offensive thrust of the movement is still further enhanced.

We believe that it is for all of these reasons that Angela's arrest is directly attributable to her tireless commitment to the defense of the Soledad Brothers and other political prisoners, and her efforts to expose the prison system. She incurs the special wrath of the ruling circles as a Black woman, a radical intellectual and a Communist.

Many people in the progressive and radical movements have tended, especially in recent months as the repression has become particularly intense, to view this intensity as a measure of the fascist nature of the government. That increasingly drastic political reprisals and increasingly open terror reveal fascist trends at the heart of ruling circles cannot be denied. The gravity of these trends must never be underestimated.

As Marxists, however, we view fascism not only in terms of the terrorist methods to which it has recourse, for these may be present before the fascist ararngement is consolidated. Fascism represents the triumph of the counter-revolution, that is, fascism is the preventive counter-revolution to the socialist transformation of society. With the advent of fascism the exploitation of the working class is infinitely more intense and buttressed by extreme forms of terrorist suppression.

For this reason it is essential to view fascist tendencies in terms of their specific challenge to working people; and in the United States, their specific challenge in the first place to the most exploited and at the same time most radical and politically conscious section of the working class—the Black, Puerto Rican and Chicano communities. Therefore, and we have tried to emphasize this throughout, the pivotal struggle to be waged among working people is the open, aggressive, uncompromising battle against all manifestations of racism.

Further, our view of the dimensions of repression must be developed in order to see the Nixon administration's attack on the collective bargaining rights of the workers (through, for example, its suspension of the Bacon-Davis Act as an overt threat to the construction workers to sign a contract or else) as an essential aspect of the fascistic thrust. So also is the administration's emergency legislation to crush the railroad workers strike; or its use of the National Guard to deal with the postal workers strike (where the most militant rank and file leadership was provided by Black workers).

It seems clear, certainly on the basis of historical evidence, that the advent of fascism is not a single event—a sudden coup d'etat —but rather a protracted social process. The maturation of fascist tendencies is a correlative to the maturation of the revolutionary process, both arising out of the acute and general crisis of the social order. The fascist thrust must be resisted in its incipient stages by the broadest possible coalition, before it has an opportunity to consolidate its power; and the democratic, radical essence of the anti-fascist movement is likewise the prerequisite for the success of the revolutionary movement.

Georgi Dimitrov, at the Seventh Congress of the Communist International (1935), while addressing himself to the rise of fascism in a particular historical period, nevertheless issued a warning that strikes us as remaining valid for our own time: "[The revolutionary proletariat] . . . must not allow fascism to take it unawares, it must not surrender the initiative to fascism, but must inflict decisive blows on it before it can gather forces, it must not allow fascism to consolidate its position, it must repel fascism wherever and whenever it rears its head, it must not allow fascism to gain new positions . . ."

The government's repression today has been met with substantial popular resistance—both spontaneous and organized. The revolt at San Rafael, from which the charges against Angela stem, must be seen as a response to the unrestrained brutality and the most severe forms of political repression in prisons. Ever greater numbers of people are beginning to involve themselves in organized mass forms of struggle. Tangible though still partial victories have been won through the successful combination of legal and political strategies which seek to utilize all existing constitutional channels and to create new ones, while simultaneously seeking to gain the widest possible support in the community.

The stunning dismissal of murder and conspiracy charges against leaders of the Black Panther Party, Ericka Huggins and Bobby Seale, by a Superior Court judge in New Haven, Connecticut, after their trial ended in a hung jury, is illustrative of the kind of legal and political struggle which can be waged. Likewise, the acquittal of the Panther 21 in New York and the reversal of the conviction of Black Panther Party Minister of Defense Huey P. Newton (though only a partial victory because he now faces a second trial on the same charges) are indicative of the extent of the popular resistance. We do not believe, however, that these victories reflect judicial fairness or impartiality, as the *New York Times* confidently asserted in an editorial following the acquittal of the Panther 21. On the contrary, the victories came in spite of the incredible obstacles placed in front of the defense. These obstacles, including in many instances the psychological and physical abuse of the defendants and their attorneys, are directly attributable to the promotion of racist hysteria, anti-communism and jingoism, and the frightful erosion of constitutional rights and provisions, inspired, in particular, by the President of the United States, his Vice-President, the Attorney-General and the Director of the FBI. These actions have turned seemingly ordinary, innocuous judicial proceedings and administrative hearings into political tribunals.

The courtroom victories thus far are the result of uncompromising and relentless resistance: one which succeeded in altering the political consciousness of the jurors in particular, and the communities in general; one which politically, organizationally and legally at every point and opportunity, sought to counter the calculated assault of the government.

In spite of these achievements, the main repressive thrust continues. Arrests and prosecutions of political activists are much in evidence. Officially-sanctioned attacks against the organized trade union movement grow more intense. The United States continues its aggression in Indochina. The officially-directed assaults against the educational system—the colleges and universities in particular —continues. Police violence in the ghettos and barrios is, if anything, escalating.

Still, in the midst of such a severe repression the acquittals and dismissals demonstrate that the popular resistance has succeeded in creating a political context counterposed to the government's hysteria. This was demonstrated in the case of Bobby Seale and Ericka Huggins and in the recent dismissal of murder charges against three Soledad prisoners, James Wagner, Roosevelt Williams and Jesse Lee Phillips, who were accused of killing a white prison guard at Soledad. Their attoorney explained that the prosecution's case ". . . just fell apart at the seams. It was a fabrication from the beginning. It was a result of the need of the prison authorities to get a conviction . . ."

A critical aspect of this movement to free political prisoners is seen not only in its ability to free the individual victims of the repression. Even more, due to its relationship to the liberation movements and the revolutionary and democratic movements, the political ramifications of each victory transcend its immediate objective to free specific individuals. This dynamic is illustrated to some degree by the partial victories won in the 1930's during the struggle to free the Scottsboro Boys.*

---

* Nine Black youths were arrested in Jackson County, Alabama in March 1931 and charged with the rape of two white girls. Their innocence was incontestable and a worldwide campaign was conducted to save their lives (upon conviction they had been sentenced to die in the electric chair) and ultimately to secure their freedom. This mass movement to free the Scottsboro Boys initiated a series of reforms in criminal procedures which persisted for some twenty years. The two most important cases were *Norris v.*

Today—forty years later, when the crisis facing the U.S. social order is even more profound and the revolutionary and national liberation movements in the U.S. and the world are infinitely more powerful—it is clear that the political dynamics of the movement to free political prisoners can far exceed its previous impact. It is in this light especially, that we may view Angela's defense as a pivotal case with political implications which transcend the liberation of a single individual.

We believe that the most pressing political necessity is the consolidation of a United Front joining together all sections of the revolutionary, radical and democratic movements. Only a united front—led in the first place by the national liberation movements and the working people—can decisively counter, theoretically, ideologically and practically, the increasingly fascistic and genocidal posture of the present ruling clique.

We believe that there is already evidence that such a Front is emerging. Black, Puerto Rican and Chicano communities are responding with ever greater force to official repression. Large sections of the peace movement, and some significant sections of the labor movement have embraced the struggle to free political prisoners; and in the San Francisco Bay Area efforts have been made to launch a Political Prisoners Solidarity Committee. Many organizations, including the Communist Party have recognized the need for and consciously projected the formation of such a United Front. The repression cuts across ideological boundaries. To succeed the resistance must do likewise. We must seek a unity of action, even as we maintain our organizational identities and agree to disagree on particular issues.

In this spirit we have included a variety of political perspectives in the selections presented here, while at the same time seeking

---

Alabama (1935) and *Powell v. Alabama* (1939). In the first case the United States Supreme Court ordered new trials for defendants Haywood Patterson and Clarence Norris on grounds that Blacks had for years been barred from jury duty in Jackson and Morgan counties, Alabama, where the Scottsboro trials occurred, and the exclusion constituted a violation of the Fourteenth Amendment to the US Constitution. *Powell v. Alabama,* involving Ozie Powell, another of the Scottsboro defendants, established the principle that in a capital prosecution the state must provide the indigent defendant with counsel.

to preserve a thematic unity of resistance—to racial and national oppression, to the war in Indochina, to repression and to the prison system as it is presently constituted. In that spirit we have also tried to expose the contrivance of the government's charges against Angela, and to convey the breadth of support her defense has already achieved.

Finally, it is our hope that this book will contribute in some way towards the crystallization of a United Front by helping to expose the bestiality of the prison system; and by establishing in factual and concrete detail the extent of the political repression in the United States which has already claimed dozens of lives and imprisoned thousands of people.

ANGELA Y. DAVIS

BETTINA APTHEKER

June, 1971

I

Political Prisoners, Prisons and Black Liberation

1

An Open Letter to My Sister, Angela Davis

by James Baldwin

November 19, 1970

Dear Sister:

One might have hoped that, by this hour, the very sight of chains on Black flesh, or the very sight of chains, would be so intolerable a sight for the American people, and so unbearable a memory, that they would themselves spontaneously rise up and strike off the manacles. But, no, they appear to glory in their chains; now, more than ever, they appear to measure their safety in chains and corpses. And so, *Newsweek,* civilized defender of the indefensible, attempts to drown you in a sea of crocodile tears ("it remained to be seen what sort of personal liberation she had achieved") and puts you on its cover, chained.

You look exceedingly alone—as alone, say, as the Jewish housewife in the boxcar headed for Dachau, or as any one of our ancestors, chained together in the name of Jesus, headed for a Christian land.

Well. Since we live in an age in which silence is not only criminal but suicidal, I have been making as much noise as I can, here in Europe, on radio and television—in fact, have just returned from a land, Germany, which was made notorious by a silent majority not so very long ago. I was asked to speak on the case of Miss Angela Davis, and did so. Very probably an exercise in futility, but one must let no opportunity slide.

I am something like twenty years older than you, of that generation, therefore, of which George Jackson ventures that "there are no healthy brothers—*none at all.*" I am in no way equipped to dispute this speculation (not, anyway, without descending into what, at the moment, would be irrelevant subtleties) for I know too well what he means. My own state of health is certainly precarious enough. In considering you, and Huey, and George and (especially) Jonathan Jackson, I began to apprehend what you may have had in mind when you spoke of the uses to which we could put the experience of the slave. What has happened, it seems to me, and to put it far too simply, is that a whole new generation of people have assessed and absorbed their history, and, in that tremendous action, have freed themselves of it and will never be victims again. This may seem an odd, indefensibly impertinent and insensitive thing to say to a sister in prison, battling for her life— for all our lives. Yet, I dare to say, for I think that you will perhaps not misunderstand me, and I do not say it, after all, from the position of a spectator.

I am trying to suggest that you—for example—do not appear to be your father's daughter in the same way that I am my father's son. At bottom, my father's expectations and mine were the same, the expectations of his generation and mine were the same; and neither the immense difference in our ages nor the move from the South to the North could alter these expectations or make our lives more viable. For, in fact, to use the brutal parlance of that hour, the interior language of that despair, he was just a nigger—a nigger laborer preacher, and so was I. I jumped the track but that's of no more importance here, in itself, than the fact that *some* poor Spaniards become rich bull fighters, or that *some* poor Black boys become rich—boxers, for example. That's rarely, if ever, afforded the people more than a great emotional catharsis, though I don't mean to be condescending about that, either. But when Cassius Clay became Muhammed Ali and refused to put on that uniform (and sacrificed all that money!) a very different impact was made on the people and a very different kind of instruction had begun.

The American triumph—in which the American tragedy has always been implicit—was to make Black people despise themselves.

When I was little I despised myself, I did not know any better. And this meant, albeit unconsciously, or against my will, or in great pain, that I also despised my father. *And* my mother. *And* my brothers. *And* my sisters. Black people were killing each other every Saturday night out on Lenox Avenue, when I was growing up; and no one explained to them, or to me, that it was *intended* that they should; that they were penned where they were, like animals, in order that they should consider themselves no better than animals. Everything supported this sense of reality, nothing denied it: and so one was ready, when it came time to go to work, to be treated as a slave. So one was ready, when human terrors came, to bow before a white God and beg Jesus for salvation—this same white God who was unable to raise a finger to do so little as to help you pay your rent, unable to be awakened in time to help you save your child!

There is always, of course, more to any picture than can speedily be perceived and in all of this—groaning and moaning, watching, calculating, clowning, surviving, and outwitting, some tremendous strength was nevertheless being forged, which is part of our legacy today. But that particular aspect of our journey now begins to be behind us. The secret is out: we are men!

But the blunt, open articulation of this secret has frightened the nation to death. I wish I could say, "to life," but that is much to demand of a disparate collection of displaced people still cowering in their wagon trains and singing "Onward Christian Soldiers." The nation, *if* America is a nation, is not in the least prepared for this day. It is a day which the Americans never expected or desired to see, however piously they may declare their belief in progress and democracy. Those words, now, on American lips, have become a kind of universal obscenity: for this most unhappy people, strong believers in arithmetic, never expected to be confronted with the algebra of their history.

One way of gauging a nation's health, or of discerning what it really considers to be its interests—or to what extent it can be considered as a nation as distinguished from a coalition of special interests—is to examine those people it elects to represent or protect it. One glance at the American leaders (or figure-heads) conveys that America is on the edge of absolute chaos, and also suggests the future to which American interests, if not the bulk of the American people, appear willing to consign the Blacks. (Indeed, one look at our past conveys that.) It is clear that for the bulk of our (nominal) countrymen, we are all expendable. And Messrs. Nixon, Agnew, Mitchell, and Hoover, to say nothing, of course, of the *Kings' Row* basket case, the winning Ronnie Reagan, will not hesitate for an instant to carry out what they insist is the will of the people.

But what, in America, is the will of the people? And who, for the above-named, *are* the people? The people, whoever they may be, know as much about the forces which have placed the above-named gentlemen in power as they do about the forces responsible for the slaughter in Vietnam. The will of the people, in America, has always been at the mercy of an ignorance not merely phenomenal, but sacred, and sacredly cultivated: the better to be used by a carnivorous economy which democratically slaughters and victimizes whites and Blacks alike. But most white Americans do not dare admit this (though they suspect it) and this fact contains mortal danger for the Blacks and tragedy for the nation.

Or, to put it another way, as long as white Americans take refuge in their whiteness—for so long as they are unable to walk out of this most monstrous of traps—they will allow millions of people to be slaughtered in their name, and will be manipulated into and surrender themselves to what they will think of—and justify—as a racial war. They will never, so long as their whiteness puts so sinister a distance between themselves and their own experience and the experience of others, feel themselves sufficiently human, *sufficiently worthwhile,* to become responsible for themselves, their leaders, their country, their children, or their fate. They will perish (as we once put it in our Black church) in their sins—that is, in their delusions. And this is happening, needless to say, already, all around us.

Only a handful of the millions of people in this vast place are aware that the fate intended for you, Sister Angela, and for George Jackson, and for the numberless prisoners in our concentration camps—for that is what they are—is a fate which is about to engulf them, too. White lives, for the forces which rule in this country, are no more sacred than Black ones, as many and many a student is discovering, as the white American corpses in Vietnam prove. If the American people are unable to contend with their elected leaders for the redemption of their own honor and the lives of their own children, we, the Blacks, the most rejected of the Western children, can expect very little help at their hands: which, after all, is nothing new. What the Americans do not realize is that a war between brothers, in the same cities, on the same soil, is not a *racial* war but a *civil* war. But the American delusion is not only that their brothers all are white but that the whites are all their brothers.

So be it. We cannot awaken this sleeper, and God knows we have tried. We must do what we can do, and fortify and save each other —*we* are not drowning in an apathetic self-contempt, we *do* feel ourselves sufficiently worthwhile to contend even with inexorable forces in order to change our fate and the fate of our children and the condition of the world! We know that a man is not a thing and is not to be placed at the mercy of things. We know that air and water belong to all mankind and not merely to industrialists. We know that a baby does not come into the world merely to be the instrument of someone else's profit. We know that democracy does not mean the coercion of all into a deadly—and, finally, wicked—mediocrity but the liberty for all to aspire to the best that is in him, or that has ever been.

We know that we, the Blacks, and not only we, the Blacks, have been, and are, the victims of a system whose only fuel is greed, whose only god is profit. We know that the fruits of this system have been ignorance, despair, and death, and we know that the system is doomed because the world can no longer afford it —if, indeed, it ever could have. And we know that, for the perpetuation of this system, we have all been mercilessly brutalized, and have been told nothing but lies, lies about ourselves and our kinsmen and our past, and about love, life, and death, so that both soul and body have been bound in hell.

The enormous revolution in Black consciousness which has occurred in your generation, my dear sister, means the beginning or the end of America. Some of us, white and Black, know how great a price has already been paid to bring into existence a new consciousness, a new people, an unprecedented nation. If we know, and do nothing, we are worse than the murderers hired in our name.

If we know, then we must fight for your life as though it were our own—which it is—and render impassable with our bodies the corridor to the gas chamber. For, if they take you in the morning, they will be coming for us that night.

Therefore: peace.

BROTHER JAMES

2

Political Prisoners, Prisons and Black Liberation

Despite a long history of exalted appeals to man's inherent right of resistance, there has seldom been agreement on how to relate *in practice* to unjust, immoral laws and the oppressive social order from which they emanate. The conservative, who does not dispute the validity of revolutions deeply buried in history, invokes visions of impending anarchy in order to legitimize his demand for absolute obedience. Law and order, with the major emphasis on order, is his watchword. The liberal articulates his sensitiveness to certain of society's intolerable details, but will almost never prescribe methods of resistance which exceed the limits of legality—redress through electoral channels is the liberal's panacea.

In the heat of our pursuit for fundamental human rights, Black people have been continually cautioned to be patient. We are advised that as long as we remain faithful to the *existing* democratic order, the glorious moment will eventually arrive when we will come into our own as full-fledged human beings.

But having been taught by bitter experience, we know that there is a glaring incongruity between democracy and the capitalist economy which is the source of our ills. Regardless of all rhetoric to the contrary, the people are not the ultimate matrix of the laws and the system which govern them—certainly not Black people and other nationally oppressed people, but not even the mass of whites. The people do not exercise decisive control over the determining factors of their lives.

Official assertions that meaningful dissent is always welcome, provided it falls within the boundaries of legality, are frequently a smokescreen obscuring the invitation to acquiesce in oppression. Slavery may have been unrighteous, the constitutional provision for the enslavement of Blacks may have been unjust, but conditions were not to be considered so unbearable (especially since they were profitable to a small circle) as to justify escape and other acts proscribed by law. This was the import of the fugitive slave laws.

Needless to say, the history of the United States has been marred from its inception by an enormous quantity of unjust laws, far too many expressly bolstering the oppression of Black people. Particularized reflections of existing social inequities, these laws have repeatedly borne witness to the exploitative and racist core of the society itself. For Blacks, Chicanos, for all nationally oppressed people, the problem of opposing unjust laws and the social conditions which nourish their growth, has always had immediate practical implications. Our very survival has frequently been a direct function of our skill in forging effective channels of resistance. In resisting, we have sometimes been compelled to openly violate those laws which directly or indirectly buttress our oppression. But even when containing our resistance within the orbit of legality, we have been labelled criminals and have been methodically persecuted by a racist legal apparatus.

Under the ruthless conditions of slavery, the Underground Railroad provided the framework for extra-legal anti-slavery activity pursued by vast numbers of people, both Black and white. Its functioning was in flagrant violation of the fugitive slave laws; those who were apprehended were subjected to severe penalties. Of the innumerable recorded attempts to rescue fugitive slaves from the clutches of slave-catchers, one of the most striking is the case of Anthony Burns, a slave from Virginia, captured in Boston in 1853. A team of his supporters in attempting to rescue him by force during the course of his trial, engaged the police in a fierce courtroom battle. During the gun fight a prominent abolitionist, Thomas Wentworth Higginson, was wounded. Although the rescuers were unsuccessful in their efforts, the impact of this incident ". . . did more to crystallize Northern sentiment against slavery than any other except the exploit of John Brown, 'and this was the last time a fugitive slave was taken from Boston. It took 22 companies of state militia, four platoons of marines, a battalion of United States artillerymen, and the city's police force . . . to ensure the performance of this shameful act, the cost of which, to the Federal government alone, came to forty thousand dollars.' " [1]

Throughout the era of slavery, Blacks as well as progressive whites recurrently discovered that their commitment to the anti-slavery cause frequently entailed the overt violation of the laws of the land. Even as slavery faded away into a more subtle yet equally pernicious apparatus to dominate Black people, 'illegal' resistance was still on the agenda. After the Civil War, the Black Codes, successors to the old slave codes, legalized convict labor, prohibited social intercourse between Blacks and whites, gave white employers an excessive degree of control over the private lives of Black workers, and generally codified racism and terror. Naturally, numerous individual as well as collective acts of resistance prevailed. On many occasions, Blacks formed armed teams to protect themselves from white terrorists who were, in turn, protected by law enforcement agencies, if not actually identical with them.

By the second decade of the twentieth century, the mass movement headed by Marcus Garvey, proclaimed in its Declaration of Rights that Black people should not hesitate to disobey all discriminatory laws. Moreover, the Declaration announced, they should utilize all means available to them, legal or illegal, to defend themselves from legalized terror as well as Ku Klux Klan violence. During the era of intense activity around civil rights issues, systematic disobedience of oppressive laws was a primary tactic. The sit-ins were organized trangressions of racist legislation.

All these historical instances involving the overt violation of the laws of the land converge around an unmistakable common denominator. At stake has been the collective welfare and survival of a people. There is a distinct and qualitative difference between one breaking a law for one's own individual self-interest and violating it in the interests of a class or a people whose oppression is expressed either directly or indirectly through that particular law. The former might be called a criminal (though in many in-

[1] William Z. Foster, *The Negro People in American History,* International Publishers, New York, 1954, pp. 169–170 (quoting Herbert Aptheker).

stances he is a victim), but the latter, as a reformist or revolutionary, is interested in universal social change. Captured, he or she is a political prisoner.

The political prisoner's words or deeds have in one form or another embodied political protests against the established order and have consequently brought him into acute conflict with the state. In light of the political content of his act, the 'crime' (which may or may not have been committed) assumes a minor importance. In this country, however, where the special category of political prisoners is not officially acknowledged, the political prisoner inevitably stands trial for a specific criminal offense, not for a political act. Often the so-called crime does not even have a nominal existence. As in the 1914 murder frame-up of the IWW organizer, Joe Hill, it is a blatant fabrication, a mere excuse for silencing a militant crusader against oppression. In all instances however, the political prisoner has violated the unwritten law which prohibits disturbances and upheavals in the status quo of exploitation and racism. This unwritten law has been contested by actually and explicitly breaking a law or by utilizing constitutionally protected channels to educate, agitate and organize the masses to resist.

A deep-seated ambivalence has always characterized the official response to the political prisoner. Charged and tried for a criminal act, his guilt is always political in nature. This ambivalence is perhaps best captured by Judge Webster Thayer's comment upon sentencing Bartolomeo Vanzetti to 15 years for an attempted payroll robbery: "This man, although he may not have actually committed the crime attributed to him, is nevertheless morally culpable, because he is the enemy of our existing institutions." [2] (The very same judge incidentally, sentenced Sacco and Vanzetti to death for a robbery and murder of which they were manifestly innocent.) It is not surprising that Nazi Germany's foremost constitutional lawyer, Carl Schmitt, advanced a theory which generalized this *a priori* culpability. A thief, for example, was not necessarily one who has committed an overt act of theft,

---

[2] Louis Adamic, *Dynamite: The History of Class Violence in America,* Peter Smith, Gloucester, Mass., 1963, p. 312.

but rather one whose character renders him a thief (*wer nach seinem wesen ein Dieb ist*). Nixon's and J. Edgar Hoover's pronouncements lead one to believe that they would readily accept Schmitt's fascist legal theory. Anyone who seeks to overthrow oppressive institutions, whether or not he has engaged in an overt illegal act, is *a priori* a criminal who must be buried away in one of America's dungeons.

Even in all Martin Luther King's numerous arrests, he was not so much charged with the nominal crimes of trespassing, disturbance of the peace, etc., but rather with being an enemy of Southern society, an inveterate foe of racism. When Robert Williams was accused of a kidnapping, this charge never managed to conceal his real offense—the advocacy of Black people's incontestable right to bear arms in their own defense.

The offense of the political prisoner is his political boldness, his persistent challenging—legally or extra-legally—of fundamental social wrongs fostered and reinforced by the state. He has opposed unjust laws and exploitative, racist social conditions in general, with the ultimate aim of transforming these laws and this society into an order harmonious with the material and spiritual needs and interests of the vast majority of its members.

Nat Turner and John Brown were political prisoners in their time. The acts for which they were charged and subsequently hanged, were the practical extensions of their profound commitment to the abolition of slavery. They fearlessly bore the responsibility for their actions. The significance of their executions and the accompanying widespread repression did not lie so much in the fact that they were being punished for specific crimes, nor even in the effort to use their punishment as an implicit threat to deter others from similar *armed* acts of resistance. These executions and the surrounding repression of slaves, were intended to terrorize the anti-slavery movement in general; to discourage and diminish both legal and illegal forms of abolitionist activity. As usual, the effect of repression was miscalculated and in both instances, anti-slavery activity was accelerated and intensified as a result.

Nat Turner and John Brown can be viewed as examples of the political prisoner who has actually committed an act which is defined by the state as "criminal." They killed and were consequently tried for murder. But did they commit murder? This raises the question of whether American revolutionaries had *murdered* the British in their struggle for liberation. Nat Turner and his followers killed some 65 white people, yet shortly before the Revolt had begun, Nat is reputed to have said to the other rebelling slaves: "Remember that ours is not war for robbery nor to satisfy our passions, it is a *struggle for freedom*. Ours must be deeds not words." [3]

The very institutions which condemned Nat Turner and reduced his struggle for freedom to a simple criminal case of murder, owed their existence to the decision, made a half century earlier, to take up arms against the British oppressor.

The battle for the liquidation of slavery had no legitimate existence in the eyes of the government and therefore the special quality of deeds carried out in the interests of freedom was deliberately ignored. There were no political prisoners, there were only criminals; just as the movement out of which these deeds flowed was largely considered criminal.

Likewise, the significance of activities which are pursued in the interests of liberation today is minimized not so much because officials are unable to *see* the collective surge against oppression, but because they have consciously set out to subvert such movements. In the Spring of 1970, Los Angeles Panthers took up arms to defend themselves from an assault initiated by the local police force on their office and on their persons. They were charged with criminal assault. If one believed the official propaganda, they were bandits and rogues who pathologically found pleasure in attacking policemen. It was not mentioned that their community activities—educational work, services such as free breakfast and free medical programs—which had legitimized them in the Black community, were the immediate reason for which the wrath of the police had fallen upon them. In defending themselves from the attack waged by some 600 policemen (there were only 11 Panthers in the office) they were not only defending their lives, but even more important their accomplishments in the Black

---

[3] Herbert Aptheker, *Nat Turner's Slave Rebellion*, Grove Press, N.Y. 1968, p. 45. According to Aptheker these are not Nat Turner's exact words.

community surrounding them and in the broader thrust for Black Liberation. Whenever Blacks in struggle have recourse to self-defense, particularly armed self-defense, it is twisted and distorted on official levels and ultimately rendered synonymous with criminal aggression. On the other hand, when policemen are clearly indulging in acts of criminal aggression, officially they are defending themselves through 'justifiable assault' or 'justifiable homicide.'

The ideological acrobatics characteristic of official attempts to explain away the existence of the political prisoner of do not end with the equation of the individual political act with the individual criminal act. The political act is defined as criminal in order to discredit radical and revolutionary movements. A political event is reduced to a criminal event in order to affirm the absolute invulnerability of the existing order. In a revealing contradiction, the court resisted the description of the New York Panther 21 trial as 'political,' yet the prosecutor entered as evidence of criminal intent, literature which represented, so he purported, the political ideology of the Black Panther Party.

The legal apparatus designates the Black liberation fighter a criminal, prompting Nixon, Agnew, Reagan *et al.* to proceed to mystify with their demagogy millions of Americans whose senses have been dulled and whose critical powers have been eroded by the continual onslaught of racist ideology.

As the Black Liberation Movement and other progressive struggles increase in magnitude and intensity, the judicial system and its extension, the penal system, consequently become key weapons in the state's fight to preserve the existing conditions of class domination, therefore racism, poverty and war.

In 1951, W.E.B. Du Bois as Chairman of the Peace Information Center, was indicted by the Federal government for "failure to register as an agent of a foreign principle." In assessing this ordeal which occurred in the ninth decade of his life, he turned his attention to the inhabitants of the nation's jails and prisons:

> What turns me cold in all this experience is the certainty that thousands of innocent victims are in jail today because they had neither money nor friends to help them. The eyes of the world were on our trail despite the desperate efforts of press

and radio to suppress the facts and cloud the real issues; the courage and money of friends and of strangers who dared stand for a principle freed me; but God only knows how many who were as innocent as I and my colleagues are today in hell. They daily stagger out of prison doors embittered, vengeful, hopeless, ruined. And of this army of the wronged, the proportion of Negroes is frightful. We protect and defend sensational cases where Negroes are involved. But the great mass of arrested or accused Black folk have no defense. There is desperate need of nationwide organizations to oppose this national racket of railroading to jails and chain gangs the poor, friendless and Black.[4]

Almost two decades passed before the realization attained by Du Bois on the occasion of his own encounter with the judicial system achieved extensive acceptance. A number of factors have combined to transform the penal system into a prominent terrain of struggle, both for the captives inside and the masses outside. The impact of large numbers of political prisoners both on prison populations and on the mass movement has been decisive. The vast majority of political prisoners have not allowed the fact of imprisonment to curtail their educational, agitational and organizing activities, which they continue behind prison walls. And in the course of developing mass movements around political prisoners, a great deal of attention has inevitably been focused on the institutions in which they are imprisoned. Furthermore the political receptivity of prisoners—especially Black and Brown captives—has been increased and sharpened by the surge of aggressive political activity rising out of Black, Chicano and other oppressed communities. Finally, a major catalyst for intensified political action in and around prisons has emerged out of the transformation of convicts, originally found guilty of criminal offenses, into exemplary political militants. Their patient educational efforts in the realm of exposing the specific oppressive structures of the penal system in their relation to the larger oppression of the social system have had a profound effect on their fellow captives.

[4] *Autobiography of W. E. B. Du Bois,* International Publishers, New York, 1968, p. 390.

The prison is a key component of the state's coercive apparatus, the overriding function of which is to ensure social control. The etymology of the term 'penitentiary' furnishes a clue to the controlling idea behind the 'prison system' at its inception. The penitentiary was projected as the locale for doing penitence for an offense against society, the physical and spiritual purging of proclivities to challenge rules and regulations which command total obedience. While cloaking itself with the bourgeois aura of universality—imprisonment was supposed to cut across all class lines, as crimes were to be defined by the act, not the perpetrator —the prison has actually operated as an instrument of class domination, a means of prohibiting the have-nots from encroaching upon the haves.

The occurrence of crime is inevitable in a society in which wealth is unequally distributed, as one of the constant reminders that society's productive forces are being channeled in the wrong direction. The majority of criminal offenses bear a direct relationship to property. Contained in the very concept of property, crimes are profound but suppressed social needs which express themselves in anti-social modes of action. Spontaneously produced by a capitalist organization of society, this type of crime is at once a protest against society and a desire to partake of its exploitative content. It challenges the symptoms of capitalism, but not its essence.

Some Marxists in recent years have tended to banish 'criminals' and the lumpenproletariat as a whole from the arena of revolutionary struggle. Apart from the absence of any link binding the criminal to the means of production, underlying this exclusion has been the assumption that individuals who have recourse to anti-social acts are incapable of developing the discipline and collective orientation required by revolutionary struggle.

With the declassed character of lumpenproletarians in mind, Marx had stated that they are as capable of "the most heroic deeds and the most exalted sacrifices, as of the basest banditry and the dirtiest corruption." [5] He emphasized the fact that the Provisional Government's Mobile Guards under the Paris Com-

---

[5] Karl Marx: *The Class Struggle in France* in *Handbook of Marxism,* International Publishers, New York: 1935, p. 109.

mune—some 24,000 troops—were largely formed out of young lumpenproletarians from 15 to 20 years of age. Too many Marxists have been inclined to overvalue the second part of Marx's observation—that the lumpenproletariat is capable of the basest banditry and the dirtiest corruption—while minimizing or indeed totally disregarding his first remark, applauding the lumpen for their heroic deeds and exalted sacrifices.

Especially today when so many Black, Chicano and Puerto Rican men and women are jobless as a consequence of the internal dynamic of the capitalist system, the role of the unemployed which includes the lumpenproletariat in revolutionary struggle must be given serious thought. Increased unemployment, particularly for the nationally oppressed, will continue to be an inevitable by-product of technological development. At least 30 per cent of Black youth are presently without jobs. In the context of class exploitation and national oppression it should be clear that numerous individuals are compelled to resort to criminal acts, not as a result of conscious choice—implying other alternatives—but because society has objectively reduced their possibilities of subsistence and survival to this level. This recognition should signal the urgent need to organize the unemployed and lumpenproletariat, as indeed the Black Panther Party as well as activists in prison have already begun to do.

In evaluating the susceptibility of the Black and Brown unemployed to organizing efforts, the peculiar historical features of the U.S., specifically racism and national oppression, must be taken into account. There already exists in the Black and Brown communities, the lumpenproletariat included, a long tradition of collective resistance to national oppression.

Moreover, in assessing the revolutionary potential of prisoners in America as a group, it should be borne in mind that not all prisoners have actually committed crimes. The built-in racism of the judicial system expresses itself, as Du Bois has suggested, in the railroading of countless innocent Blacks and other national minorities into the country's coercive institutions.

One must also appreciate the effects of disproportionally long prison terms on Black and Brown inmates. The typical criminal mentality sees imprisonment as a calculated risk for a particular

criminal act. One's prison term is more or less rationally predictable. The function of racism in the judicial-penal complex is to
shatter that predictability. The Black burglar, anticipating a 2 to
4 year term may end up doing 10 to 15 years, while the white
burglar leaves after two years.

Within the contained, coercive universe of the prison, the captive is confronted with the realities of racism, not simply as individual acts dictated by attitudinal bias; rather he is compelled
to come to grips with racism as an institutional phenomenon collectively experienced by the victims. The disproportionate representation of the Black and Brown communities, the manifest
racism of parole boards, the intense brutality inherent in the
relationship between prison guards and Black and Brown inmates
—all this and more cause the prisoner to be confronted daily,
hourly, with the concentrated, systematic existence of racism.

For the innocent prisoner, the process of radicalization should
come easy; for the 'guilty' victim, the insight into the nature of
racism as it manifests itself in the judicial-penal complex can lead
to a questioning of his own past criminal activity and a re-evalua-
tion of the methods he has used to survive in a racist and exploitative society. Needless to say, this process is not automatic, it does
not occur spontaneously. The persistent educational work carried
out by the prison's political activists plays a key role in developing the political potential of captive men and women.

Prisoners—especially Blacks, Chicanos, and Puerto Ricans—
are increasingly advancing the proposition that they are *political*
prisoners. They contend that they are political prisoners in the
sense that they are largely the victims of an oppressive politico-
economic order, swiftly becoming conscious of the causes underlying their victimization. The Folsom Prisoners' Manifesto of
Demands and Anti-Oppression Platform attests to a lucid understanding of the structures of oppression within the prison—structures which contradict even the avowed function of the penal
institution: "The program we are submitted to, under the ridiculous title of rehabilitation, is relative to the ancient stupidity of
pouring water on the drowning man, in as much as we are treated
for our hostilities by our program administrators with their hostility as medication." The Manifesto also reflects an awareness

that the severe social crisis taking place in this country, predicated in part on the ever-increasing mass consciousness of deepening social contradictions, is forcing the political function of the prisons to surface in all its brutality. Their contention that prisons are being transformed into the "fascist concentration camps of modern America," should not be taken lightly, although it would be erroneous as well as defeatist in a practical sense, to maintain that fascism has irremediably established itself.

The point is this, and this is the truth which is apparent in the Manifesto: The ruling circles of America are expanding and intensifying repressive measures designed to nip revolutionary movements in the bud as well as to curtail radical-democratic tendencies, such as the movement to end the war in Indochina. The government is not hesitating to utilize an entire network of fascist tactics, including the monitoring of congressmen's telephone calls, a system of 'preventive fascism,' as Marcuse has termed it, in which the role of the judicial-penal systems looms large. The sharp edge of political repression, cutting through the heightened militancy of the masses, and bringing growing numbers of activists behind prison walls, must necessarily pour over into the contained world of the prison where it understandably acquires far more ruthless forms.

It is a relatively easy matter to persecute the captive whose life is already dominated by a network of authoritarian mechanisms. This is especially facilitated by the indeterminate sentence policies of many states, for politically conscious prisoners will incur inordinately long sentences on their original conviction. According to Louis S. Nelson, warden of San Quentin Prison, ". . . if the prisons of California become known as 'schools for violent revolution,' the Adult Authority would be remiss in their duty not to keep the inmates longer." (S.F. *Chronicle,* May 2, 1971). Where this is deemed inadequate, authorities have recourse to the whole spectrum of brutal corporal punishment, including out and out murder. At San Quentin, Fred Billingslea was teargassed to death in February, 1970. W. L. Nolan, Alvin Miller, and Cleveland Edwards were assassinated by a prison guard in January, 1970 at Soledad Prison. Unusual and inexplicable suicides have occurred with incredible regularity in jails and prisons throughout the country.

It should be self-evident that the frame-up becomes a powerful weapon within the spectrum of prison repression, particularly because of the availability of informers, the broken prisoners who will do anything for a price. The Soledad Brothers and the Soledad 3 are leading examples of frame-up victims. Both cases involve militant activists who have been charged with killing Soledad prison guards. In both cases, widespread support has been kindled within the California prison system. They have served as occasions to link the immediate needs of the Black community with a forceful fight to break the fascist stronghold in the prisons and therefore to abolish the prison system in its present form.

Racist oppression invades the lives of Black people on an infinite variety of levels. Blacks are imprisoned in a world where our labor and toil hardly allow us to eke out a decent existence, if we are able to find jobs at all. When the economy begins to falter, we are forever the first victims, always the most deeply wounded. When the economy is on its feet, we continue to live in a depressed state. Unemployment is generally twice as high in the ghettos as it is in the country as a whole and even higher among Black women and youth. The unemployment rate among Black youth has presently skyrocketed to 30 per cent. If one-third of America's white youth were without a means of livelihood, we would either be in the thick of revolution or else under the iron rule of fascism. Substandard schools, medical care hardly fit for animals, over-priced, dilapidated housing, a welfare system based on a policy of skimpy concessions, designed to degrade and divide (and even this may soon be cancelled)—this is only the beginning of the list of props in the overall scenery of oppression which, for the mass of Blacks, is the universe.

In Black communities, wherever they are located, there exists an ever-present reminder that our universe must remain stable in its drabness, its poverty, its brutality. From Birmingham to Harlem to Watts, Black ghettos are occupied, patrolled and often attacked by massive deployments of police. The police, domestic caretakers of violence, are the oppressor's emissaries, charged with the task of containing us within the boundaries of our oppression.

The announced function of the police, 'to protect and serve the people,' becomes the grotesque caricature of protecting and preserving the interests of our oppressors and serving us nothing but injustice. They are there to intimidate Blacks, to persuade us with their violence that we are powerless to alter the conditions of our lives. Arrests are frequently based on whims. Bullets from their guns murder human beings with little or no pretext, aside from the universal intimidation they are charged with carrying out. Protection for drug-pushers, and Mafia style exploiters, support for the most reactionary ideological elements of the Black community (especially those who cry out for more police), are among the many functions of forces of law and order. They encircle the community with a shield of violence, too often forcing the natural aggression of the Black community inwards. Fanon's analysis of the role of colonial police is an appropriate description of the function of the police in America's ghettos.

It goes without saying that the police would be unable to set into motion their racist machinery were they not sanctioned and supported by the judicial system. The courts not only consistently abstain from prosecuting criminal behavior on the part of the police, but they convict, on the basis of biased police testimony, countless Black men and women. Court-appointed attorneys, acting in the twisted interests of overcrowded courts, convince 85 per cent of the defendants to plead guilty. Even the manifestly innocent are advised to cop a plea so that the lengthy and expensive process of jury trials is avoided. This is the structure of the apparatus which summarily railroads Black people into jails and prisons. (During my imprisonment in the New York Women's House of Detention, I encountered numerous cases involving innocent Black women who had been advised to plead guilty. One sister had entered her white landlord's apartment for the purpose of paying rent. He attempted to rape her and in the course of the ensuing struggle, a lit candle toppled over, burning a tablecloth. The landlord ordered her arrested for arson. Following the advice of her court-appointed attorney, she entered a guilty plea, having been deceived by the attorney's insistence that the court would be more lenient. The sister was sentenced to three years.)

The vicious circle linking poverty, police, courts and prison is an integral element of ghetto existence. Unlike the mass of whites, the path which leads to jails and prisons is deeply rooted in the imposed patterns of Black existence. For this very reason, an almost instinctive affinity binds the mass of Black people to the political prisoners. The vast majority of Blacks harbor a deep hatred of the police and are not deluded by official proclamations of justice through the courts.

For the Black individual, contact with the law-enforcement-judicial-penal network directly or through relatives and friends, is inevitable because he is Black. For the activist become political prisoner, the contact has occurred because he has lodged a protest, in one form or another, against the conditions which nail Blacks to this orbit of oppression.

Historically, Black people as a group have exhibited a greater potential for resistance than any other part of the population. The ironclad rule over our communities, the institutional practice of genocide, the ideology of racism have performed a strictly political as well as an economic function. The capitalists have not only extracted super profits from the underpaid labor of over 15 per cent of the American population with the aid of a superstructure of terror. This terror and more subtle forms of racism have further served to thwart the flowering of a resistance, even a revolution which would spread to the working class as a whole.

In the interests of the capitalist class, the consent to racism and terror has been demagogically elicited from the white population, workers included, in order to more efficiently stave off resistance. Today, Nixon, Mitchell and J. Edgar Hoover are desperately attempting to persuade the population that dissidents, particularly Blacks, Chicanos, Puerto Ricans, must be punished for being members of revolutionary organizations; for advocating the overthrow of the government; for agitating and educating in the streets and behind prison walls. The political function of racist domination is surfacing with accelerated intensity. Whites, who have professed their solidarity with the Black Liberation Movement and have moved in a distinctly revolutionary direction, find themselves targets of the self same repression. Even the anti-war movement, rapidly exhibiting an anti-imperialist consciousness, is falling victim to government repression.

Black people are rushing full speed ahead towards an understanding of the circumstances which give rise to exaggerated forms of political repression and thus an overabundance of political prisoners. This understanding is being forged out of the raw material of their own immediate experiences with racism. Hence, the Black masses are growing conscious of their responsibility to defend those who are being persecuted for attempting to bring about the alleviation of the most injurious immediate problems facing Black communities and ultimately to bring about total liberation through armed revolution, if it must come to this.

The Black Liberation Movement is presently at a critical juncture. Fascist methods of repression threaten to physically decapitate and obliterate the movement. More subtle, yet not less dangerous ideological tendencies from within threaten to isolate the Black movement and diminish its revolutionary impact. Both menaces must be counteracted in order to ensure our survival. Revolutionary Blacks must spearhead and provide leadership for a broad anti-fascist movement.

Fascism is a process, its growth and development are cancerous in nature. While today, the threat of fascism may be primarily restricted to the use of the law-enforcement-judicial-penal apparatus to arrest the overt and latent revolutionary trends among nationally oppressed people, tomorrow it may attack the working class en masse and eventually even moderate democrats. Even in this period, however, the cancer has already commenced to spread. In addition to the prison army of thousands and thousands of nameless Third World victims of political revenge, there are increasing numbers of white political prisoners—draft resisters, anti-war activists as the Harrisburg 8, men and women who have involved themselves on all levels of revolutionary activity.

Among the further symptoms of the fascist threat are official efforts to curtail the power of organized labor, such as the attack on the manifestly conservative construction workers and the trends towards reduced welfare aid. Moreover, court decisions and repressive legislation augmenting police powers such as the Washington no-knock law, permitting police to enter private dwellings without warning and Nixon's 'Crime Bill' in general—can eventually be used against any citizen. Indeed congressmen are already protesting the use of police-state wire-tapping to survey their activities. The fascist content of the ruthless aggression in Indochina should be self-evident.

One of the fundamental historical lessons to be learned from past failures to prevent the rise of fascism is the decisive and indispensable character of the fight against Fascism in its incipient phases. Once allowed to conquer ground, its growth is facilitated in geometric proportion. Although the most unbridled expressions of the fascist menace are still tied to the racist domination of Blacks, Chicanos, Puerto Ricans, Indians, it lurks under the surface wherever there is potential resistance to the power of monopoly capital, the parasitic interests which control this society. Potentially it can profoundly worsen the conditions of existence for the average American citizen. Consequently, the masses of people in this country have a real, direct and material stake in the struggle to free political prisoners, the struggle to abolish the prison system in its present form, the struggle against all dimensions of racism.

No one should fail to take heed of Georgi Dimitrov's warning: "Whoever does not fight the growth of fascism at these preparatory stages is not in a position to prevent the victory of fascism, but, on the contrary, facilitates that victory." (Report to the VIIth Congress of the Communist International, 1935.) The only effective guarantee against the victory of fascism is an indivisible mass movement which refuses to conduct business as usual as long as repression rages on. It is only natural that Blacks and other Third World peoples must lead this movement, for we are the first and most deeply injured victims of fascism. But it must embrace all potential victims and most important, all working class people, for the key to the triumph of fascism is its ideological victory over the entire working class. Given the eruption of a severe economic crisis, the door to such an ideological victory can be opened by the active approval or passive toleration of racism. It is essential that white workers become conscious that historically through their acquiescence in the capitalist-inspired oppression of Blacks they have only rendered themselves more vulnerable to attack.

The pivotal struggle which must be waged in the ranks of the working class is consequently the open, unreserved battle against entrenched racism. The white worker must become conscious of the threads which bind him to a James Johnson, Black auto worker, member of UAW, and a political prisoner presently facing charges for the killings of two foremen and a job setter.[6] The merciless proliferation of the power of monopoly capital may ultimately push him inexorably down the very same path of desperation. No potential victim of the fascist terror should be without the knowledge that the greatest menace to racism and fascism is unity!

MARIN COUNTY JAIL

May, 1971

[6] See Chapter Five on political prisoners for the details of James Johnson's case.

II

The Prison System

3

The Social Functions of the Prisons in the United States

by Bettina Aptheker

Officially it is maintained that there are no prisons in the United States. There is a Department of Corrections, and there are "correctional facilities" equipped with "educational programs," "vocational training" and the necessary "psychiatric therapy." There are also no prisoners in the United States; there are only "inmates." There are most certainly no *political* prisoners in the United States; only "terrorists" and those who "perpetrate criminal violence"—which is known in the international arena as "criminal communist aggression."

The semantic somersaults of the prison and State bureaucracy serve a calculated and specific ideological function. Once we penetrate this linguistic shield we have the key to understanding the social and political functions of the prison system.

The dominant theoretical assumption among social and behavioral scientists in the United States today is that the social order is functionally stable and fundamentally just.

This is a very basic premise because it means that the theory *must* then assume the moral depravity of the prisoner. There can be no other logical explanation for his incarceration. It is precisely this alleged depravity that legitimates custody. As George Jackson put it: "The textbooks on criminology like to advance the idea that the prisoners are mentally defective. There is only the merest suggestion that the system itself is at fault . . ." [7] Indeed, the

[7] George Jackson, *Soledad Brother,* Bantam Books, New York, 1970, p. 29.

assistant warden at San Quentin, who is by profession a clinical psychologist, tells us in a recent interview that prisoners suffer from "retarded emotional growth." The warden continues: "The first goal of the prison is to isolate people the community doesn't want at large. Safe confinement is the goal. The second obligation is a reasonably good housekeeping job, the old humanitarian treatment concept." [8] That is, once the prisoner is adequately confined and isolated, he may be treated for his emotional and psychological maladies—which he is assumed to suffer by virtue of the fact that he is a prisoner. We have a completely circular method of reasoning. It is a closed-circuit system from which there is no apparent escape.

The alleged criminal characteristics of the prisoner must, in accord with this logical sequence, arise from *within* the prisoner himself—the prisoner is "crime-prone" like some people are supposed to be "accident-prone." In the nineteenth century, leading theorists put forth the idea that the criminal had certain *physical* characteristics which shaped his destiny of crime, e.g. slanted eyes and a broad forehead. The alleged depravity and criminality of the poor—because they are poor—is an even older theme in class society, e.g. the ancient idea of the "dangerous poor"; and the oft-repeated phrase of the Founding Fathers, "the rich, the well-born and (therefore) the able." Now our leading penologists and criminologists are much more subtle and sophisticated. They have a veneer of humanitarian instinct but it quickly falls away revealing the racist, anti-human core.

Now, it is argued, the criminal may look like anybody else; but he has acquired certain *psychological* characteristics which dictate his pattern of criminal behavior. To "unacquire" these characteristics a leading behavioral scientist, James V. McConnell, explains that: "We have but two means of educating people or rats or flatworms—we can either reward them or punish them . . ." [9] The treatment for what McConnell calls "brainwashing the criminals" to ultimately restructure their entire per-

[8] See the especially good article by Jessica Mitford, "Kind and Usual Punishment: The California Prisons," *The Atlantic Monthly,* March 1971.

[9] James V. McConnell, "Brainwashing the Criminals," *Psychology Today,* April 1970, Vol. 3, No. 11.

sonality is an alternating sequence of reward and punishment (including especially so-called Shock Treatment) until the prisoner has "learned" what the society defines as non-criminal behavior.

The source of criminality then is psychological rather than social. The solution to the problem is obvious: quarantine the afflicted individuals; then subject them to treatment. Hence we have *correctional* facilities rather than prisons; and we have *inmates* (as in any asylum for the insane) rather than prisoners.

As Herbert Marcuse has so aptly described it: "The language of the prevailing Law and Order, validated by the courts and by the police, is not only the voice but also the deed of suppression. This language not only defines and condemns the Enemy, it also *creates* him; and this creation is not the Enemy as he really is but rather as he must be in order to perform his function for the Establishment . . ." [10]

In this instance the Enemy is the criminal or the prisoner. The single most important thing to understand in all of this is that the behavioralist view of the criminal *has nothing to do with breaking the law*. Let us explain this with some well-known statistics.[11]

First, it is a matter of common knowledge that only a small number of law violations is detected and reported. Further, even of reported violations only a small percentage actually result in police investigations and arrest.

Second, 90 per cent of all criminal defendants in the United States today *plead guilty without a trial* because they cannot afford a lawyer, and hope for judicial leniency.

Third, 52 per cent of all people in county and city jails have not been convicted of any crime; they simply cannot afford bail. Many will spend months and even years in jail, awaiting trial.

Fourth, between 30–50 per cent of the prisoners in various cities and states are Black and Brown, while Black people, for example, constitute about 15 per cent of the total population. In the State prisons in California there are 28,000 prisoners, 45 per cent of whom are classified as "non-white."

It should be perfectly clear that thousands upon thousands of

---

[10] Herbert Marcuse, *Essay on Liberation,* Beacon Press, Boston, 1970, p. 74.
[11] *Time* magazine, "U.S. Prisons: Schools for Crime," January 18, 1971.

people presently in jail and prison have broken no laws whatsoever.

The conclusion from all of this is apparent. Professor Theodore Sarbin of the University of California criminology department put it very well: ". . . membership in the class of people known as 'law-breakers' *is not* distributed according to economic or social status, but membership in the class 'criminals' *is* distributed according to social or economic status. . . ." [12]

Example: the ten executives of the General Electric Company convicted in 1961 of price-fixing involving tens of millions of dollars are law-breakers, and some of them actually served some months in prison. Still, the society does not consider them criminals.

By way of contrast, a Chicano or Black youth alleged to have stolen 10 dollars from a grocery store is not only considered a criminal by the society, but this assumption allows the police to act with impunity. They may shoot him down in the street. Chances are it will be ruled justifiable homicide in a coroner's inquest.

What then is the political function of the criminal and the prisoner as they are created and described by the bourgeois penologists and criminologists?

Consider penology as one aspect of the theory and practice of containment on the domestic front; that is, consider penology as the confinement and treatment of people who are *actually or potentially* disruptive of the social system.

In an increasing number of ways the entire judicial and penal system involving the police, the courts, the prisons and the parole boards has become a mechanism through which the ruling powers seek to maintain their physical and psychological control, or the threat of control, over millions of working people, especially young people, and most especially Black and Brown young people. The spectre of the prisons, the behavioral psychologists, the Adult Authority, the judicial treadmill, haunts the community.

Examine for a moment the operations of the Adult Authority. In California roughly 97 per cent of the male prisoners are even-

---

[12] Theodore R. Sarbin, "The Myth of the Criminal Type," Monday Evening Papers #18, Center for Advanced Studies, Wesleyan University, 1969.

tually released from prison—all of them via parole. A man is sentenced to a term in prison. In addition to whatever time he actually serves in prison, he is released on parole for five, even ten or more years. The conditions of his parole are appalling. For example, he can be stopped and searched at any time; his house can be entered without a warrant; he needs the permission of his parole officer to borrow money, to marry, to drive a car, to change his job, to leave the country, and so forth. If parole is revoked the prisoner is returned to custody without trial to complete his full sentence. Members of the Adult Authority are appointed by the Governor. They are answerable to no one. This, combined with California law which allows "indeterminate sentences" for felony convictions, e.g. one year to life imprisonment, gives the parole board incredible powers.

This entire complex is a system of tyranny under which an ever-increasing number of working people—again especially Black and Brown people—are forced to live. As such, it is a prelude to fascism. Indeed, Professor Herbert Packer of the Stanford Law School is exactly right in his conclusion that ". . . the inevitable end of the behavioral view is preventive detention . . ." [13]

For once you accept the behavioralist view of the criminal as morally depraved or mentally defective it is perfectly logical to preventively detain *all* persons who manifest such tendencies and are therefore *potential* criminals. Thus, in April 1970 a leading physician and close associate of President Nixon proposed that the government begin the mass testing of 6 to 8 year old children to determine if they have criminal-behavior-tendencies. He then suggested "treatment camps" for the severely disturbed child and the young hard-core criminal.

Even more consequential in terms of their potential political impact are the proposals of Edward C. Banfield, a professor of Urban Government at Harvard, and the chairman of President Nixon's task force on the Model Cities Program. Professor Banfield has recently written a book entitled: *The Unheavenly City: The Nature and Future of Our Urban Crisis*. Banfield's analysis of the urban crisis exactly coincides with the behavioralists' view

[13] Herbert L. Packer, "Crimes of Progress," *New York Review of Books*, October 23, 1969.

of the criminal. That is, the cause of the urban crisis lies with the existence of what Banfield calls the "lower classes" who are poverty-prone. These lower classes are of course working people, and Black and Brown people in particular. They are, Banfield would have us believe, morally depraved and mentally defective. For example, Banfield describes people of the lower classes (quoting from different passages in his book) as: "feeble . . . suspicious and hostile, aggressive yet dependent . . . no attachment to community, neighbors or friends . . . lives in the slum and sees little or no reason to complain . . . does not care how dirty and dilapidated his housing is . . . nor does he mind the inadequacy of such public facilities as schools, parks and libraries . . . features that make the slum repellent to others actually please him . . . prefers near-destitution, without work to abundance with it . . . the morality of lower-class culture is preconventional, which means that the individual's actions are influenced not by conscience but only by a sense of what he can get away with. . . ." [14]

Banfield's description of the lower class is in fact a description of the criminal. And it is precisely at this moment when the description of the lower class and the description of the criminal *coincide* that we have a central aspect of the ideological basis for fascism and genocide. This is exactly Banfield's program.

Summarizing the most salient points in Banfield's program we find these proposals: that the government avoid all rhetoric holding out high expectations for resolving the urban crisis or any of its aspects; that it try to reduce unemployment by eliminating all minimum-wage laws and by repealing all laws which give trade unions "monopolistic powers," e.g. the closed shop; that the government abolish all child labor laws and cut compulsory education from 12 to 9 years; that it change poverty definitions from those which encompass relative standards of living to a "fixed standard" and that it encourage or require all persons who fall into this fixed poverty standard to live in an institution or semi-

---

[14] Edward C. Banfield, *The Unheavenly City: The Nature and Future of Our Urban Crisis,* Little, Brown, Boston 1970, pp. 53, 62, 112, 122, 163 and 211 respectively. See the review/essay of this book by Herbert Aptheker, "Banfield: The Nixon Model Planner," *Political Affairs,* December 1970.

institution; that the government institute vigorous birth control measures for the incompetent poor and send their children to public nurseries; that the government intensify police control and specifically permit the police to 'stop and frisk' and to make misdemeanor arrests on probable cause; that the government speed-up trials and the punishment process; and that the government "abridge to an appropriate degree the freedom of those who in the opinion of a court are extremely likely to commit violent crimes . . ." [15]

This is a *fascist* program. It is a *genocidal* program.

Aspects of it are already to be found in Nixon's Organized Crime Control Bill signed in to law in October (1970). For example, this bill provides for a special category of 'criminals' known as "special dangerous offenders." Such a person is defined, in part, as an offender who has been convicted of two or more offenses of a kind punishable by death or impronment for one year, one of which offenses occurred within the past five years and for one of which he has been imprisoned. As the *New Republic*'s columnist, TRB noted: "That's a curious juxtaposition— 'punishable by death or imprisonment for more than one year.' Quite a range, eh?" The "special dangerous offender" can be imprisoned for 20 years at the discretion of the judge, regardless of the proscribed punishment for the original offense for which he was brought to trial.

Here then lies the final significance of a mass political movement to expose the prisons and free the prisoners. The issue is not only reform, but also to mount a struggle to abolish the present functions and foundations of the prison system, an effort which can finally succeed only with the abolition of capitalism. For, as Engels observed more than a century ago, the prison system under capitalism is overwhelmingly a repressive institution, an appendage of its state apparatus employed to maintain exploitative and oppressive social conditions. Of course, what reforms can be won in day to day battle on the legal and political front will be important concessions. But the point is to attack the whole foundation—all the assumptions—involved in main-

[15] Ibid., pp. 245–246.

taining a rehabilitative prison system which must assume the moral and mental defectiveness of its victims, in the midst of a morally bankrupt, racist, defective and generally deteriorating social order. To do this now is to launch a front-line offense against the increasingly fascistic thrust of the present Administrations in Washington and Sacramento.[16] For the movement to abolish the present functions of the prison system attacks a basic ideological pillar of fascism at its root.

It is on the basis of these realities that we in the radical and revolutionary movements must broaden and develop our concept of the political prisoner. For the prison system and its various appendages such as the Adult Authority is increasingly used as a political instrument of mass intimidation, subversion, manipulation and terror against working people and the Black and Brown communities, *as a whole.*

In this regard we may consider four groupings of prisoners who are prisoners by virtue of their political views and activities or are specially victimized on the basis of class, racial and national oppression. First, of course, there are those who become effective political leaders in their communities, and therefore become the victims of politically-inspired police frameups. They are not imprisoned for any violations of law; but for their political beliefs. Such political prisoners include Bobby Seale, Ericka Huggins, Reies Tijerina and Angela Davis. There is a second, though similar category of political prisoner; that is, those who have committed various acts of civil disobedience, or refused, for example, to be inducted into the Armed Forces. They are in technical violation of various laws; but their violations were clearly political acts, and they are political prisoners. Such political prisoners include the Berrigan Brothers, and many thousands of draft resisters. Moreover, there are many in the liberation movements who engage in specific acts of resistance or armed self-defense—both within and outside the prisons—which may constitute violations of law. These actions are politically conceived and engendered by the overt acts of brutality, terror and suppression inside the prisons, and in the ghettos and barrios.

[16] See, Susan Castro, "Line of Defense Against Fascism," *People's World,* June 1970, p. 10.

Third, there are many thousands of originally non-political people who are the victims of class, racial and national oppression. Arrested for an assortment of alleged crimes, and lacking adequate legal or political redress they are imprisoned for long years, in violation of fundamental civil and human rights though they are innocent of any crime.

Finally there are many in prison who have committed various offenses, but who, in the course of their imprisonment, and due to the social conditions they experience begin to develop a political consciousness. As soon as they give expression to their political views they become victims of politically-inspired actions against them by the prison administration and the parole boards. They too may become victims of politically inspired frameups within the prison. There are today many who were either never guilty of any crime at all, or were guilty of some offense, and later developed a political consciousness. These include the Soledad Brothers, Ruchell Magee, and the Folsom Strikers.

The intensification of the oppressive functions of the prison system and the emergence of the liberation movements on a new level in the Sixties create the basis for a change in the political consciousness of people in the communities. More and more people have begun to understand the practical consequences of the prison—police—judicial apparatus. It is this fact which now offers us new opportunities to secure greater and greater mass opposition to the frameups and jailings of all political prisoners.

Further, it is precisely this intensification of the socially-oppressive function of the prison system, and the stunning rise of the liberation movements, that creates the basis for a political consciousness among the prisoners *as a whole* leading to individual acts of resistance and other forms of struggle, including mass political work stoppages by the prisoners and temporarily taking over prison facilities. The greatest achievment of this movement is its growing awareness of the *class* nature of the prison system. In this way it has been able to unite Black, Brown and white prisoners around specific demands such as we saw in the magnificent Manifesto of the Folsom Prisoners.

The development of a mass movement to free all political prisoners represents the emergence of another front—another aspect—

of the growing coalition of all oppressed and exploited peoples against capitalist rule.

If we begin to grapple with some of these developments; if we begin to see the relationship between the prison system and fascist ideology and program; if we begin to see that we must develop our concept of the political prisoner; and if we begin to see the relationship between containment at home and counter-insurgency and aggression abroad—then, we will have opened up whole new avenues for legal and political defense involving many thousands of people which will, in fact, constitute an important part of a peoples' offensive against the Nixon-Reagan-Agnew axis.

Seize the Time!

4

Prisoners
in Rebellion

For Black youth throughout the United States, Huey P. Newton, the Minister of Defense of the Black Panther Party, is a radiant leader, a bold fighter, a hero and a genuine brother. They identify with the battle he has fought against the forces of racism and reaction. They identify with his principled revolutionary struggle against a system which ineluctably spells misery and destitution for the mass of Black people.

Very early, the Black Panther Party played a decisive part in unleashing the new tide of Black militancy. In the Fall of 1966, Brother Huey, together with Brother Bobby Seale and Brother Bobby Hutton (later assassinated by Oakland policemen) established the groundwork for the Party. After formulating a basic 10-point program for the Black Liberation struggle (calilng for full employment, housing, education, the cessation of police hostilities, and an end to the railroading of Black men and women into jails and prisons), they began to take action. Their first step was an attempt to deal with one of the most immediate and most injurious symptoms of oppression—police brutality.

Armed with law books, rifles, shotguns and pistols, they patrolled Oakland's Black community, monitoring the police, observing arrests and informing brothers and sisters of their rights. Their vigilance produced a marked decrease in police harrassment and brutality. Black people in Oakland, California were impressed.

The increasing influence of the Black Panther Party in the Black community, their vehement defense of the rights of their

49

people inevitably engendered violent, hysterical reactions in the police force and in government.

On October 28, 1967, a policeman radioed to his headquarters that he was following a 'panther car.' Shortly afterwards Brother Huey had been shot four times in the stomach. One cop was dead, another wounded. Huey P. Newton was charged with murder.

The Black Panther Party spearheaded a nationwide Free Huey campaign, as they continued to increase in size and influence. The impact of this movement, coupled with Brother Huey's manifest innocence, resulted in his acquittal on the murder charges, but, in what was clearly a political compromise, he was convicted of manslaughter and sentenced from 2 to 15 years in prison. Governor Reagan had made no secret of his attitude toward the Panthers.

As the Free Huey movement continued to gain support, the courts could no longer blatantly disregard the interests of justice and the demands of the people. In the summer of 1970, Brother Huey's conviction was reversed on an appeal, and he was released on bail pending the outcome of a new trial.

Temporarily free after almost three years' imprisonment, Brother Huey's first remarks expressed a renewed commitment on his behalf and on behalf of his party to energetically struggle for the liberation of all political prisoners.

The following article was written in captivity.

Prison, Where Is Thy Victory?

BY HUEY P. NEWTON

When a person studies mathematics, he learns that there are many mathematical laws which determine the approach he must take to solving the problems presented to him. In the study of geometry, one of the first laws a person learns is that "the whole is not greater than the sum of its parts." This means simply that one cannot have a geometrical figure such as a circle or a square which in its totality, contains more than it does when broken down into smaller parts. Therefore, if all the smaller parts add up to a certain amount, the entire figure cannot add up to a larger amount. The prison cannot have a victory over the prisoner, because those in charge take the same kind of approach and assume if they have the whole body in a cell that they have there all that makes up the person. But a prisoner is not a geometrical figure, and an approach which is successful in mathematics, is wholly unsuccessful when dealing with human beings.

In the case of the human, we are not dealing only with the single individual, we are also dealing with the ideas and beliefs which have motivated him and which sustain him, even when his body is confined. In the case of humanity the whole is much greater than its parts, because the whole includes the body which is measurable and confineable, and also the ideas which cannot be measured and which cannot be confined. The ideas are not only within the mind of the prisoner where they cannot be seen nor controlled, the ideas are also within the mind of the prisoner where they cannot be within the people. The ideas which can and will sustain our movement for total freedom and dignity of the people, cannot be imprisoned, for they are to be found in the people, all the people, wherever they are. As long as the people live by the ideas of freedom and dignity there will be no prison which can hold our movement down. Ideas move from one person to another in the association of brothers and sisters who recognize that a most evil system of capitalism has set us against each other, when our real enemy is the exploiter who profits from our poverty. When we realize such an idea then we come to love and appreciate our brothers and sisters who we may have seen as enemies, and those exploiters who we may have seen as friends are revealed for what they truly are to all oppressed people. The people are the idea, the respect and dignity of the people, as they move toward their freedom, is the sustaining force which reaches into and out of the prison. The walls, the bars, the guns and the guards can never encircle or hold down the idea of the people. And the people must always carry forward the idea which is their dignity and their beauty.

The prison operates with the idea that when it has a person's body it has his entire being—since the whole cannot be greater than the sum of its parts. They put the body in a cell, and seem to get some sense of relief and security from that fact. The idea of prison victory then, is that when the person in jail begins to act, think, and believe the way they want him to, then they have won the battle and the person is then "rehabilitated." But this cannot be the case, because those who operate the prisons, have failed to examine their own beliefs thoroughly, and they fail to understand the types of people they attempt to control. Therefore, even when the prison thinks it has won the victory, there is no victory.

There are two types of prisoners. The largest number are those who accept the legitimacy of the assumptions upon which the society is based. They wish to acquire the same goals as everybody else, money, power, greed, and conspicuous consumption. In order to do so, however, they adopt techniques and methods which the society has defined as illegitimate. When this is discovered such people are put in jail. They may be called "illegitimate capitalists" since their aim is to acquire everything this capitalistic society defines as legitimate. The second type of prisoner, is the one who rejects the legitimacy of the assumptions upon which the society is based. He argues that the people at the bottom of the society are exploited for the profit and advantage of those at the top. Thus, the oppressed exist, and will always be used to maintain the privileged status of the exploiters. There is no sacredness, there is no dignity in either exploiting or being exploited. Although this system may make the society function at a high level of technological efficiency, it is an illegitimate system, since it rests upon the suffering of humans who are as worthy and as dignified as those who do not suffer. Thus, the second type of prisoner says that the society is corrupt and illegitimate and must be overthrown. This second type of prisoner is the political prisoner. They do not accept the legitimacy of the society and cannot participate in its corrupting exploitation, whether they are in the prison or on the block.

The prison cannot gain a victory over either type of prisoner no matter how hard it tries. The "illegitimate capitalist" recognizes that if he plays the game the prison wants him to play, he will have his time reduced and be released to continue his activities. Therefore, he is willing to go through the prison programs and do the things the prison authorities want to hear. The prison assumes he is "rehabilitated" and ready for the society. The prisoner has really played the prison's game so that he can be released to resume pursuit of his capitalistic goals. There is no victory, for the prisoner from the git-go accepted the idea of the society. He pretends to accept the idea of the prison as a part of the game he has always played.

The prison cannot gain a victory over the political prisoner because he has nothing to be rehabilitated from or to. He refuses to accept the legitimacy of the system and refuses to participate. To participate is to admit that the society is legitimate because of its exploitation of the oppressed. This is the idea which the political prisoner does not accept, this is the idea for which he has been imprisoned, and this is the reason why he cannot cooperate with the system. The political prisoner will, in fact, serve his time just as will the "illegitimate capitalist." Yet the idea which motivated and sustained the political prisoner rests in the people; all the prison has, is a body.

The dignity and beauty of man rests in the human spirit which makes him more than simply a physical being. This spirit must never be suppressed for exploitation by others. As long as the people recognize the beauty of their human spirits and move against suppression and exploitation, they will be carrying out one of the most beautiful ideas of all time. Because the human whole is much greater than the sum of its parts. The ideas will always be among the people. The prison cannot be victorious because walls, bars and guards cannot conquer or hold down an idea.

Prisoners from New York to California, in city jails and state and federal penitentiaries have organized massive protests against the inhuman and brutal conditions of their existence. The single greatest achievement of their collective resistance has been the growing unity of Black, Brown and White prisoners, for the fomenting of racial hatreds by the prison authorities has been the main bulwark of the uncurbed terror.

The formation of a chapter of the Black Panther Party inside

San Quentin, of a Chicano prisoners' organization, also at San Quentin, of prisoners' unions at the Men's Colony in San Luis Obispo and Folsom Prison in California, attest to the politicalization of thousands of prisoners. Indeed, during all of the rebellions across the country, the prisoners have indicated that their oppression is not simply a matter of overcrowded prisons, filthy conditions and guard brutality: but that it is centered in the institutionalized racism and class discrimination of the judicial system itself. Behind their concrete demands for relief there is a radical political consciousness.

The solitary confinement of prisoners for months and even years, often generates a tendency toward individual acts of resistance. However, mass, collective, organized rebellions are also now much in evidence, and the attempted rescue by Jonathan Jackson of three Black prisoners from the Marin County Court House on August 7, 1970—while involving only a few individuals—had a dramatic impact on this mass movement inside the prisons.

A rebellion at Long Island City Prison in New York touched off a five-day, city-wide revolt from October 1 through October 6, 1970. Over 2,000 prisoners took part in the uprisings, which were finally crushed by police acting on the authority of the Mayor, John Lindsay, who broke off negotiations with representatives of the prison rebels. Police armed with clubs, teargas, guns and acetylene torches moved into the Queens Men's House of Detention in Kew Gardens and the Brooklyn Men's House of Detention. The several hundred prisoners at each jail, who had seized control of various floors, were overpowered and beaten.

Within a month similar revolts broke out in several California prisons including Folsom, San Quentin, Soledad and the Men's Colony at San Luis Obispo. At Folsom Prison the men began a work stoppage on November 3, 1970 involving 2,100 out of 2,400 prisoners. Two days into the strike the warden locked all prisoners into their cells. Prison authorities then unleashed a reign of terror—the men called it "night riding." Guards were given unlimited powers. They beat prisoners and made them stand outside naked all night.

The strike was broken when four strike leaders—two white, one Black and one Chicano—were transferred out of Folsom and

scattered to other prisons throughout the state. Then prison authorities placed 52 other strikers—considered to be "hard core"—in
"the hole," solitaray confinement in small, dark rooms with cement
floors and a hole in the floor for the toilet, which can be flushed
only from the outside. These cells have no beds and the diet consists of bread and water.

Then guards went into the cells and used whatever force was
required to make prisoners work. The warden told the prisoners
that refusal to work might result in denial of parole.

The prisoners made 31 demands, which were ignored by prison
authorities but gained considerable support on the outside. A press
conference was held in San Francisco on November 6, at which
representatives of several labor, medical, legal and ex-prisoner
groups voiced their support for the strike.

Among the supporting organizations was the San Francisco-
Bay Area Chapter of the National Lawyers Guild, Local 1570 of
the American Federation of Teachers, Local 1695 of the State,
County and Municipal Employees, the Medical Committee for Human Rights, and Local 535 of the Social Service Union, as well as
a number of leading trade unionists.

"Although each of the sponsors supports all of the demands of
the striking prisoners," the press release said, "each emphasizes a
particular interest.

"The National Lawyers Guild pledges to provide full legal assistance to protect strikers from any form of retaliatory repression that
may be used by prison authorities to break the strike or to prevent
future prisoner organization. The Guild also pledges to take affirma-
tive legal steps to obtain the prisoners' demands.

"Ex-prisoner groups co-sponsoring this conference have a very
personal interest in participating, since they consist of human beings
who already have been processed by the prison system, and stig-
matized by it.

"Labor groups and leaders have joined in support to protest the
unacceptable wages and working conditions of their fellow workers who are compelled to labor in prison industries.

"Medical groups have joined to expose the inadequate medicine
practiced upon inmates."

A message from a Folsom prisoner, dated Nov. 4, the second

day of the strike, shows something of the prison atmosphere. Here are excerpts:

"We have had three or four incidents where individuals have been committed to isolation for discussing the strike and for circulating literature in this area. As it (the strike) is escalated and the anxieties rise a little higher, we do expect more suppression from the administration. We have been peaceable and orderly; we don't desire destructive things, we don't want a violent thing. We really want to raise the issue on a peaceful level.

"We feel that although we are in prison, we should not be denied all rights and privileges of citizens. We feel that the conditions of prison life have been ignored too long. We call for all people who are concerned about the welfare and conditions of prisoners throughout the state, people who are concerned about the escalating violence perpetrated upon inmates in prison, who care about what the American doctrine stands for, to raise these issues.

"The accusation that this has been instigated by outside instigators is ridiculous, because the inside people are the people who composed the Manifesto, the inside people are the ones who are requesting the support of the outside people regarding the situation inside."

In his message the prisoner doubts the warden's claim that he never received the demands. They were, he says, mailed to the warden on October 29, and also to the head of the Department of Corrections.

He also says that the prisoners selected four persons outside the prison to represent them in negotiations with authorities. They were Attorney Charles Garry, Sal Candeleria of the Brown Berets, Huey P. Newton of the Black Panther Party, and John Irwin of the Coordinating Council on Prison and Parole Reform, "because we love and respect them, and we feel that these people or any representatives of these people will do what is just and right by all."

The Folsom Prisoners Manifesto and Anti-Oppression Platform printed below, constituted the grievances and demands of the striking men.

The Folsom Prisoners Manifesto of Demands and Anti-Oppression Platform

WE THE IMPRISONED MEN OF FOLSOM PRISON SEEK AN END TO THE INJUSTICE SUFFERED BY ALL PRISONERS, REGARDLESS OF RACE, CREED, OR COLOR.

The preparation and content of this document has been constructed under the unified efforts of all races and social segments of this prison.

We the inmates of Folsom Prison totally and unlimitedly support the California state wide prison strike on November 3, 1970, under the united effort for designated change in administrative prison practice and legislative policy.

It is a matter of documented record and human recognition that the administrators of the California prison system have restructured the institutions which were designed to socially correct men into the FASCIST CONCENTRATION CAMPS OF MODERN AMERICA.

DUE TO THE CONDITIONAL FACT THAT FOLSOM PRISON IS ONE OF THE MOST CLASSIC INSTITUTIONS OF AUTHORITATIVE INHUMANITY UPON MEN, THE FOLLOWING MANIFESTO OF DEMANDS IS BEING SUBMITTED:

1. We demand the constitutional rights of legal representation at the time of all Adult Authority hearings, and the protection from the procedures of the Adult Authority whereby they permit no procedural safeguards such as an attorney for cross examination of witnesses, witnesses in behalf of the parolee, at parole revocation hearings.

2. We demand a change in medical staff and medical policy and procedure. The Folsom Prison Hospital is totally inadequate, understaffed, prejudicial in the treatment of inmates. There are numerous "mistakes" made many times, improper

and erroneous medication is given by untrained personnel. The emergency procedures for serious injury are totally absent in that they have no emergency room whatsoever; no recovery room following surgery, which is performed by practitioners rather than board member surgeons. They are assisted by inmate help neither qualified, licensed, nor certified to function in operating rooms. Several instances have occurred where multiple injuries have happened to a number of inmates at the same time. A random decision was made by the M.D. in charge as to which patient was the most serious and needed the one surgical room available. Results were fatal to one of the men waiting to be operated upon. This is virtually a death sentence to such a man who might have otherwise lived.

3. We demand adequate visiting conditions and facilities for the inmates and families of Folsom prisoners. The visiting facilities at this prison are such as to preclude adequate visiting for the inmates and their families. As a result the inmates are permitted two hours, two times per month to visit with family and friends which of course has to be divided between these people. We ask for additional officers to man the visiting room five days per week, so that everyone may have at least four hours visiting per month. The administration has refused to provide or consider this request in prior appeals using the grounds of denial that they cannot afford the cost of the extra officers needed for such a change. However, they have been able to provide twelve new correctional officers to walk the gun rails of this prison, armed with rifles and shotguns during the daytime hours when most of the prison population is at work or attending other assignments. This is a waste of the taxpayers' money, and a totally unnecessary security precaution.

4. We demand that each man presently held in the Adjustment Center be given a written notice with the Warden of Custody's signature on it explaining the exact reason for his placement in the severely restrictive confines of the Adjustment Center.

5. We demand an immediate end to indeterminate Adjustment

Center terms to be replaced by fixed terms with the length of time to be served being terminated by good conduct and according to the nature of the charges, for which men are presently being warehoused indefinitely without explanation.

6. We demand an end to the segregation of prisoners from the mainline population because of their political beliefs. Some of the men in the Adjustment Center are confined there solely for political reasons and their segregation from other inmates is indefinite.

7. We demand an end to political persecution, racial persecution, and the denial of prisoners' right to subscribe to political papers, books, or any other educational and current media chronicles that are forwarded through the United States Mail.

8. We demand an end to the persecution and punishment of prisoners who practice the constitutional right of peaceful dissent. Prisoners at Folsom and San Quentin Prisons, according to the California State Penal Code, cannot be compelled to work, as these two prisons were built for the purpose of housing prisoners and there is no mention of prisoners being required to work on prison jobs in order to remain on the mainline and/or be considered for release. Many prisoners believe their labor power is being exploited in order for the State to increase its economic power and continue to expand its correctional industries which are million dollar complexes, yet do not develop working skills acceptable for employment in the outside society, and which do not pay the prisoner more than the maximum sixteen cents per hour wage. Most prisoners never make more than six or eight cents per hour. Prisoners who refuse to work for the two to sixteen cent pay rate, or who strike, are punished and segregated without the access to privileges shared by those who work. This is class legislation, class division, and creates class hostilities within the prison.

9. We demand an end to the tear-gassing of prisoners who are locked in their cells. Such action led to the death of Willie

Powell in Soledad Prison in 1968, and of Fred Billingslea on February 25, 1970 at San Quentin Prison. It is cruel and unnecessary.

10. We demand the passing of a minimum and maximum term bill which calls for an end to indeterminate sentences whereby a man can be warehoused indefinitely, rehabilitated or not. That all prisoners have the right to be paroled after serving their minimum term instead of the cruel and unusual punishment of being confined beyond his minimum eligibility for parole, and never knowing the reason for the extension of time, nor when his time is completed. The maximum term bill eliminates indefinite life time imprisonment where it is unnecessary and cruel. Life sentences should not confine a man for longer than ten years, as seven years is the statute for a considered lifetime out of circulation and if a man cannot be rehabilitated after a maximum of ten years of constructive programs, etc., then he belongs in a mental hygiene center, not a prison. Rescind Adult Authority Resolution 171, arbitrary fixing of prison terms.

11. We demand that industries be allowed to enter the Institutions and employ inmates to work eight hours a day and fit into the category of workers for scale wages. The working conditions in prisons do not develop working incentives parallel to the money jobs in the outside society, and a paroled prisoner faces many contradictions on the job that adds to his difficulty to adjust. Those industries outside who desire to enter prisons should be allowed to enter for the purpose of employment placement.

12. We demand that inmates be allowed to form or join Labor Unions.

13. We demand that inmates be granted the right to support their own families. At present thousands of welfare recipients have to divide their checks to support their imprisoned relatives who without the outside support could not even buy toilet articles or food. Men working on scale wages could support themselves and families while in prison.

14. We demand that correctional officers be prosecuted as a matter of law for shooting inmates, around inmates, or any

act of cruel and unusual punishment where it is not a matter of life or death.

15. We demand that all institutions that use inmate labor be made to conform with the state and federal minimum wage laws.

16. We demand that all condemned prisoners, avowed revolutionaries and prisoners of war be granted political asylum in the countries under the Free World Revolutionary Solidarity Pact, such as Algeria, Russia, Cuba, Latin America, North Korea, North Vietnam, etc., and that prisoners confined for political reasons in this country, until they can be exchanged for prisoners of war held by America, be treated in accord with the 1954 Geneva Convention; that they and their personal property be respected, that they be permitted to retain possession of personal property and that they not be manacled.

17. We demand an end to trials being held on the premises of San Quentin Prison, or any other prison without a jury of peers—as required by the United States Constitution—being picked from the country of the trial proceedings; peers in this instance being other prisoners as the selected jurors.

18. We demand an end to the escalating practice of physical brutality being perpetrated upon the inmates of California State Prisons at San Quentin, Folsom, and Soledad prisons in particular.

19. We demand that such celebrated and prominent political prisoners as Reis Tijerina, Ahmad Evans, Bobby Seale, Chip Fitzgerald, Los Siete, David Harris, and the Soledad Brothers, be given political asylum outside this country as the outrageous slandering of the mass media has made it impossible either for a fair trial or for a safe term to be served in case of conviction, as the forces of reactions and repressions will be forever submitting them to threats of cruel and unusual punishment and death wherever they are confined and throughout the length of their confinement.

20. We demand appointment of three lawyers from the California Bar Association for full time positions to provide legal assistance for inmates seeking post-conviction relief, and to act

as liaison between the administration and inmates for bringing inmate complaints to the attention of the administration.

21. We demand update of industry working conditions to standards as provided for under California law.

22. We demand establishment of inmate workers insurance plan to provide compensation for work related accidents.

23. We demand establishment of unionized vocational training program comparable to that of the Federal Prison System which provides for union instructors, union pay scale, and union membership upon completion of the vocational training course.

24. We demand annual accounting of Inmate Welfare Fund and formulation of an inmate committee to give inmates a voice as to how such funds are used.

25. We demand that the Adult Authority Board appointed by the Governor be eradicated and replaced by a parole board elected by popular vote of the people. In a world where many crimes are punished by indeterminate sentences, where authority acts with secrecy and vast discretion and gives heavy weight to accusations by prison employees against inmates, inmates feel trapped unless they are willing to abandon their desire to be independent men.

26. We strongly demand that the State and Prison Authorities, conform to recommendation #1 of the "Soledad Caucus Report," to wit:

   "That the State Legislature create a fulltime salaried board of overseers for the State Prisons. The board would be responsible for evaluating allegations made by inmates, their families, friends, and lawyers against employees charged with acting inhumanely, illegally, or unreasonably. The board should include people nominated by a psychological or psychiatric association, by the State Bar Association or by the Public Defenders Association, and by groups of concerned, involved laymen."

27. We demand that prison authorities conform to the conditional requirements and needs as described in the recently released Manifesto from the Folsom Adjustment Center.

29. We demand that the California Prison System furnish Folsom

Prison with the services of Ethnic Counselors for the needed special services of Brown and Black population of this prison.

30. We demand an end to the discrimination in the judgement and quota of parole for Black and Brown People.

We the men of Folsom Prison have been committed to the State Correctional Authorities by the people of this society for the purpose of correcting what has been deemed as social errors in behavior, errors which have classified us as socially unacceptable until re-programmed with new values and a more thorough understanding of our roles and responsibilities as members of the outside community. The structure and conditions of the Folsom Prison program have been engraved on the pages of this manifesto of demands with the blood, sweat, and tears of the inmates of this prison.

The program which we are committed to under the ridiculous title of rehabilitation is likened to the ancient stupidity of pouring water on the drowning man, in as much as our program administrators respond to our hostilities with their own.

In our efforts to comprehend on a feeling level an existence contrary to violence, we are confronted by our captors with violence. In our effort to comprehend society's code of ethics concerning what is fair and just, we are victimized by exploitation and the denial of the celebrated due process of law.

In our peaceful efforts to assemble in dissent as provided under the nation's United States Constitution, we are in turn murdered, brutalized, and framed on various criminal charges because we seek the rights and privileges of *all american people*.

In our efforts to keep abreast of the outside world, through all categories of news media, we are systematically restricted and punished by isolation when we insist on our human rights to the wisdom of awareness.

III

Realities
of Repression

5

Trials of
Political Prisoners Today

The case descriptions which follow have been assembled for the
purpose of providing a glimpse of the concrete dimensions of
political repression in the United States today. By no means does
this account pretend to be comprehensive. To be reflective of the
reality of repression, these cases must be multiplied a thousand-
fold—and many times more—when we consider that the army of
Blacks, Chicanos, Puerto Ricans immured in the nation's dungeons are largely victims of an exploitative, racist socio-economic
arrangement.

The vast majority of these cases have been publicized through
mass political defense campaigns. While there are many more
which have been brought to light in this way, we must infer that
where such movements are lacking the names of innumerable
political prisoners are lost in obscurity.

An attempt has been made to select representative cases. They
all involve individuals and groups presently imprisoned or under
indictment.

Political prisoners discussed elsewhere in the body of this book
—the Soledad Brothers, Ruchell Magee, Ericka Huggins, Bobby
Seale, etc.—have been excluded.

Represented are Blacks, Chicanos, Puerto Ricans, Indians,
Whites, both men and women, students, workers and the unemployed. Political prisoners who have been manifestly framed as
reprisals for their successful community organizing constitute the
largest proportion of cases described. But there are also the individuals such as war resisters as well as men and women who have
participated in armed acts of resistance, who are technically in

violation of the law. Included are prisoners who have attained political maturity during the course of their imprisonment for non-political crimes and against whom prison authorities have consequently launched political vendettas.

Finally the legion of victims has incorporated the colossal multitude of Third World men and women, of whom many are innocent, but even the 'guilty' among them receive punishments that far outweigh their crimes.

The prosecution of Marie Hill, sentenced to die, in a small Southern city, at 15 years' old is perhaps the most outrageous case of them all.

THE BLACK PANTHER PARTY

Among movement people, the mere mention of political repression almost inevitably conjures up images of scores of Panthers killed, hundreds imprisoned, hundreds more pursued and plagued by police. This is indeed the inevitable treatment to be accorded a party arrogantly declared by the F.B.I. to be the gravest threat to domestic peace.

In this collection of case descriptions, it is impossible to even scratch the surface of the devastating, legally sanctioned assault on the Black Panther Party. A simple cataloging of all the presently incarcerated or charged political prisoners who are members of the party or were members at the time of their arrest would require volumes.

During the two-and-a-half year period beginning in May, 1967, there occurred over 1000 arrests and 19 killings of Panthers including the brutal police assassinations of Mark Clark and Fred Hampton in Chicago, Illinois in Dec. 1969 as they slept. Statistics of repression compiled for this period by Attorney Charles Garry, Chief Counsel for the Party, reveal the following: over 125 charges of conspiracy (to bomb, murder, steal, commit arson); over 152 charges alleging offenses of a violent nature such as murder, arson, battery, many stemming from police attacks on Panther members and officers; over 150 charges involving weapons; over 129 charges involving theft or stolen property; over 35 charges of disorderly conduct, loitering, etc.; over 39 charges of resisting arrest; over 24 narcotics charges; 4 selective service cases; and numerous other charges.

Recently the charges of criminal anarchy and advocating the overthrow of the government by force were invoked against five members of the Black Panther Party's National Committee to Combat Fascism in New Orleans, Louisiana.

Presently a case is pending against Panther leader Huey P. Newton, Minister of Defense, now charged with manslaughter; and charges against David Hilliard, the chief of staff, for 'threatening the life of the President,' were dismissed, while he has just been convicted for offenses stemming from the April 6, 1968 Oakland police attack during which Bobby Hutton was killed.

Numerous Panthers are presently scattered throughout the California Prison System, having been convicted in connection with the same police raid, which followed Dr. Martin Luther King's assassination by two days. When Oakland police, aware that a party meeting was in progress, launched a heavy armed attack on the meeting place, the brothers had no alternative but to defend themselves. They eventually surrendered, however, and as one of the Black policemen present later confirmed, Bobby Hutton was murdered, unarmed, his hands in the air.

Charles Bursey, convicted as a result of this incident, began his 2 to 15 year prison term at San Quentin. The prison authorities' decision to isolate the Panthers from one another as well as from the broader captive population caused him to be transferred to a work camp in Susanville, California.

In April, 1971, he was invited to speak for the Susanville Afro-American Cultural Group before a gathering of La Raza Unida, a Chicano prison organization. The need for Chicano-Black unity in the struggle to effect a restructuring of the prison system was the dominant theme of his talk.

The prison system thrives on racial separation and hostility. Frequently, racial conflict is provoked and urged by the administrators, to avoid being the targets of hostility themselves.

A few days after this speech, Brother Bursey was charged with 'racial agitation,' drugged (potent tranquilizing medication was substituted for his regular sinus pills), and forcibly transferred to San Quentin. There, on the verge of collapse, he was placed in a strip cell—a bare cubicle without even a cot or a blanket.

Charles Bursey is but one of the innumerable imprisoned members of the Black Panther Party on whom racist guards practice their techniques of terror. During the Spring of 1971, prisoners announced the formation of a chapter of the Black Panther Party within San Quentin's walls, a cadre which would work in conjunction with a newly organized Chicano revolutionary group. Repeated acts of unprovoked harassment and brutality have been experienced by both groups.

One of the most thorough attempts to decimate the party and disrupt its activities at the height of its development was the indictment of the Panther 21. Their case merits a detailed description. (Some of the defendants who apparently adhere to the political line of the International Section, headed by Eldridge Cleaver, are no longer members of the Oakland-directed party.)

On April 1, 1969, 21 members of the New York chapter of the Black Panther Party were accused in a 30 count indictment of conspiracy to bomb a police station, a section of the New Haven Railroad, four mid-town Manhattan department stores and the Bronx Botanical Gardens. When the trial drew to a close and virtually no concrete evidence had been produced, unless by some wild stretch of the imagination, three pieces of pipe, not rigged as bombs, could have accomplished all this.

Strictly an offense of intent, the charges have been backed up by the exceedingly imaginative testimony of paid police infiltrators.

The defendants who surrendered themselves or were captured had bail set at $100,000 each or no bail at all.

Such brutal treatment was bestowed upon Lee Berry, an epileptic, that he experienced recurrent seizures, contracted pneumonia and developed an abscess on his lung. Seven months elapsed before he was removed from his cell in a New York jail and transferred to a hospital. Because of the severe damage to his health, his case had to be severed from the rest.

Joan Bird was declared to be a defendant in the 21 case on the basis of an indictment brought against her the previous January. Charged with driving a car from which shots were fired at a police station, she was ruthlessly beaten and tortured at the time of her arrest.

> ". . . They put handcuffs on me and turned me over face down on the ground and my hands cuffed behind me. Then they began to kick me and walk on my back and legs. Then McKenzie put a gun to my head and stated: 'I ought to kill you, you motherfucker,' then proceeded to take my right hand fingers and bend them back and said, 'you better talk or I'll break your fingers.' Then they were all talking about how they should take me to the woods in the park and shoot me and nobody would know the difference. I screamed."

By coercion they drove her to sign a confession.

The in-court protests of many of the defendants who felt their rights were being trampled upon led the judge to disregard their right to a speedy trial. He ordered the proceedings discontinued until they would swear themselves "prepared to participate in a trial according to the American system of justice."

In May of 1971, the trial at last drew to a close.[17] Most of the defendants had been in jail, unconvicted of any crime, for over two years. Of the four released on bail, Michael Tabor and Richard Moore were first reported to be in Algeria, apparently persuaded that justice would not prevail.

Throughout the country Panthers are awaiting trial. Community organizers with the Party's National Committee to Combat Fascism in New Orleans have been accused of various offenses deriving from a police attack on the housing project where they had organized a movement to resist forced evictions. In Philadelphia, as a result of a police assault on the Party office, Panthers have been charged with a wide range of offenses. Brothers and sisters of the Detroit Branch have been accused of killing a policeman.

One of the most recent police raids occurred in Winston-Salem, North Carolina. Four brothers—the High Point Four—who had helped to establish a Free Breakfast for Children Program and a

---

[17] On May 13, 1971, all 13 remaining defendants were acquitted of all charges by the jury which deliberated for 2½ hours.

Liberation School, stand accused of conspiracy to commit murder and assault on a police officer with intent to kill. The brothers who range in age from 16 to 19, had attempted to repel an attack on their offices in February, 1971.

From the draconian responses of police forces, systematic and undoubtedly calculated, it can only be inferred that the Panthers are victims of an official, nation-wide conspiracy to destroy their party.

AHMED EVANS

"White racism is essentially responsible for the explosive mixture which has been accumulating in our cities since the end of World War II."

—KERNER COMMISSION REPORT, 1968.

Cleveland, Ohio is one of the numerous major cities whose Black populations have spontaneously given aggressive expression to frustrations engendered by thwarted desires to lead decent lives free of want and misery. The election of a Black mayor could not gratify basic material needs which have so long remained unfulfilled.

In July, 1968, a rebellion lasting five full days erupted in Glenville, a Black community in Cleveland. The immediate catalyst was an incident involving Ahmed Evans and his militant community organization. Centered around Brother Evans' Afro Culture Shop and Bookstore, the group stressed Black identity and the need to forcefully respond to the urgent problems confronting Cleveland's Black population. In this respect, they openly advocated self-defense and were known to be in possession of legally purchased weapons.

During this period of grass roots militancy among Blacks and the white establishment's hysterical reaction to Black Power, Brother Evans' organization was naturally the object of police harassment, intimidation and concerted attempts to crush it. Three times the city forced the bookstore to close down.

On July 23, after the Cleveland police force had ordered intensive moving surveillance of all members of the group, Brother Evans appealed to a Black councilman to persuade the police to discontinue their harassment. Within minutes after the councilman left Ahmed's house, the area was swarming with trigger happy policemen, firing at every shadow they detected. An hour later 7 were dead and 15 wounded. For five days, Black rage could not be restrained.

Ahmed Evans and four others were charged with first degree murder—three policemen and a tow truck operator had been among the dead.

Ten months later Brother Evans was tried by an all white jury in a city whose total population of 800,000 includes 300,000 Blacks, in a city among whose 2,186 man police force, only 165 Blacks could be counted. He was found guilty under an Ohio law which requires no proof that he ever pulled a trigger; he was convicted on circumstantial evidence, police testimony and allegations of paid police informers. Before being sentenced to death, he unwaveringly declared his innocence, proclaiming at the same time that "the electric chair or fear won't stop the Black man today."

Brother Ahmed Evans waits on Ohio Penitentiary's Death Row while his case is appealed and the July 23 Defense Committee leads a mass campaign to save his life, to set him and the other defendants free.

SOLEDAD 3 [18]

California is celebrated for its enlightened approach to penology. If the most progressive network of prisons in the country is supposed to be found in this state, then other prison systems must be worse than Auschwitz. By now, the officially fostered racial con-

[18] All charges against the Soledad 3 were dismissed in May 1971, after the prosecution's star witness admitted on the stand that he had given perjured testimony in exchange for an early parole. This is now an official confirmation of our contention that Black political activists in prison are frequently framed.

flict, the numerous efforts of prison guards to buy the murders of politically undesirable inmates at Soledad Prison are well-known. It has also been disclosed in a report to the California legislature by the legislature's Black caucus that Black inmates in the notorious O-wing, Soledad's maximum security row, find cleanser, crushed glass, spit, urine and feces in their food.

On January 13, 1970 three Blacks, widely known for their aggressive political stance, were ruthlessly murdered by a prison guard during an exercise period. The guard found dead shortly after this incident was used as an excuse to indict three more Black activists—The Soledad Brothers—for murder.

Following the killing of another guard in July of that year fifteen inmates were held for 49 days in solitary confinement during which they were fiercely interrogated and prohibited any communication with the outside. Seven Black men were subsequently charged with murder: Jesse Phillips, Jimmy James, O. C. Allen, Jimmy Wagner, Roosevelt Williams, Alfred Dunn and Walter Watson. They were all known to be militant advocates of Black Liberation and all faced indeterminate sentences with a maximum of life. Consequently, like George Jackson and Ruchell Magee, they were charged with penal code 4500, assault on a non-inmate by a life termer, carrying a mandatory death penalty.

The prison authorities as it was recently revealed in court let it be known that an automatic parole and five hundred dollars were being offered as reward to anyone who would testify against the brothers. Apparently they were not as successful as they hoped, for a few months later charges were dismissed against four of the seven. Yet, the authorities are still determined to convict Brothers Phillips, Wagner and Williams.

Monterey County Judge Gordon Campbell has refused to appoint counsel acceptable to the brothers and in fact their present court-appointed lawyers have indicated their unwillingness to take the case. Incidentally, Campbell is the judge who reportedly announced after the assassination of Martin Luther King that Dr. King got what he deserved. Further revealing his racism he had also admonished Black and Chicano spectators at a Soledad Brothers hearing to conduct themselves properly, not as if they were in a pool hall or at a barbecue table.

In another incident of official harassment directed against the Soledad 3, the brothers were teargassed in their cells when they refused to submit to a blood-test without prior consultation with their attorneys. The tests were administered after they fell unconscious. It may not have been a sheer coincidence that the following day the Soledad Brothers—Jackson, Cluchette and Drumgo—were attacked by prison guards in open court in San Francisco.

HUGO PINELL

Hugo Pinell, a 26 year old Black man from Nicaragua, lives in Soledad Prison's O-wing, the infamous maximum security row where guards offer white prisoners freedom in return for killing militant Blacks. Two white inmates have attested to this in court.

In November, 1970, at the height of political activity in California's prisons, Brother Pinell was one of the leading organizers of a hunger strike among the inmates in O-wing. They were demanding three meals a day, daily one and a half hour exercise periods, the right to read and the right to representation on the disciplinary board. During the strike, twelve inmates were summoned before the disciplinary board, charged with destroying property—Brother Pinell was the sole Black. In an attempt to break the Black-White-Chicano solidarity manifested in the strike, the board found him innocent, the rest guilty.

He assessed this experience in a letter to attorney Fay Stender: "Yes, they were trying to frame me and cross me at the same time. Frame? Well, if I came back up and told the Blacks that the administration was really favoring us, and not to get mixed up in anything in coalition with the other ethnic groups because we finally got what we want, what do you think will happen? True enough, separation, and back to the gutter, 'inmate vs. inmate'."

No special insight is required in order to understand why Hugo Pinell, in March 1971, was charged with killing a guard. He is another political prisoner, like the Soledad Brothers and the Soledad 3 who has been singled out for extinction.

H. RAP BROWN

As chairman of SNCC (Student Non-Violent Coordinating Committee), Rap Brown delivered numerous speeches in Black communities throughout the country during the period in which intense urban rebellions occurred in virtually every major city in the nation. Although the Kerner Commission Report later affirmed that white racism had to be held responsible for the rebellions, Brother Rap was repeatedly singled out as having incited Black people to revolt. His life was continually disrupted by recurring official attempts to silence him.

In 1967, Rap was indicted for riot, inciting to arson following a fiery speech to Black residents of Cambridge, Maryland. The pretext for these charges was the burning of a school near the spot where Rap had spoken which had occurred after Rap had already left Cambridge. The District Attorney in Cambridge has been widely quoted as saying that he had no proof for the arson charge —it was a ploy designed to bring the F.B.I. into the case.

In early August, 1967, Rap carried a .30 M-1 carbine during flights from New York to New Orleans, New Orleans to Atlanta and Atlanta to New York. On each occasion he checked the gun with the captain who kept it in the cockpit. Following the trips, he was arrested for unlawful transportation of a weapon in interstate commerce while under indictment for a felony. This charge, which virtually no one had previously heard of, was clearly dug out of the books for the purpose of silencing Rap once more.

Out on bail for both charges, Rap traveled to the west coast in February, 1968 to confer with his attorney; while there, he was a surprise speaker of a birthday celebration for Huey P. Newton, the then imprisoned Minister of Defense of the Black Panther Party. This was used as an excuse to revoke his bail on the New Orleans gun charge—the U.S. Attorney claimed that he should have requested the permission of the court before his trip.

New bail was fixed in the exorbitant sum of $50,000 and he was further charged with "threatening" the Black F.B.I. agent who had reported on his speech in California. With the addition of the $50,000 for this charge, bringing the total to one hundred thousand dollars the use of the bail as ransom to gag Black activists could no longer be disguised. Rap refused to leave jail on such outrageous terms and began a fast which lasted 46 days— until his original bail of fifteen thousand dollars was reinstated by a Federal Court of Appeals.

Although he was acquitted of transporting the weapon from New York to New Orleans, he was strangely convicted of returning to New York with the gun and given the maximum penalty of 5 years in jail and two thousand dollars fine. This case is on appeal.

The Maryland charges have yet to be brought to trail and Rap has not been seen or heard from since two of his friends and fellow SNCC members, Ralph Featherstone and Che Payne were killed when their car was bombed near Bel Air, Maryland where Rap's trial was to take place on March 9, 1970. It is not known whether Rap is dead or alive.

LEE OTIS JOHNSON

A former SNCC field secretary is serving a 30 year sentence in Houston, Texas on charges of possession and sale of marijuana— allegedly *one* joint.

In March, 1968, a Black policeman was ordered to infiltrate the Houston Chapter of SNCC where Lee Otis Johnson was a key organizer. Some weeks later, he was indicted on the marijuana charges, two days after he had vigorously criticized the mayor and the Police Chief at a memorial meeting for Martin Luther King. The police contended that he had given the undercover agent one joint. When an all-white jury convicted him, imposing an incredible 30 year sentence the District Attorney commented that "One could reasonably argue that Lee Otis Johnson received less than he deserved."

It had been an open secret that Houston authorities were determined to crush the burgeoning political activity in the Black community. In Brother Johnson's case, the transformation of the courts into an overt instrument of political repression is patently and outrageously exposed. In his own words, "I'm a Political

Prisoner, victimized for none other than my organizing influential and effective Human Rights activities to cure the conspicuous and detestable ills of this society."

ALABAMA BLACK LIBERATION FRONT

Birmingham Alabama's Black community has long lived under the threat of racist terror and officially sanctioned violence. The bombing of the 16th Street Baptist Church in 1963 which left four young sisters dead brutally unmasked Southern racism for the eyes of the world to behold.

On September 1, 1970, 23 members of a sheriff's posse converged upon a house where five members of the Alabama Black Liberation Front were visiting and without warning, riddled the house with bullets. Even according to police testimony, there had been no immediate provocation, not one shot fired from the house. The occupants, including the two wounded and a pregnant ABLF member were forced to crawl out on their stomachs.

Wayland Bryant, Ronald Williams and Harold Robertson were charged with assault with intent to murder. All three were held for 16 days in a single 3x10 cell containing only one cot and no linen. During this time they received half-rations of food and were allowed communications with no one, not even their lawyer.

The charges against Brother Robertson were eventually dropped, but only for the purpose of illegally extraditing him to New York on a parole violation charge. He was removed to New York without benefit of the normal extradition proceedings, although he had refused to waive his right to a hearing.

The ABLF had previously been the target of persistent police harassment and Brother Bryant and Brother Williams had been named in Birmingham newspapers as local leaders of the Black Panther Party. If convicted, they can receive a 20 year prison sentence; their only crime will have been their energetic efforts to build a revolutionary mass movement among the victims of poverty and racism.

WALTER COLLINS

Walter Collins is a Black organizer for the Southern Conference Educational Fund (SCEF) which has its main offices in Louisville, Kentucky. He is also an anti-war activist, who began organizing opposition to the Vietnam war in 1966 in the Black community of New Orleans.

In what has become a common procedure since the mid-1960's, Brother Collins was subsequently reclassified from a 2-S (student deferment) to a 1-A (person subject to being drafted at any time) by the draft board as a result of his political activity.

He challenged that classification right up to the Supreme Court on what is, legally, an established recognized defense.

His draft board is all-white; the chairman of the board did not live in the county (as provided by law), four of the five members did not live in the area, and the board clerk told Collins it wouldn't do any good to file for a conscientious objector status.

Draft resisters have won cases on all of these counts and it seemed assured that Brother Collins would be freed of a five year sentence and a five thousand dollar fine for refusing to be inducted.

However, the US Supreme Court refused to review his conviction, thereby putting its stamp of approval on the sentence. Just 11 days after the Supreme Court's refusal to hear the case Brother Collins was arrested (on November 27, 1970) to begin serving his time.

His arrest and incarceration came in the midst of his attorneys' attempts to file an appeal, to which they're legally entitled within 35 days of the Court's action.

The response to what is becoming the major example of preferential treatment to get Blacks, particularly Black political activists, to the front lines in Vietnam or into jail, is building.

Brother Collins is being used as an example to others. He not only works for SCEF, but is Southern regional director for the National Association of Black Students (NABS) and was setting up a southern regional office for the Central Committee of Conscientious Objectors. He was also organizing a network of Black draft counselors throughout the South.

Three white draft resisters who won their cases before the Supreme Court attempted to file amicus briefs before that Court on Brother Collins' behalf.

It was refused by the Court clerk because none of the three were lawyers and the brief was not professionally prepared.

The three then sent the text of the brief with personal letters to each of the justices. Part of the brief read: "It is an obvious fact that the Selective Service System is being used as a means of repression and control in the Black community.

"The number of young, active Black voices who have been suddenly drafted when they speak out against repression in the past few years can be explained in no other way.

"Our victories in the face of Black defeats," their petition said, "contradicts everything we are trying to make our lives stand for."

On December 10, 1970, Human Rights Day, a delegation of Black and white citizens from various national organizations called on the Justice Department, the White House and the national headquarters of the Selective Service System. They brought petitions with 12,000 signatures calling for presidential amnesty for Brother Collins and all other draft resisters.

There has been no response from the Nixon administration and Brother Collins is presently imprisoned in a federal pententiary. Meanwhile, with the initiative of SCEF, a National Committee to Free Black Draft Resisters is being organized.

CONNIE TUCKER

Drug charges are frequently used to frame political activists, to silence them and isolate them from the community. Both Martin Sostre and Lee Otis Johnson are serving long prison sentences, having been convicted on fabricated drug charges.

Connie Tucker, a 20 year old organizer in Florida's Black communities, has been sentenced to 5 years in prison for possession of marijuana. Two white defendants in court on the same day on the same charge were given suspended sentences. Florida state chairman of JOMO—the Junta Of Militant Organizations—she had been the object of repeated police attacks since she began organizing in Florida in 1969. Shortly before her arrest, the detective who staged the marijuana raid had boasted to two of her friends that he would see to it that Sister Tucker did time in prison.

Although none of the marijuana was produced during the trial—(only two papers in which they claimed it had been smoked) and despite the no-drug policy of JOMO, she was convicted and given the maximum sentence. JOMO, which is waging a national campaign for the freedom of Sister Tucker, has expressed fears for her life. Many of their leaders have been threatened and the Lowell Women's Prison where she is being held, is located in Ocala, Florida, a city known to be the headquarters of Florida's Ku Klu Klan. Three years ago a Black woman prisoner was murdered there under the pretext that she was attempting to escape.

NORMA GIST

Undoubtedly there are thousands upon thousands of Black, Chicano, and Puerto Rican community leaders in small towns from the Deep South to the Northwest who are scorned, harassed and legally punished by local representatives of the establishment. Most of these cases are never reported outside an extremely small circle.

One such case involves a Black woman, an active community leader in Idabelle, Oklahoma. Norma Gist has played a leading role in the movement to prevent the closing down of the Black Idabelle School district and its merger with another district. An inevitable consequence of her aggressive leadership, the school authorities have declared war on Sister Gist.

When her seven year old child was repeatedly beaten during the fall of 1970 by his school principal, it was clear that this was an attempt to chastize Sister Gist. She was particularly anguished by the beatings because her son had a hernia as well as other medical problems. Her renewed appeals to the principal to refrain from beating her son were all to no avail.

Upon hearing of the last beating, which was especially severe, she once more approached the principal, who this time used overly abusive language and made overt threats on her person. Sister Gist, overwrought and desperately seeking to protect herself and her child pulled out her gun and slightly wounded him in the arm. Immediately afterwards, she turned herself in at the police station.

After being held in jail for thirty days without bail and without access to a lawyer, she was tried and convicted of attempted murder even though the principal had suffered an insignificant injury. Her sentence was ten years.

For the moment, Sister Gist is out of jail pending the outcome of her appeal. A defense movement is being organized throughout Oklahoma's Black communities. Sister Gist and others are assiduously working to kindle support around her case and for all victims of Oklahoma's repression.

JAMES JOHNSON

The complex realities of American racism emanate from the basic fact of the overexploitation of Black workers at the point of production. Capitalists not only reap enormous super profits from underpaid Black labor, but use racism as a divisive factor to stave off a united, revolutionary working class movement.

Chrysler Corporation's Eldon Road gear and axle plant in Detroit is notorious for its ruthless treatment of 6,000 overwhelmingly Black workers. Lay-offs, speed-ups, frequent fatal accidents and intolerable working conditions in general create an exceedingly tense atmosphere in that plant. As a direct outcome of these conditions, James Johnson, a Black Eldon worker and member of the United Auto Workers Union is presently on trial for the murders of two foremen and a job setter.

In the brake and shoe department where Brother Johnson worked loading the conveyor belt, he was forced to labor at an inhuman pace since the conveyor belt operated with such speed that brake shoes were thrown all over the floor. Such unbearable conditions had already provoked rank and file strike actions.

As a result of an auto accident, Brother Johnson had been instructed by his physician to take time off from work, but Chrysler doctors ordered him to return. This prompted him to take his two weeks vacation. Upon his return, he was summarily fired. When the Union had him reinstated, foremen persistently harassed him and eventually transferred him with a pay cut to the brake ovens, an area where the average temperature is 120°F.

Johnson's protests led management to fire him for 'insubordination' and on July 15, 1970, he was escorted out of the plant by armed guards. Shortly afterwards, he returned with a carbine, indicating that he was seeking the general foreman. During the subsequent events, his own foreman, a second foreman and a job setter who had attempted to disarm him were killed.

James Johnson refused to be dehumanized and destroyed by a merciless, racist system. He was a political prisoner and in the words of his attorney, "This is a political trial, of a system that can drive a worker to such a point in his fight against oppression and inhuman working conditions . . . It's not James Johnson that is on trial, it is the system that creates such terrible conditions that a worker lashes out."

James Johnson has been found not guilty by reason of insanity, a condition, according to his lawyers, which was a direct outgrowth of the oppressive circumstances surrounding his job.

MARTIN SOSTRE

A few years ago, Martin Sostre, a Black Puerto Rican, opened the Afro-Asian Bookstore in a Black community in Buffalo, New York. He had worked in a steel mill in order to raise money for the operation of the Bookstore and community center. F.B.I. and local police surveillance and harassment became more intense as people began to relate to the center and the regularly scheduled educational activities it sponsored.

In the summer of 1967, the Black community in Buffalo erupted in rebellion. During the three days of the uprising, Brother Sostre allowed his store to be used as a haven for those who were fleeing tear gas and bullets. This was apparently the incident which stamped him as an enemy to be destroyed in the eyes of the police.

On July 4, the police raided the store, arresting Brother Sostre as well as a co-worker, Geraldine Robinson. Brother Sostre was charged with riot, arson, possession of narcotics and assault. His case finally came to trial in March 1968 after he had spent almost eight months in jail because of an outrageous bail set by the court. During his confinement the heads of the police department, and the Buffalo news media repeatedly proclaimed his guilt, and whipped up a racist hysteria among Buffalo's white citizenry. Brother Sostre's trial lasted three days. Manifestly innocent of the drug charges, he was nevertheless convicted of possession and sale of narcotics and given a sentence of 30 to 41 years. The jury was all-white.

This was not his first experience in prison—he had been incarcerated from 1952 to 1964. Even then he had been the target of political reprisals for he was denied parole in 1957 after he challenged the composition of the all-white parole board.

In prison on the most recent charges he has continued his educational work among prisoners. This brought him harsh punishment —373 successive days he was kept in solitary confinement. His release from isolation came as a result of a suit he filed against the State of New York for cruel and unusual punishment. As a result of that suit Brother Sostre was awarded thirteen thousand dollars in damages for his treatment in Green Haven, N.Y. State Prison. The Judge also ruled that the prison officials were forbidden to return him to solitary confinement without an impartial due process hearing; the Judge ordered a halt to prison censorship of his correspondence with attorneys, courts and public officials.

The most recent development in his case may very well lead to his release from prison. The state's star witness has retracted his testimony. This principal prosecution witness, Arto (Toby) Williams, has signed an affidavit recanting his court testimony in which he claimed to have bought heroin on July 15, 1967 from Brother Sostre. Attorneys for Brother Sostre filed a motion for a new trial on April 19 (1971) on the basis of the affidavit. Their motion is pending, and Brother Sostre remains in prison—now about to begin his fifth year of confinement.

LUIS TALAMANTEZ

Minor scuffles and fights are naturally common occurrences in jails and prisons where conditions of confinement raise the tension level exceedingly high. Although the rise in political consciousness among prisoners has brought about a marked decrease in internecine hostility, the fights are still inevitable. They are generally accepted by prison officials as part of the routine, just as the minor disciplinary measures they mete out for such incidents are routine. When, in fact, prisoners channel their aggression towards one another, the officials feel relatively comfortable, having less to fear themselves.

Luis Talamantez was involved in one such scuffle, yet he has received no minor punishment. He is presently facing the gas chamber or life imprisonment as the possible outcome of a trial on charges of assault. An excerpt from one of his letters should convince us that he is one of the many prison victims of political persecution: "I am a 20th century revolutionario [who belongs] to a world state with no barriers to the brotherhood of man, I do not belong to the American fascist state." He believes that La Raza must play a significant part in overthrowing the American government, "the enemy of the whole world."

Like so many other captives, Talamantez acquired his political understanding and first expressed his commitment while in prison. He has been in San Quentin since 1965 serving time for two armed robbery convictions. San Quentin officials are determined that he either leaves in a coffin or not at all.

LOS SIETE DE LA RAZA

San Francisco's Mission District, like ghettos and barrios throughout the country, is always teeming with white policemen, charged with preserving the status quo of misery. On May 1, 1969, Mario Martinez had planned to take three brothers, Jose Rios, Babe Menedez and Gary Lescallett to register at the College of San Mateo. Together with Gio Lopez, they were stopped by two plainclothes policemen who claimed they were investigating a burglary. Every barrio inhabitant knows that he is always susceptible to being ordered to submit himself to police investigation. A scuffle occurred; when it terminated one cop was dead, the other wounded, both shot with the wounded cop's gun, and the five brothers had left the scene.

They were subsequently charged, along with two brothers, Nelson Rodriguez and Tony Martinez, who were not even on the scene, with murder, assault and burglary. Eventually, all except Gio Lopez, who is presently in Cuba, surrendered themselves.

The Martinez brothers and Brother Rodriguez had been enrolled in the College Readiness Program at San Mateo College and were recognized student and community leaders. In 1968 they were involved in agitation to prevent a cutback in funds for the program. Brother Rodriguez was expelled for his leadership in the San Mateo College strike which coincided with the Third World Liberation Front Strike at San Francisco State College.

In their community street organizing, they attempted to kindle interest in education. The dead cop, who was well acquainted with their activities, had once told them, "We know you guys want to overthrow the government, but you're not going to do it while we're around."

Following their arrests, a massive campaign in their defense was launched. The 'Free Los Siete' signs throughout the Mission District indicated the strong sentiment of the people. It was revealed at the trial, which lasted from June to November, 1970, that the wounded cop had actually pulled the trigger. Yet their acquittal must be attributed to the intense mass activity around the case.

Brother Tony Martinez and Brother Rodriguez were acquitted of all charges, but the jury was hung with respect to the burglary charges for the remaining four. Exasperated by this defeat, the prosecutor immediately filed charges of armed robbery and car theft against all the brothers in connection with an incident which occurred during their original flight. (They had been certain they would not receive a fair trial.)

Brothers Lescallett and Menedez were arrested in April, 1971 for still another armed robbery. The whereabouts of the remaining four, who did not appear for a hearing on the first robbery charge, are not known.

Their defense committee, also called Los Siete de la Raza, continues to work for the freedom of the two imprisoned brothers. In addition they operate a free medical clinic and La Raza Legal

Defense which deals with the daily incidents of police brutality and the numerous cases of Chicanos who are railroaded into jails and prisons.

REIES TIJERINA

Since the Treaty of Guadalupe Hidalgo between Mexico and the United States in 1848, Mexican-Americans have lost over 4,000,-000 acres of land-grant territory in the Southwest. The Chicano demand for lands illegally wrested from their ancestors received militant expression as early as 1963 in the Alianza Federale de Mercedes. This mass movement, deeply rooted in the rural population in northern New Mexico was headed by Reies Tijerina. In 1966, it was estimated that the organization had a membership of over 14,000 families.

An extensive range of tactics was employed by the Alianza, from demonstrations and protest marches to mass, armed occupation of the lands they claimed. In October, 1966 they took over Carson National Forest, the old San Joaquin del Rio de Chama land grant. After it was renamed the People's Republic of San Joaquin, the Alianzans arrested two forest rangers for trespassing and their jeeps were confiscated.

The day before the Alianza's national conference was scheduled to take place in June, 1967, it was arbitrarily pronounced an unlawful assembly by the local District Attorney, who threatened to arrest all the participants. That same day he rounded up 18 Alianzans on charges which were clearly fabricated. The District Attorney's actions, undisguised violations of the Alianzan's constitutional rights, prompted other members to plan a citizen's arrest. Twenty armed men, deputized by the People's Republic of San Joaquin, descended upon Tiera Amarrillo courthouse and seeking the District Attorney, whom they never located, held it for 90 minutes. In the course of the raid, a policeman went for his gun and he and the local jailor were wounded. An undersheriff and a reporter were escorted away from the scene, but later released. Ten Alianzans were brought up on charges.

When Brother Tijerina was tried for kidnapping in 1968, he acted as his own attorney and as a consequence of his compelling political defense as well as the mass defense waged by the Alianza, he was acquitted. The presiding judge, a Chicano whose father as governor of New Mexico had staunchly defended the rights of his people, gave an unprecedented instruction to the jury: ". . . anyone, including a state police officer, who intentionally interferes with a lawful attempt to make a citizen's arrest does so at his own peril, since the arresting citizens are entitled under the law to use whatever force is reasonably necessary to defend themselves in the process of making said citizen's arrest."

The verdict was a tremendous victory, not only for the Alianza, for whom the citizen's arrest was an important tool, but for the movement everywhere. New Mexico authorities, however, had further plans to silence Tijerina. In June, 1969, he was rearrested on charges stemming from the 1966 Carson National Forest incident. Convicted of assault on the two forest rangers, who had not been harmed at all and arson in connection with a forest sign which his wife, Patsy had admittedly burned, he received two and three year sentences for the respective charges. His wife was never brought to trial.

While in Federal prison he was charged with a new set of offenses arising from the Tiera Amarrillo courthouse raid, among them, assault on the jailor. Speedily convicted, he received concurrent prison terms of one to five and two to ten years. At present, Brother Tijerina is still doing time for the Carson National Forest incident, imprisoned in a Federal medical facility in Springfield, Missouri. His health has seriously deteriorated and the alleged medical treatment he is receiving for a malignant tumor in his throat has apparently worsened his condition. All efforts to obtain outside medical aid have so far proved futile. The authorities who originally refused to release him on bail because he was "a danger to the community," are preparing the way towards his total elimination.

LOLITA LEBRON

The heroic Puerto Rican Independence struggle has claimed innumerable lives and many partisans are presently being held captive in U.S. prisons.

Seventeen years ago on March 1, 1954 while the Organization of American States, the U.S. dominated organ of imperialism in Latin America, was in session in Caracas, Venezuela, four Puerto Rican partisans staged a raid on the House of Representatives in Washington. They were attempting to dramatically force the attention of the world on the callous oppression of the Puerto Rican people.

Lolita Lebron, a Puerto Rican living in New York, led other members of their independence organization in this offensive. Standing in the spectators gallery, they opened fire on the congress while a resolution concerning Mexican migrant voters was being put to a vote. This moment was apparently chosen to demonstrate their solidarity with all oppressed peoples in Latin America.

At the time of the shooting, the Puerto Rican flag was raised amid cries of "Long Live Puerto Rico." Five congressmen were wounded.

Sister Lebron, sentenced from 25 to 65 years in prison, is still behind bars in a Federal prison in Virginia. The three brothers are in Leavenworth.

This incident was similar to the attempt three and a half years earlier in November, 1951, by two Puerto Rican nationalists to kill President Truman. Gurselio Torresola was killed, and Oscar Collazo was sentenced to death. Truman later commuted his sentence to life and he is presently in prison.

The Young Lords Party, a revolutionary Puerto Rican organization is seeking to wage a mass campaign around Lolita Lebron, Oscar Collazo and other partisans of the independente movement imprisoned in the U.S.

PUYALLUP 59

Native Americans in Tacoma, Washington have been waging an aggressive and resolute struggle around issues central to their survival. In flagrant violation of the 1853 Treaty of Medicine Creek, the Fish and Game Authority, at the behest of commercial fishing interests, has severely restricted the Indians' rights to fish for salmon in the Puyallup and Nisqually Rivers.

In July, 1970 a Fish Camp was established on Puyallup reservation land under the leadership of Survival of American Indians. On September 9, State and City police staged a raid, shooting, tear-gassing and beating the fishermen and women. Fifty-nine were arrested, among them a few white supporters—and were held on charges ranging from unlawful assembly, inciting to riot and failure to disperse to assault and possession of arms.

At their arraignment, the defendants were chained in groups of ten—an appropriate expression of the U.S. government's centuries-old genocidal treatment of Native Americans. The chief prosecutor of the case, a co-owner of a sports fisherman resort which caters to salmon fishermen, is in no position to pretend he will mete out justice. Only eight of the defendants have been tried as yet; the trials are expected to continue through the fall of '71.

The Indians have been subjected to persistent intimidation, sabotage and violence by local sports fishermen and vigilante groups. In January, 1971, Hank Adams, one of the fifty-nine defendants and director of Survival of American Indians was shot in the stomach as he sat in his car beside the river where his nets had been cast.

Johnvigel Orlando Chiquiti, who acted as his own attorney during the first trial was told that the nature of the land and the Indians' relation to the land could not be discussed in court. He replied: "If the nature of the land is not admissible then I am not admissible. The earth is my mother. When I die I return to my mother. You pour feces in our sacred river, filthy smoke in our sky. The wrong people are in court. Someone wants our land, someone wants our fish."

HARRISBURG 8

J. Edgar Hoover's pronouncements do not easily engender shock. His ultra-rightist hysteria is widely known. Having pursued Communists, Black activists, he has now launched a vendetta against the anti-war movement. In November, 1970, testifying before a Senate appropriations sub-committee, Hoover announced "an incipient plot on the part of an anarchist group" to blow up government underground heating systems in Washington. He additionally accused them of planning to kidnap a highly placed government official, demanding a cessation of the bombing in Indochina and the release of all political prisoners as ransom. This anarchist group was supposed to consist of priests, nuns, teachers, students, led by two priests, Philip and Daniel Berrigan.

The two brothers were already serving prison terms for anti-war activity at a Federal prison in Danbury, Connecticut. In 1967, Philip and others had poured their blood over draft records stored in the Baltimore Selective Service Headquarters stating that "we pour [our blood] upon these draft files to illustrate that with them and these offices begins the pitiful waste of American and Vietnamese blood ten thousand miles away." He, his brother and 9 others burned 1-A draft records in 1968 in Catonsville, Maryland. Philip is serving a six year sentence, Daniel a three year term.

As a consequence of Hoover's charges, an enormous public outcry was heard. Representative William R. Anderson (D-Tenn.) publicly criticized Hoover for operating with "tactics reminiscent of McCarthyism, using newspaper headlines and scare dramatics rather than the due process of law. . ." Nixon, of course, revealed his approval of Hoover's action.

Under the pressure of numerous demands to either repudiate his irresponsible accusations of known advocates of non-violence or formerly bring charges, Hoover elected to prepare the way for what even the St. Louis *Post-Dispatch* has called one of the flimsiest indictments on record. In January, six persons were indicted for conspiracy to kidnap Henry A. Kissinger, and to blow up the heating systems of Federal buildings in Washington: Dr. Eqbal Ahmad, Father Philip Berrigan, Sister Elizabeth McAlister, Father Neil McLoughlin, Anthony Scoblick (a married priest), and Father Joseph Wenderoth. Seven others, including Daniel Berrigan, were named as co-conspirators, though not defendants.

Implicitly confirming the tenuousness of the charges, a new indictment was returned in April, dropping the names of three co-conspirators not charged and reducing the kidnap conspiracy charge which carried a maximum sentence of life to the one with a five year maximum. However, in an attempt to broaden the attack on the anti-war movement, the defendants were further accused of plans to destroy draft records in several cities and two more defendants were named: Mrs. Mary Cain Scoblick (a former nun) and John Theodore Glick.

The significance of the attack on the Harrisburg 8 must be sought within the context of the rapidly expanding use of the judiciary to arrest the development of all forms of opposition to government policy. The increasing recourse to conspiracy laws— vague crimes of intent which require no overt illegal activity— marks a definite deterioration in the judicial system, a fascist weapon which can be used against any American citizen. As Eqbal Ahmad has observed, "Our trial will force us again to demonstrate our capacity for continued resistance against the injustice and the erosion of democratic processes in the United States today."

KENT STATE UNIVERSITY

As the student protests have grown so has the repression meted out to the students. It is now not unusual to hear of police and National Guard troops shooting students. In Berkeley in May 1969 over 100 students were shot by the police—one died, another blinded for life. The incident became known as the Battle for People's Park. Police have not hesitated to shoot into student dormitories in the dead of night; or into crowds of unarmed students in the course of peaceful protests. This has been particularly evident at predominantly Black or all-Black institutions, for example, the shootings at the State University of Ohio; Texas Southern University; or the Orangeburg Massacre in Orangeburg, South Carolina. In May 1970 two Black students were shot and killed by police at Jackson State College in Mississippi. In all of these incidents the police have ultimately found themselves absolved of any guilt.

On May 4, 1970, at the height of nationwide student strikes against the U.S. invasion of Cambodia, four students at Kent State University in Ohio were shot and killed and several others were wounded by National Guard troops who fired point blank into a crowd of unarmed students. Five months later the Ohio State Grand Jury which investigated the entire incident, absolved the National Guard of any responsibility saying that the May 4 protests "constituted a riot" and that the National Guardsmen "fired their weapons in the honest and sincere belief . . . that they would suffer serious bodily injury had they not done so." The Grand Jury's report flatly contradicted the report of the Presidential Commission on Campus Unrest which called the shootings "unwarranted and inexcusable."

The Ohio Grand Jury in October 1970 instead indicted 25 people on the campus, singling out known political activists, for first degree riot, second degree riot, arson and assault, and set bail at between one thousand and seven thousand dollars for each person.

Among the first persons arrested were Craig Morton, President of the student body; Dr. Thomas S. Lough, an associate professor of sociology; Kenneth Hammond, a former SDS (Students for a Democratic Society) organizer, and now with the Kent Liberation Front; Alan Corfora and Joe Lewis both of whom were among the nine students wounded.

In addition, the campus community at Kent is facing other repressive actions: two court injunctions prohibiting demonstrations or criticism of the Grand Jury report; and a new repressive state law providing punishment for anyone who creates a "substantial risk" of campus disruption; stricter university regulations limiting the right to protest; and a right-wing bombing of a building that housed offices of the Black United Students.

President Nixon gave personal sanction to the actions of the Grand Jury when he appeared October 20 at a rally in Columbus, Ohio, campaigning on behalf of Senator Robert Taft (running for Governor—he was defeated in November, 1970). Nixon said: "All over this country today, we see a rising tide of terrorism, of crime and on the campuses of our universities we have seen those who instead of engaging in peaceful dissent, engage in violence."

Trials of the Kent students are pending.

JOHN SINCLAIR

John Sinclair was a key organizer of the White Panther Party in Detroit. As a result of his radical political and cultural activities he was framed by the police on various drug charges—an increasingly common police tactic to suppress dissident individuals and groups.

Today, John Sinclair, 29 years old, is serving a sentence in Michigan prisons for a term of nine-and-a-half to ten years (the maximum allowed by Michigan State law, after being convicted in July, 1969 with having given 2 marijuana cigarettes to an under-cover police agent who posed as his friend in the privacy of Sinclair's home. The original charge was sale of marijuana. But, it was dismissed when a judge held that Sinclair was unlawfully entrapped into giving the cigarettes to the undercover agent. Yet, the same illegal evidence was used to convict him of the possession charge.

Sinclair's request for bail pending appeal of his conviction was denied by the sentencing judge who said:

"John Sinclair has been out to show that the law means nothing to him, and to his ilk. And that they can violate the law with impunity. . . . Well, the time has come. The day has come. And you may laugh, Mr. Sinclair, but you will have a long time to laugh about it."

Persons convicted of violent crimes, persons claimed to be part of organized criminal syndicates are granted bail pending appeal as a matter of course in Michigan. But, so far the Michigan appellate courts have denied bail to Sinclair. His conviction was affirmed by one Michigan appeals court, and he is now appealing to the Michigan Supreme Court. His chief lawyer, Justin C. Ravitz has argued in the appeal that,

"Marijuana is not on trial here. John Sinclair is not on trial. What is really on trial is the integrity and independence of the judiciary."

Shortly after his conviction, law enforcement officers sought to guard against a reversal of Sinclair's conviction and his freedom. They pulled out a confirmed and unstable addict on whose testimony they charged Sinclair with conspiracy to bomb a CIA office in Ann Arbor, Michigan. Sinclair had met the witness only once or twice in passing, he did not even know of the existence of the CIA office, and the bombing alleged in the indictment against him occurred more than a year before the witness sought to implicate Sinclair. This charge is pending in the federal courts. It will be dismissed unless the United States Supreme Court reverses a ruling by the lower courts that there was illegal wiretapping of one of Sinclair's co-defendant's.

Michigan prison officials banished him to a maximum security institution in the most remote part of the state, and they have sought to isolate him from other prisoners. Yet, John Sinclair has remained resolute. While legal action is being taken to secure his release, he has brought to public attention the inhuman and degrading conditions prevailing in Michigan's prisons and jails. Recently, he participated as a party to a suit in which a Michigan court has ordered that the largest pretrial detention facility in Michigan be closed unless officials remedy its abominable conditions in the next several months.

MARIE HILL

Seventeen year old Marie Hill has lived on death row in a North Carolina prison for over two years. She is without doubt a political prisoner, not because she has been involved in political actions against the Establishment, but rather because the State of North Carolina, through a political act of terror, has condemned her to die. Marie Hill is Black. Like millions of Black people, she was an easy target, particularly in a small southern city, of the racist-inspired, draconian efforts of police, judges and juries to assert their supremacy.

From 1930 to 1969, out of a total of 3,817 executions, 2,066 involved Black people—well over 50 per cent when Blacks constitute some 15 per cent of the population.

Sister Hill was arrested in October, 1968 in South Carolina, and at the age of 15 charged with the murder of a white grocery store proprietor in Rocky Mountain, North Carolina. The unfolding of events in the aftermath of the arrest is a classic study in the transformation of the law-enforcement-judicial network into a tool of terror against Blacks.

She was coerced into signing a confession, without having received the advice of an attorney, a confession she later repudiated, saying, "I had no choice." Ill-informed of her right to resist extradition, she was speedily transported to North Carolina. Intensive in-custody interrogation—inherently coercive—with no accompanying attempt to apprise her of her right to remain silent led her to break down once again. This throng of white policemen even tricked her into waiving a preliminary hearing.

A week had already passed before she was permitted to speak to her parents or even confer with her attorney.

On December 17, 1968, she was brought to trial. The prosecution had no evidence of her guilt save her own confession which she vigorously repudiated on the witness stand. The state could not even offer proof that she had been present at the scene of the killing and although the prosecutor referred to objects touched by the perpetrator of the crime, no fingerprints were produced.

After two days, Marie Hill, then 15 years of age, was found guilty of first degree murder and was sentenced to die.

In their appeal to the U.S. Supreme Court, her lawyers have stated: "Such a penalty—not law, but Terror—is the instrument of totalitarian government. It is a cruel and unusual punishment, forbidden by the Eighth Amendment."

Emmett Till was lynched outside the law, Marie Hill is being lynched under the color of law.

6

Bobby Seale
and Ericka Huggins

Bobby Seale and Ericka Huggins, leaders of the Black Panther Party, recently stood trial in New Haven, Connecticut each charged with two capital offenses: murder and conspiracy to commit murder. After their six-month-long trial finally ended in a hung jury, the judge, in a landmark decision on May 25, 1971, dismissed all charges against Bro. Bobby and Sister Ericka, maintaining that given the extensive and exaggerated press coverage, especially in New Haven, it would be impossible for them to receive a fair trial.

Bobby Seale was first arrested on August 19, 1969 on conspiracy charges stemming from the demonstrations in Chicago in August 1968 at the Democratic Party National Convention. Bro. Bobby was abducted by Federal authorities and taken to Chicago to stand trial. The proceedings began before his attorney, Charles Garry, who was ill and hospitalized, could attend the trial. Bro. Bobby vigorously asserted his constitutional right to act as his own counsel or to have counsel of his own choosing. For these protests he was brutally gagged, bound and beaten in the courtroom. His case was arbitrarily severed from the seven other defendants and he received a four year prison sentence for contempt of court. Subsequently the government dropped the conspiracy charges against Bro. Bobby (but not the contempt charges) for "lack of sufficient evidence." Arrested on new charges of murder, arising out of the death of a Connecticut member of the Panther Party, Alex Rackley, Bro. Bobby had remained in custody for almost two years, convicted of absolutely nothing. Following the dismissal of the Connecticut charges Bro. Bobby was finally released from custody on bail over the government's objection, pending the outcome of appeals for his Chicago contempt citation, and the efforts of California authorities to revoke his probation from a previous arrest in that state.

Ericka Huggins had been in custody since the Spring of 1969. Her husband Jon Huggins had been murdered by police agents in Los Angeles on January 17, 1969. She has a daughter, Mai, who is now 2½ years old. This beautiful Black sister has been a leading organizer for the Black Panther Party both in Los Angeles and in her home State of Connecticut.

Brother Bobby and Sister Ericka maintained their innocence throughout the long ordeal of the trial. Court testimony during their trial revealed that Rackley was in fact killed by a self-admitted police agent, George Dams. Both Brother Bobby and Sister Ericka were clearly the victims of a police-FBI inspired racist plot designed to deal yet another repressive blow to the Black Panther Party. Ericka Huggins' poems, written in prison, are an eloquent testimony to her humanity; her spirit; and her devotion to the revolutionary movement.

> tall
> skinny
> plain
>
> tall
> skinny
> plain i am
> ericka, 22,
> fuzzy hair
> droopy eyes
> long feet
>
> > i love people
> > love nature
> > love love
> > i am a revolutionary
> > nothing special
> > > one soul

one life   willing
to give it
ready to die . . .

noises
sounds
unspoken words
feelings repressed because
the prison walls are also
soul walls
barriers
if only all barriers could be removed
and we could walk/ talk/ sing
be . . .
free of all psychological, spiritual
political, economic
boundaries
all of us all the freedom lovers of
the world but especially
right now—prisoners.

*21 december 1970
7 p.m.   niantic*

for paula:
(who ran from the camp
and was eventually caught)

hopes that render me speechless
fly through my soul
the reality of now is
too much to accept the
racism, fascism and oppression
we suffer / have suffered is
numbing my soul
if it is true that they
have stifled your attempt

91077

to breathe air and see
life and be a part of the
chaos that is the streets
then i cry inside
because no one will
    understand outside tears
    for you—or those like you—
    strange it is for you for i only
know your face and soul   personalities
        sometimes
        don't matter . . .
  but that's good enough   you are a
    part of me sister-love   the part of me
that has been and will one day be . . .
    every door is not locked

29 december 1970
after 9 p.m.

love spelled the same but meaning
    spiritually much more
      meaning that we realize the creative
    forces to be energy and that we as a
    part of that must
      come together
      come
    together
wow—there are tears in my laughter

17 december 1970, 6 p.m.
niantic prison

On Sunday, the 13th of December, the
New Haven Women's Liberation Rock Band
played a concert at Niantic State Prison.

reflections on Sunday:

sounds that come from the soul are always
   the same
           free
           open sounds
           giving
the kind that reach out and touch—

that's what our sisters did / minimum
touching maximum / showing oppression
           and the wish for its
      removal . . .
   feeling those sounds
   seeing them felt on others
   watching faces smile
   really smile for the first time in months—
getting high—on the natural power of the
people to resist/to smile/to laugh/to sing/
           shout/love/give
           ever here!!!
wild hair, funky guitar
long hair funky voice (someone said
      bessie smith came to mind)
      hair—all lengths, legs, arms, smiles, music—
         SISTERS—and us . . .
      raggedy peacoats, cotton dressed, rocking,
                           swaying
                           screaming

        enjoying it—
        crying too—even if not too many
let the tears fall free
. . . us—black/brown/white/poor—SISTERS
and it was all a total exchange
        of energy
communication
even if we did not share words
we all knew their soul-sounds were

saying
we understand
we know
we can see what amerika is doing
to you—mother/daughter/child/woman
     of oppression—

we can see, they sung
and our voices answered their guitars,
horns flute-voice-cowbell-tambourene demand for freedom with an unspoken right on
. . . a feeling there that one day—soon—
     all people will be free . . . and
                    we left
                    stronger
able to smile (for a moment) . . .
till we returned to
rules that degrade
schedules that destroy sanity
racism that they cannot see
sexism that rapes us of our womanhood . . .

and the locks, keys, windows, walls, doors,
     threats
     warnings
     bribes that harden our hearts and
chain our souls . . .
     the time
         must be
             seized
                 venceremos!

                the oldness of new things
                fascinate me like a new
                feeling about love about people
                snow, highways that
          sparkle at night, talk,

laughter . . .
that old longing for freedom
   that this place constantly
renews—it all makes
me know that humankind
has longed to be free ever forever
since its break from the
whole
      maybe the longing for
      freedom will soon make
      others homesick for our
      natural state in / with
      earth, air, fire, water
         not dead
         but living
         not asking for freedom—
         but free—

for connie, a rollingstone

      if there is cosmic beauty
      then your face holds it
      if there is human understanding
then your soul is capable of it
if a mind ever thought of freedom
yours has flown to where freedom
lives and has drifted back
here to tell your body about it
and you long for it
         i can see it in your eyes
         aquarius sister-love
         i can see it . . . you
         must know that one
         day we will all
           be
         FREE

whiz ,whir, spin
flow melt fly
      float
      blend
      become
      be . . . but not until
   the people are free
   not until there is time
   to take time to be *free*
   if that makes sense
          free to exchange energy
             communicate
          productively create.
        i must not forget that i can
      not love everyone now, that putting
    the real truth into practice now will only
   disillusion those who take it for its verbal value
  i must wait to really smile inside and pass it on
  i must reject the silly feeling to jump, scream, enjoy the cosmos
disoriented as it is now—not until we have all evolved more
not until there are no more incarnations of hitler unevolved
not until the racism/oppression that has raped our souls
has been destroyed then we can all whiz, whir, spin
          flow, melt, fly
            float
            blend
            become
            be . . .

for sam a brother* / friend of the people
i remember now that sam used to call me sweet sister
and his voice had a ring to it like music / sort of a
soft-fast-hardworking voice (always a smile to it tho)
     that's how his soul was—soft yet strong

* (Sam Napier was murdered by police agents in New York City, April 17, 1971. He was a member of the Black Panther Party, and circulation manager for the Party's Intercommunal News Service. He leaves a wife, Pauline Napier, and two children, Stag and Huey.)

fast, yet not by bypassing the
needs of the people / the FREE-dom of the people /
    hardworking—yes he was
the sweet engraved in the issues of our
paper—in good times / in hard, bitter, bad times . . .
    he is not/ nor will be forgotten—he was
too symbolic of all we stand for dedication,
    love for the people self less ness
seems as tho he was taken away so unnecessarily
seems as tho we've got a lot to learn about this struggle of ours
seems as tho this country, amerikkka, wants to wipe out
  all the samual napiers
    jonathan jacksons
    bobby seales of the whole world
seems as tho we have a WHOLE LOT of work to do
    love to give
    freedom to give. Good brother
. . . i cannot be there/ bobby cannot so—on that, i place
a kiss on your forehead and a dandelion in your hand
(a dandelion because they grow wild/free/rebellious over the
      earth)
(like the people—poor people/ oppressed people.)
. . . this may be said many times, but it is sincere—
. . . you will not be forgotten, we love you, sweet brother
    we love you/

    . . . ericka

A Message from Prison

In February 1971 an anti-war conference was held in Ann Arbor,
Michigan to launch nationwide support for the "People's Peace
Treaty" which had been signed earlier by students from Vietnam
and from the United States. Brother Bobby and Sister Ericka sent
this taped message to the conference.

Brother Bobby:

To make this racist railroading trial of Sister Ericka and myself a focal point to further educate the people, massive demonstrations should occur around the end of the trial. There must also be teach-ins of people's revolutionary ideology—on inter-communalism and the work that political prisoners do and did before being incarcerated.

Ericka and I feel that the demonstrations at the end of our trial should mark a massive national beginning of a struggle to free all political prisoners and prisoners of war throughout the country.

We must educate the people more broadly about the people's revolutionary movement, and about the people's struggle to end war, racism and repression. Of course, we revolutionary, peace-loving people who want to end war, racism and repression know the general outlines of what we must attempt to do to help make a peace-loving society and world. We must make more widely known what we believe in for the people, all the people, beyond our beautiful rhetoric of "All Power to the People."

The youth in America with their peace-loving states of mind and a loving will to see that all forms of exploitation, oppression, war and racism end—really are America. Humane people. The other is Amerikkka . . . an American nightmare, not the "American Dream."

The American Dream is for world peace and an end to oppression and racism; this American Dream lies buried within the 60% of the population under 30 years of age. (Oh, I'm not 34 years old! Being on death row right now and looking back on the ten years I've been in the struggle, I feel like a new born adolescent with vigor and love for the people in the whole world.)

I saw on the eleven o'clock news where Sister Angela Davis has beautifully taken the position of defending herself with the assistance of fine lawyers. That is right, right, right on time! She's out of sight. Beautiful, full womanhood, revolutionary mind, heart and soul. It seems like it might be summer before that fascist railroad starts . . .

. . . Regular communications to Ericka and me would be good.

We do feel that we have some significant things to say with respect to rallying and mobilizing the people around political prisoners.

Sister Ericka:

Bobby's said what's important; educating the people about all political prisoners of our war against oppression. No heroes, no rhetoric, but massive educational rallies and street politicizing, showing how POW's are examples of the situation every one of us face.

And we have to do it with love, you know, and the understanding that we need more than just movement people and sympathizers at these rallies. We need whole families of people. Young, old, black, brown, red, yellow, beige, whatever. Male, female, gay— everybody. Because everybody is faced with Amerikan oppression and all of us are the America that will be, you dig it? So we all really have to get to work and focus on the people, not individuals.

Marin County jail
San Rafael, California
May 2, 1971

A Letter from Angela

Dearest Ericka, Sister, Comrade,

All your messages have been beautiful and inspiring.

It's been a long time—over two years—since our last meeting. I recall, however, as if it were yesterday, that cold, rainy evening, submerged under sadness and rage, those agonizing hours we were stationed in the parking lot outside Sybil Brand, anxiously awaiting your release from jail. The outrageous assassination of John and Bunchy had come so unexpectedly, engendering an atmosphere of shock, incredulity and ungovernable anger. But our paramount concern was you Ericka. Your husband, closest comrade in struggle, your love, the father of Mai, your new-born child, had just been slain by the bullets of our foes. You had been immediately arrested on a manifestly fabricated charge—conspiracy to retaliate, or something equally ridiculous. We were hurting with your pain.

While we watched your approach—you were now walking through the jail's iron gates—our silence was throbbing with inexpressible pain. And as we were desperately searching for words to convey our unyielding solidarity, it was your strong, undaunted voice that broke the silence. *You* were asking us why we appeared so thoroughly dejected. Had we forgotten the infinite fortitude the long struggle ahead would require? Your unflinching determination as you clenched your fist and said, 'All Power to the People,' prompted me to think to myself, this must be the strongest, most courageous Black woman in America.

It was then that I realized that the guardians of this depraved, racist order would never be satisfied until they contained your strength, until they isolated you from our people. When a few months later the news of your arrest in New Haven reached us, I was appalled, though in light of your magnificent work in the New Haven Black community, as before in Los Angeles, I was not terribly surprised.

Just recently I read in the Newsletter covering the progress of your trial that on account of F.B.I. agents' immunity to subpoenas, their heavy involvement in the case would remain obscure. Couple the attempt to conceal the role of the F.B.I. in the events preceding your arrest with the announcement a few months later by J. Edgar Hoover that the Black Panther Party is "without question, the greatest threat to the internal security of this country" and the real conspirators should emerge with striking clarity.

As long as sisters and brothers like you and Bobby continue to articulate the deepest instinctive feelings of oppressed people and to illuminate the path towards concrete expression of our grievances and our demands for revolutionary change, our adversaries will not fail to rave about threats to their internal security. And actually, this is the way it should be.

This is all I'm trying to say: we know why you have been locked up behind the walls of Niantic State Farm for over two years and we know why Bobby has been thrown into dungeon after dungeon, from Chicago to San Francisco to New Haven. Black people—not simply Black people, but people of all colors and all nations— are swiftly becoming conscious of the critical importance of freeing you and Bobby.

I've been trying to keep abreast of developments in your trial as well as less available details of the happenings in your life at Niantic State Farm. The interview in this week's issue of the Black Panther Party newspaper with the two sisters recently released from the prison was tremendously moving. Their utter respect for you, for the ideas and ideals you represent, the leadership you have given the sisters at Niantic, all this was unmistakably clear—the radiant presence I recall so vividly from the days we worked together in Los Angeles. I thought the idea of Sisterlove Collective positively powerful: the mere notion of sharing among prisoners militates all the internal hostilities officials invariably attempt to engender.

You must know I've been in total isolation since I was extradicted from New York to San Rafael. I miss the sisters in New York a great deal—the discussions, the clandestinely organized demonstrations, their warmth, their instinctive grasp of the concrete realities of oppression. I miss the pictures of you and other revolutionary heroes and heroines torn from contraband newspapers and pasted on cell walls with institutional lye soap.

So much work remains to be done around prisons in general— pending revolutionary change, we have to raise the demand that prisons in their present form be abolished. As an inevitable by-product of a male-oriented society and consequently still largely male-oriented movement—which women however are increasingly contesting—sufficient attention has not been devoted to women in prison.

I have often heard the rumor that as compared to men's prisons, women's institutions are humanely benign, the gravest problem being the tendency to 'baby' the women captives. This is a myth which must be immediately smashed. Perhaps it is true that white middle-class women, if they are arrested at all, are given preferential treatment, but for the vast majority of women prisoners— who are Black, Chicano and Puerto Rican—the notion of mildness in the midst of coercion is a blatant misrepresentation.

In the women's House of Detention in New York, at least 95% of the prisoners were Black and Puerto Rican. On my floor, approximately 50 of us—two corridors—would take meals together. At no time during my imprisonment were there more than 6 white women in this group and 4 of them had been arrested for political offenses! Though there were a few openly sympathetic Black matrons (who, for example, would smuggle in to us political literature much in demand), treatment in general was far from delicate.

At the time of my arrest the whole building was astir with talk of demonstrations around all sorts of issues. The grievances advanced by the men in the Tombs were all equally reflective of conditions in the Women's House. As a retaliatory measure, the jail officials ordered all the women in a number of floors locked up in their miniscule cells (9' x 5' for two persons) for well over a week. (During this period they had shut me away in the psychiatric ward and later in total isolation.) All personal effects, down to cigarettes, toothbrushes and clothes were confiscated. Linen was removed from the bunks. The sisters were left in their cells with nothing but the night gowns they were wearing, the bare, cold, plastic-covered mattresses and the hordes of roaches and mice. This is not to mention the women who were taken to 4-A (the disciplinary block) or the sister who was so badly beaten by male guards that she had to spend two or three weeks in Bellevue Hospital. This is supposed to be mild treatment? That myth must definitely be shattered.

And the innocents—not just the victims of politically-inspired frameups—but the innocents whose sole crime is their color and their accidental birth into a racist universe. A sister who lived two cells away from me (her name was Helen) had been in the House of D for *18* months on a murder charge about which she had absolutely no knowledge. After 18 months of imprisonment with an exorbitant bail tantamount to no bail at all, the prosecutor decided to dismiss the charges for lack of evidence and as the result of a man's having confessed to the offense. Elated, Helen returned from court that day announcing that she would at last be able to walk under the sun once more. Her next court date, a week away, would mark her final day in the House of D. The entire floor celebrated her victory. The next week, amid tears and joy, she left us saying she would return soon to scream up at us from Greenwich Village sidewalk below.

That evening however her victory had proved to be short-lived, for the court van brought her back with the rest of the sisters and with her story of a new D.A. in the case. He wanted her to plead guilty to a lesser charge, "attempted manslaughter" after which he would credit her with time already served as the sentence. He was afraid, it seems, that once all charges were dismissed, she might sue for false arrest—for the 18 months the state had stolen from her life. Two months later when I left, Helen was yet in the cell two numbers away, still resolutely refusing to plead guilty for something in which she had played no part. She will be tried for murder and will doubtlessly be acquitted. But how can she ever be repaid for those long monotonous months of her life?

An inordinate amount of work around women's prisons remains to be done. As you well know, sisters behind these walls are urgently in need of outside encouragement and support. The Women's Bail Fund organized by a coalition of women's organizations in New York, whose inception was signalled by a massive people's demonstration outside the House of D, was a tremendous incentive for extensive political work inside. When I left, the entire jail was being organized, floor by floor, corridor by corridor, so that decisions concerning the women who got out on bail would be collectively made. Those who did leave would have to commit themselves to on-going work with the Fund.

Many more of these kinds of projects are needed: campaigns to uncover in their entirety the abominable conditions prevailing in women's institutions, from the inhuman circumstances of prison existence in general to the fascist techniques to which officials have recourse in attempting to create political neutrality and homogeneity.

Ultimately, we must all be liberated and as you have repeatedly insisted, only a strong people's thrust can set us free. You must be liberated, Ericka. Connie Tucker, imprisoned in Florida's Klan territory because she has been a consistent advocate of the rights and revolutionary ideals of Black people—she must be unchained. Marie Hill, sentenced to die at the age of 15 in a small racist Southern city—she must be rescued. And all our strong sisters, wherever they may be, must be enabled to enjoy the relative freedom of the streets in order to more vigorously embrace the tasks which lie ahead.

You, Ericka, have sketched the dimensions of that task better than anyone—I found this quote on the cover of an underground newspaper:

We must build a new world. All other generations have passed this responsibility on and it is time to stop the clocks and seize the time. Change, destroy and rebuild. It is time for us to build a new world free of selfishness, racism, narrow nationalism and the desire of any group to claim this world as their own. The universe belongs to the people—to love—to create—for each other.

The urgency of transforming this ideal into reality has been impressed upon us by all our fallen comrades—John, Bunchy, 'Lil Bobby, Jonathan, William Christmas, James McClain, Sam Napier. They must live again through us and our struggles. Through our children and our unborn, they must enjoy the rewards of victory— a victory towards which they have already made infinite contributions.

All my love to you, Ericka, to Bobby, to all the Sisters at Niantic.

Seize the Time!

ANGELA

IV

The Soledad Brothers
Fleeta Drumgo
John Clutchette
George Jackson

7

Letter from Fleeta

Dear Brothers and Sisters

The Department of Corrections doesn't exist! All institutions under such titles are barbaric, oppressive, racist and murderous institutions. This system of government is designed to oppress, exploit and intimidate, all that are not classified as a white Anglo-Saxon-bourgeois ruling clique. The hatred, violence and destruction imbedded in the system is the same fascist repression that is destroying the people in general, Black people in particular. Knowing this fact it is not difficult to understand that America is a prison. As Brother Huey P. Newton stated, the only difference is that one is maximum and the other minimum security.

It seems at times that the oppression and violence inflicted upon us here in the maximum security is more intense than that inflicted upon us in the minimum security, but really it's utterly impossible for me or any of us here to distinguish the oppression and violence we are all victimized by. I am constantly thinking about unemployment, under-employment, poverty and malnutrition that are the basic facts of our existence; it's this which sends persons to these concentration camps; it's this which causes so-called crime in general.

I like to express that there's a growing awareness behind the walls; we're seeing through the madness of capitalism, class interest, surplus value and imperialism, which this gestapo system perpetuates. It's this which we have to look at and understand in order to recognize the inhumanity inflicted upon the masses of the people here in America and abroad. As Brother Malcolm X once said, "We as people, as human beings have the basic human right to eliminate the conditions that have and are continuously destroying us."

The decadence and corruption in the present day society and in these concentration camps must be dealt with by the people, and the only way we can deal with it is uniting, becoming as one! Because people who are oppressed, exploited and deprived are one. What I am trying to relay is the fact that we are all prisoners, and under the yoke of fascist enslavement. Anyone who can deny this fact isn't really concerned about liberation; he considers himself free and the attitude relates directly to the petty-bourgeois class of society.

In conclusion let me say on behalf of all of us in the maximum, please don't reject and forget us, because this allows the monster to brutalize, murder and treat us inhumanly. We are of you, we love you and struggle with you.

Power to the People-Liberation in Our Time!

FLEETA DRUMGO

8

How a Prison
Picks Its Victims
by Eve Pell

Think of California's Monterey County and you'll probably imagine quaint shops in Carmel, gnarled pines hanging wind-swept above one of the most dramatic beaches on the West Coast, or exclusive mountain hide-aways for the wealthy. You may remember that Joan Baez has her school for non-violence in Monterey, that the Esalen Institute offers sessions in sensitivity training, or that hitch-hiking hippies are taking over beautiful Big Sur.

Images of the easy life come to mind quickly. But there is another side to the county not mentioned in Chamber of Commerce leaflets and not part of the tourists' beaten paths. Inland from the resorts lies the Salinas Valley, flat acres of rich farmland whose white owners once employed vigilance committees and strike-breakers to intimidate and occasionally kill migrant workers. This is the part of the county that John Steinbeck saw. South from Salinas is an even uglier reality—Soledad Prison. Here, the violence and brutality that were once part of the chaos of the Depression have been evoked again with the murders of three of the prison's Black inmates.

When Soledad (more properly known as California Training Facility at Soledad) opened in 1946, it was touted as a progressive institution. Perhaps it was, but over the years prisoners have come to know it as the "gladiator school" or the "front line" because of the intensity of the racial hostility which exists between guards and inmates, and among the inmates themselves. Letters detailing the brutality of daily life inside the prison have made their way to

inmates' families and attorneys and finally to the attention of legislators in Sacramento. Finally, in early June of this year, California
State Senator Mervyn Dymally made an inspection of the maximum
security part of the prison, accompanied by two staff members and
Bay Area attorney Fay Stender. The group wanted to distribute a
questionnaire, to be filled out and returned on the spot by prisoners
so that no one would be punished for complaining about conditions.

The plan ran afoul of Ray Procunier, Director of the California
Department of Corrections, and of the czars of the prison. "If
there's any questionnaire," said Procunier, "I'm going to put it in
there. If there's anything wrong going on down here, we want to
be the first to know about it." Dymally submitted, and after touring
the prison's O-wing, the senator's group reassembled in the
warden's office to talk over what they had learned from brief discussions with inmates. They were especially concerned about Black
prisoners' complaints about food being contaminated, urine in their
coffee and similar harassments.

"It's my opinion that the food is not being tampered with," said
Procunier. "From a management point of view, we don't want it.
There's just a bad set of feelings going around this joint." When
Dymally suggested that there must be some basis for the fact that
so many letters and complaints had mentioned this, Procunier
turned to his prison officials. "Now I want you to tell me the truth,"
he warned. "Has it ever happened that someone has urinated in
anyone's coffee?" When the four men shook their heads from side
to side in unison, he turned back, satisfied.

After they had asked a few more questions and received Procunier's arbitrary answers, Dymally's group left Soledad without
ever getting to the prison's major problem—the rampant racism
that has led to a series of murders of Black inmates and, more
recently, to the outrageous framing and prosecution of three others
who have become known as the Soledad Brothers.

A black inmate in Soledad's maximum security section wrote
recently about the racial hatred there: "On ———, A.B. and myself were transferred to Soledad Correctional Facility. We were
placed in the Max Row section, O-wing. Immediately entering
the sallyport area of this section I could hear inmates shouting
and making remarks such as, 'Nigger is a scum lowdown dog,' etc.

I couldn't believe my ears at first because I knew that if I could hear these things the officers beside me could too, and I started wondering what was going on. Then I fixed my eyes on the wing sergeant and I began to see the clear picture of why those inmates didn't care if the officials heard them instigating racial conflict. The sergeant was, and still is, a known prejudiced character towards Blacks. I was placed in cell No. ———, and since that moment up til now I have had no peace of mind. The white inmates make it a 24-hour job of cursing Black inmates just for kicks, and the officials harass us with consistency also."

On "Max Row," prisoners remain in solitary confinement in little cells like iron boxes twenty three-and-a-half hours a day. Heavy screens, not just bars, shut them in, and they are fed through holes in their respective doors.

Another prisoner wrote from O-wing about food service there: "The prison officials here stopped serving the meals and deliberately selected the Caucasian and Mexican inmates to serve the meals and they immediately proceeded to poison our meals by filling food to be issued to us with cleanser powder, crushed glass, spit, urine and feces while the officials stood by and laughed."

For many months prior to January 1970, inmates of O-wing had not been permitted to exercise in groups. The deputy super-intendent of Soledad, who has called "O" wing "a prison within a prison," explained that "difficulties between inmates had oc-curred, and fights—serious fights, assaults, assaults without weap-ons, assaults with weapons—had occurred when we attempted to permit people to exercise together." Last December, [1969] a new exercise yard was built for these inmates. It didn't open on schedule because some work remained unfinished. A Black pri-soner wrote, "I did notice that white inmates and officials were awfully cheerful for some reason or another and they continu-ously didn't forget to remind us of the yard opening soon."

In the second week of January, 13 inmates were skin-searched—stripped, their clothes examined, their buttocks parted and searched for concealed weapons. The guards found no weapons and allowed them into the yard. No guards went with them, but Guard O. G. Miller, known to be an expert marksman, was stationed in a tower 13 feet over the yard, armed with at least one loaded carbine.

Predictably, black and white inmates began to fight in the yard. Without a warning the guard in the tower fired four shots. Three Blacks—Alvin Miller, Cleveland Edwards, and W. L. Nolen— were fatally wounded, and one white was shot in the groin. At least one of the Blacks remained alive and moving. His friends wanted to get him to the prison hospital as fast as they could.

"I looked at the tower guard," one of them later explained, "and he was aiming the gun toward me and I thought then that he meant to kill me too, so I moved from the wall as he fired and went over to stand over inmate X, all the while looking the guard in the gun tower in the face. He aimed the gun at me again and I just froze and waited for him to fire, but he held his fire. After I saw he was not going to fire I pointed to where inmate X lay, with two other Black inmates bending over him, and started to walk to him very slowly. The inmate I had played handball with suggested that I take inmate X to the hospital so I kneeled so inmate X could be placed on my shoulder, then started to walk toward the door through which we had entered the yard, and the tower guard pointed the gun at me and shook his head. I stopped and begged him for approximately ten minutes to let me take X to the hospital but all he did was shake his head. Then I started forward with tears in my eyes, expecting to be shot down every second. The tower guard told me, 'That's far enough.' Then another guard gave me permission to bring X off the yard and I was ordered to lay him on the floor in the officer's area and go to my cell."

By the time this drama was completed, the wounded man was dead.

Why were these three Black men shot? W. L. Nolen had been known throughout the prison as a tough man who had maintained his identity and his pride. Cleveland Edwards, in jail for the political crime of assaulting a police officer, had also been a visible Black leader. Alvin Miller had been neither militant nor a leader, but he closely resembled the ranking Black Panther in Soledad, Earl Satcher, who was also in the exercise yard at the time of the shooting. Nolen had known that he was marked for death. He had told his father so during a recent visit. The father had tried to see the warden in order to arrange protection for his son, but the warden had been "too busy" to see him. Miller also had had a premonition of death, perhaps because of the taunting he had received from whites about the opening of the yard. One week before it opened, he wrote a farewell letter to his mother.

In a civil rights suit filed in Federal Court against prison officials Cletus Fitzharris, Superintendent; William Black, Deputy Superintendent; Clement Swagerty, Associate Warden; and O. G. Miller, Guard, attorney Melvin Belli states that "O. G. Miller maliciously shot and killed W. L. Nolen, Alvin Miller and Cleveland Edwards, because of his general hatred of persons of African descent and because of his particular hatred of one of the decedents, W. L. Nolen, who had struck O. G. Miller during a previous altercation between the two. . . .

"[Miller] knew that the possibility of serious bodily injury or death from the engaging in fisticuffs was minimal and that his shooting at the decedents' vital parts would almost certainly cause their death or serious bodily injury; yet he made the deliberate choice to shoot."

The suit further charges that prison officials "fostered" extreme racial tension in the prison by maintaining rigid segregation of the races; that they knew O. G. Miller to be prejudiced against Blacks; that they did not arrange for prompt treatment of the injured prisoners and so they are responsible for the deaths.

After these killings, the already tense atmosphere at Soledad became explosive. When the Monterey County Grand Jury held hearings at the prison to decide if charges should be filed against O. G. Miller, no Blacks who had been in the yard were permitted to testify, although some whites were. As they were being walked over to appear before the Grand Jury, they were reminded by guards, "Remember, there *was* a warning shot."

Shortly after the prison radio broadcast to the inmates at Soledad that Officer O. G. Miller had been exonerated of the murder of the three Black inmates, a white guard named John V. Mills was found dying in "Y" wing. He had been beaten and thrown from a third floor tier down into the television room 30 feet below.

Deputy Superintendent William Black stated, "We believe that the death of Officer Mills was reprisal for the death of the three Black inmates." And, as if to balance some score being kept, prison officials proceeded to find three Black suspects who, they said, had killed Mills. The accused were Fleeta Drumgo, 23; John W. Clutchette, 24; and George L. Jackson, 28. Tall and bespectacled, Jackson handles himself well. He is serving a one-year-to-life sentence for robbery and has done ten years. Although the median sentence for that crime is two-and-a-half years, the California Adult Authority has yet to set his parole date. Like the three Black inmates murdered in January, he is known throughout the prison as a Black who has held onto his identity, who has refused to lower his eyes and accept indignities. Jackson was not politically aware when he entered prison, but during the past ten years he has read extensively and has understood from his prison experiences what has happened to Black people in America. Jackson is a writer.

His father has worked hard all his life, often holding down two jobs so that his family would have enough. He preached the traditional virtues to his children, as well as faith in the American way.

Jackson's route to Soledad is a familiar trail for Blacks. Poor young Black men from the ghetto in their first brush with the law are tarred with a record they would never have if they were middle-class or white. Later on they get into suspicious circumstances and are arrested on heavier charges. They plead guilty because they can't establish innocence and already have a record; they don't get the light sentence they were given to expect, and end up in prison for long stretches.

Prison is a metaphor for the larger society, and some of the most powerful and articulate Black leaders have come up through prison systems—Eldridge Cleaver and Malcolm X, for example. Perhaps because the prison system forces definite choices upon Black men, they have to define themselves very clearly. Jackson got into trouble while he was first at Soledad because in the television room he would not sit in the back section unofficially "reserved" for Blacks. A fight broke out and authorities punished Jackson by sending him to San Quentin, where he spent two years isolated in the maximum security section.

Jackson, Drumgo and Clutchette maintain that they were nowhere near the third tier of "Y" wing when John Mills was killed, and that they are innocent. Clutchette, who was imprisoned for burglary, had already been given a parole date and was to be home on April 28. Drumgo was scheduled to appear before the Adult Authority in April and had an excellent chance of getting a release date.

Of the three inmates accused of assaulting and murdering the guard, Jackson is in a particularly strange legal situation. Because he is serving an indeterminate sentence, he is considered a "lifer," and his case falls under California Penal Code Section 4500, which provides a mandatory death sentence for any lifer convicted of assaulting a non-inmate who dies within a year. So if Jackson is convicted he must be sent to the gas chamber.

After the murder of the guard, all the inmates in "Y" wing were locked up and questioned for many days by guards, prison officials and the district attorney. From the beginning a terrible team-work began to operate against the three who had been selected as victims. No defense attorneys were present at the questioning. Prison officials never notified the families of the suspects that their sons were in trouble. Jackson, for instance, had been in court twice before his mother ever heard of his situation. John Clutchette's mother was told that her son did not need a lawyer and that she need not attend his arraignment. "Your son will advise you by mail," she was told by Lieutenant Leflores of the prison staff. However, she scurried to legislators, the NAACP and other organizations, and was able to find an attorney, Floyd Silliman of Salinas, who would help her son. Clutchette, anxious after days of questioning and solitary confinement, prepared a list of witnesses who could testify to his innocence. He attempted to give this list to his mother, breaking a prison rule which forbids giving written material to anyone but an attorney—at the time, he had no attorney. The list was discovered and taken away from him; the inmates whose names were written were transferred to other prisons. Mrs. Inez Williams, mother of Fleeta Drumgo, heard about the guard's death on the radio and phoned the prison to see whether her son was in any way involved. Prison officials assured her that the investigation was "routine" and that she had no need for worry. "The prison gets the parents' consent for having a tooth pulled, and informs the parents of other things," she said, but she was never told her son was accused of murder.

State officials dealing with this case have been passionate in their desire to keep records secret. The Adult Authority will not let George Jackson's lawyers know how they decided his status. Prison officials won't let the lawyers see all of Jackson's files or look at any of their records about the killing of the three Blacks. The State of California, as both custodian and prosecutor of the three, holds control of the witnesses and the evidence. In the person of Judge Gordon Campbell, Presiding Judge of the Superior Court of Monterey County, it is also sitting in judgment.

A small old man with a shiny bald head, Campbell sits high in his chair overlooking the court, his face often blank and preoccupied. At pre-trial hearings in March, April and May, he seemed like a Monterey version of Judge Julius Hoffman. At one hearing, the first to be packed with supporters and friends of the three defendants, he told the spectators that they probably would not like a visit from the bailiff and that they should sit quietly and not act as if they were "at a barbecue table or the local pool hall."

Campbell sometimes did the District Attorney's work for him; sometimes he even consulted him. He denied nearly all the motions made by the defense. In one instance, when the defense had asked to have a copy of the Manual for Correctional Officers at the prison, Campbell said to the D.A., "I presume you object to that." The D.A. nodded. "Motion denied," said Campbell, and the defense could not have the manual.

As soon as better-known Bay Area attorneys entered the case in late February, the judge issued an order forbidding them or the prosecution from making any statements to the press about matters relevant to the case. The attorneys were barred from the prison, unable to see the site of the murder until it had been remodeled, unable to interview witnesses. The prosecution, which had had unlimited access to the prison from the very start, refused to divulge the names of witnesses or their whereabouts until forced to do so by a court order obtained many weeks later.

None of the accused has been convicted of violent crimes or of crimes against persons. Yet they have been chained and shackled whenever they speak with visitors or attorneys; they are chained and shackled even in the courtroom itself. Chains encircle their waists and hang between their legs; cuffs bind their ankles, which are chained together, and their wrists, which are chained to the waist chains. Padlocks swing as they move. In court when friends greet them with raised fists, the three lift up their fists slightly above their waists—as far as their chains allow.

In February of 1970 when the earliest court appearances took place, families and friends of the prisoners were not present. The prisoners were driven to the courthouse from prison and were marched in chains across the sidewalk through the main entrance to the courthouse while passersby hooted at them. Since that time the case has received some publicity and has attracted a concerned and sympathetic following. Now the three are driven in a station wagon which has had special screens constructed to fit over the windows so that neither people nor cameras can intrude; they are driven directly into the basement garage of the courthouse and hustled upstairs through corridors where the public cannot go. Thus the men, who spend their other hours in solitary confinement, cannot even glimpse the crowd of their well-wishers.

People are beginning to find out who the Soledad Brothers are, and they're learning a little about what California prisons are like. But bitter winds of repression are blowing once again inside Monterey County, and it is likely that the three men will be on "Max Row" for a long time to come.

9

An Appeal

Fleeta Drumgo, George Jackson and John Cluchette are scheduled to go to trial in August, 1971. If the state of California is permitted to proceed unhampered, the outcome of that trial could be death for all three in San Quentin's gas chamber. The recently unsuccessful attempt on the part of the prosecution to change the venue of the trial to San Diego County, where the reactionary political climate would virtually guarantee their conviction, was a clear indication that the State intends to claim their lives. In an unprecedented in-court episode during a recent hearing (May 1971) they were compelled to defend themselves when they were physically attacked by San Quentin guards and San Francisco riot police.

For almost a year we have rallied around the slogan, 'Save the Soledad Brothers from Legal Lynching.' Before it is too late we must increase the momentum of that process which alone will allow us to transform this slogan into a reality—the involvement of masses of people in aggressive and creative activities which will challenge the use of the judicial system as well as the penal system as tools of political control and repression. All those who oppose the increasingly fascist features of this society—the barbarous extermination of the Indo-Chinese people, the formidable routine oppression of Black communities, the unbridled repression of revolutionaries—must become conscious of their responsibility to defeat the state's designs to legally murder the Soledad Brothers. Now is the time to intensify our efforts to build a massive popular campaign which will unconditionally demand and ultimately secure the freedom of our brothers.

Just as the defense of Ericka Huggins and Bobby Seale is central to the survival of our movement for Black Liberation, the Soledad Brothers' case, likewise possesses a special significance both for the movement and for Black people in general. Without a clear understanding of the centrality of their case, it is impossible to discern the motives underlying the government's determination to murder them and thus to affirm its ability to indiscriminately punish political activists. As ever greater sections of the Black community achieve political maturity and search for radical solutions, they will be exposed to the fascist techniques of suppression which seek confirmation in the Soledad Brothers' case.

As a consequence of the racism securely interwoven in the capitalist fabric of this society, Black people have become more thoroughly acquainted with America's jails and prisons than any other group of people in this country. Few of us indeed, have been able to escape some form of contact—direct or indirect—with these institutions at some point in our lives. We are acutely aware of the critical function of the entire network of penal institutions as a buttress assisting the ruling class to maintain its domination. Engels observed over a century ago that along with the army and the police, prisons are the essential instruments of state power. The prospect of long prison terms is meant to preserve order; it is supposed to serve as a threat to anyone who dares disturb existing social relations, whether by failing to observe the sacred rules of property or by consciously challenging the right of an unjust system of racism and domination to function smoothly.

Historically the prison system has been an integral part of our lives. Black people emerged from slavery only to encounter the prison labor system as one element of the new apparatus of exploitation. Arrested for trivial or falsified offenses, Blacks were leased out to politicians, planters, mining firms, and Northern syndicates for up to thirty years. A remnant of that era can still be detected, for example, in Arkansas' notorious Cummins' Prison Farm where prisoners work for no pay in cotton fields five and a half days a week. While more insidious forms of slave labor have persisted in the prisons, this broader social function of maintaining the existing socio-economic order has achieved monstrous proportions.

The mere fact that almost half of the twenty-eight thousand convicted felons in California's prison system are non-white—Blacks and Chicanos—is enough to reveal the intrinsic racism of the courts, Youth Authorities, and Parole Boards to which George Jackson, John Clutchette, and Fleeta Drungo fell victim at a very early age. All three were convicted of alleged 'crimes against property,' Fleeta and John of second degree burglary and George of second degree robbery. In spite of the indeterminate sentences they received (George, one to life; Fleeta six months to fifteen years; John six months to fifteen years) which made their release contingent on 'good conduct,' they refused to pattern their lives after the authoritarian behavior of the apologetic victim. Only after having conceded the state's unqualified right to dictate the principles governing their lives, would the prison officials and the Adult Authority consider them sufficiently 'rehabilitated' to warrant their release. Like so many of our brothers and sisters today they would not acquiesce in their victimization and continued to challenge the assumptions underlying this distorted concept of rehabilitation.

George, John, and Fleeta took on the perilous task of creating centers of resistance to the totalitarian prison regime and to the society fraught with irreconcilable antagonisms, which engendered repressive penal institutions as one of its bulwarks. They have continued to fight unwaveringly in the most dangerous arena of struggle in America. The mindless, sadistic guards whose carbines at any given moment could let loose bullets aimed at their brains, could not deter the Soledad Brothers from reaching out to every other inmate whose ears were receptive to their teachings on liberation.

George's book, *Soledad Brother,* declared contraband for California prisoners immediately after publication, contains a penetrating and articulate analysis of the American penal system. He elucidates the perverted relationship which locks the overseers and the subjugated, the masters and the slaves in constant conflict. This is the nature of the prisoner's unending battle for survival and dignity. He defines the structure and function of the

American prison system in the context of capitalist society, while at the same time projecting the crucial role of 'criminals' become revolutionaries in the broader liberation movement. With Ho Chi Minh, George insists that when the prison gates are flung open, the real dragon will appear, the dragon whose goal is to work for the emergence of an egalitarian Socialist order. His book is a vivid testimony of the evolution and maturation of a committed revolutionary under conditions which demand a perseverance verging on the superhuman.

It comes as no surprise that the fascist mentality of the prison authorities induces them to react with extreme panic in the face of this remarkable Black man. No wonder they have resolved to kill this man whose extraordinary ability to recognize the precise nature of his oppressors and to persuade his captive companions to embark on the correct path to liberation has not even been slightly debilitated by eleven long difficult years of imprisonment climaxed by the heroic death of his brother, Jonathan.

The three Soledad Brothers are the descendants of a long line of Black heroes, whose determination to prevail, whose persistent courage throughout our four hundred and fifty years of oppression has not been dampened by the superior physical powers of our adversaries. We can detect the fruits of their struggles in the rapidly developing liberation movements in prisons throughout the State of California. During the eleven years of George's imprisonment—eleven years of an indeterminate one to life sentence for a robbery involving seventy dollars—he has done time in practically all of California's prisons, San Quentin, Soledad, Folsom. Fleeta, who has lived over half his life in California penal institutions, has spent three and a half years in state prisons; and John, since August of 1966 has been held captive in San Quentin, Tehachipi, and Soledad.

The Soledad Brothers, having consciously relinquished their immediate self-interests of a speedy release from prison by educating and enlightening their fellow captives in the theory and practice of collective liberation, were natural targets of the fascist administrators of Soledad Prison. They have all related numerous incidents which occurred prior to this last definitive attempt to claim their lives. Fleeta was continually harassed when he refused to remove the political posters from the walls of his cell. George has said, "The only reason that I am still alive is because I take everything to the extreme, and they know it. I never let any of them get within arm's reach, and their hands must be in full view. Nothing, absolutely nothing comes as a surprise to me." (*Soledad Brother*).

Still, George has been repeatedly charged with 'crimes' resulting, for example, from the refusal to accept the racial segregation of certain prison facilities. Most of these alleged offenses which occur behind prison walls—those which do not incur the death penalty—are never tried in court. As James Park, Associate Warden at San Quentin said, in an interview with Jessica Mitford, referring to the prisoner accused of a crime: "He hasn't the right to a trial. We find him guilty or not guilty administratively." When asked how guilt is determined when no witnesses are called and no evidence presented, he said: "That's simple. We know who did it from other inmates . . . We don't have the type of case we could take to court; it would be too dangerous for our inmate-informers to have to testify." (Jessica Mitford, "Kind and Usual Punishment in California," *The Atlantic,* March 1971.)

It should be obvious that this administrative punishment can have the effect of prolonging indefinitely the sentences of prisoners who are known to espouse revolutionary causes. Of course anyone who claims to struggle for revolutionary change, anyone in fact who announces his opposition to a system of domination—the prison or the larger society—which ultimately rests on violence, is immediately labelled a criminal; that is, an advocate of violence. The Deputy Superintendent of Soledad Prison observed that: "We live at a time where there has been more violence in the streets. And we get people from the streets in here who have problems with violence. The joint is full of them." (*New York Times,* February 7, 1971). This is the technique used to justify the inordinate political repression which pervades the prisons. This is the cycle of repression which the Soledad Brothers encountered.

George's administratively determined guilt, an *a priori guilt,* was the pretext used by the Parole Board when they refused year after year to grant him a parole date. They hoped to coerce him to abdicate his revolutionary vocation, but year after year this man said with his words and actions: "Without the cold of winter, there could not be the warmth of spring. Calamity has hardened me and turned my mind to steel." (Ho Chi Minh).

On January 13, 1970 a white Soledad prison guard brutally assassinated three Black men without provocation. The murderer went unpunished for his racist deed, for the Grand Jury ruled justifiable homicide in one of the innumerable instances where grand juries have proved themselves handmaidens of official repression. On the day of the Grand Jury ruling a guard was killed. George, John, and Fleeta were elected by the Soledad Prison administrators to pay with their lives for the death of this guard. But even this is not an adequate description of the situation in which they found themselves entangled. For the death of the guard was seized upon as a convenient opportunity to kill them because of the enormous contributions they had made in heightening and intensifying political consciousness in California's prisons. Indeed the informers (whose existence Park indirectly acknowledges) who gave false testimony before the Grand Jury which indicted them were chosen to accomplish a far more profound and devastating task. Under the surface of the murder indictment lurked the real charges: revolutionary insubordination, failure to conform to the established order of things, inciting dissent, planting the seeds of liberation in the minds of their comrades in captivity.

Three Black activists had already been unceremoniously assassinated. Without incurring the suspicion of democratic-minded inhabitants of the outside world, it would be difficult to repeat this with grace. This time the legal machinery was set into motion. George, John and Fleeta would be legally assassinated. Their murder would be veiled by the external trappings of a democratic trial, but notwithstanding this formal exercise in democracy, their fate would be understood, and, as the prison officials hoped, well-taken by thousands of inmates in California's prisons. It would serve as a warning to anyone who contemplated repudiating his or her role as unfree automaton, victim, broken human being. If the fascists were correct in their calculations, the immolation of George, John and Fleeta would act as a brake on revolutionary prison activities. Strikes would subside. Rebellions would cease. There would be few remaining inmates courageous enough to utter words of liberation when it might be at the expense of their lives. These are the dynamics of terrorism. Not only the Soledad Brothers but countless other political activists in prisons have become targets of this terrorism.

Objectively seen, the insurrection of August 7, 1970, involving three San Quentin captives who were joined by Jonathan Jackson, George's younger brother, must have been an attempt to break this vicious cycle and to impress upon the world the unrestrained political repression as well as the sub-human conditions of existence which characterize prison life. The three prisoners involved— James McClain, William Christmas, and the sole survivor, Ruchell Magee, had lived and suffered under these conditions. Jonathan had experienced them vicariously. He was acutely aware of the vicious attempts to silence his brother George.

The events of August 7 forced broader sectors of the American public to become cognizant of the terror which reigns in this country's penal institutions. Evidence of its profound catalytic impact can be seen in the abundance of prison exposes which have been regularly appearing in the established press, such as a three week series of articles on California prisons in the San Francisco *Chronicle*.

The reaction of the ruling circles to the insurrection of August 7 was swift, demonstrating that they were shaken to the very core. Politicians and government officials have hastened to administer meaningless reforms in an attempt to assuage the anger of conscientious citizens. The former want to give credence to their deceptive assertions that the centuries-old tradition of brutality and terror crystallized in the prisons and now reaching the peak of Fascist political repression is merely a minor sore—to be cured with anesthetic-like reforms.

"Reforms" such as conjugal visiting programs reserved for the "good boys" are anesthetic ploys designed to divert attention from the real issues involved in the struggle against repression in the prisons. Many of these reforms will prove to be merely more subtle techniques of repression—just as the indeterminate sentence which was originally proposed in California as a policy of shorter prison terms has had precisely the opposite effect on prisoners, especially Blacks and Chicanos, who refuse to be subservient. Our response to these so-called reforms must be to push to the forefront more substantial issues which attack the very basis on which the prison system rests, such as the freedom for all political prisoners. Our slain brothers, Jonathan, Christmas, and McClain and our brother Ruchell who comes to trial with me, have brought our consciousness to the fore as to the magnitude of these tasks which lie ahead.

The Soledad Brothers, have become central figures, not only of the prison movement, but also of our wider movement for Black liberation. Their present struggle against death exemplifies the potential destiny of many more Black activists, Chicano, Puerto Rican, Asian and native American leaders, and those whites who have elected to wage a persistent battle against the most advanced capitalist society, maintained and buttressed by racism at all levels. Indeed I have learned of this first hand. Bobby and Ericka have already been confronted with this fate: just as we must fight for Bobby and Ericka's freedom in order to prevent fascism from engulfing our entire movement, so is the fight for the freedom of the Soledad Brothers vital to the survival of our ability to continue to actively struggle for revolutionary change.

George has developed an extensive theory on the nature of present-day fascism. His contention is that America has already entered a stage in which fascism has securely established itself in power. I agree with his underlying analysis, while I reject his conclusions; namely, the uncontested victory of the counter-revolution. While there can be no doubt that we are headed in a fascist direction, I do not think that fascism has yet consolidated itself in America; and as long as a vestige of the democratic process remains, then the sheer force of the people ought to be capable of freeing the Soledad Brothers as it must also free Bobby, Ericka, myself, Ruchell, and keep Huey and Los Siete free. The fact that Huey and Los Siete are on the streets at all attests to the power of the mass movement.

We should seek out all the doors which still remain ajar, however slight the opening might be. We must appeal to all people in this country and throughout the world to prove their anti-fascist commitments by struggling on all levels available to us. The movement must not be afraid to exhort people to initiate petition campaigns, mass rallies, demonstrations, block meetings. It must not be afraid to demand changes such as an end to the indeterminate sentence law and the abolition of penal code 4500 under which an inmate facing a life sentence who is convicted of assaulting a non-inmate must receive a mandatory death sentence (George's one to life sentence, supposedly a humane act on the part of the sentencing court, for he could have conceivably been released after one year, will bring him the gas chamber even if he is acquitted of the murder charges and convicted of assault).

It is the mark of an immature revolutionary to dismiss such actions as 'reformist' or 'liberal.' Such an attitude confuses the subjective consciousness of a minority of individual revolutionaries with the objective development of the masses of people. We *must* draw the masses into the arena of struggle via the mechanism of a broad defense movement. The failure to do so, justified by the claim of 'revolutionary purity,' the all or nothing stand, can too easily become a tool in the hands of our adversaries.

We cannot envision a socialist revolution in this country nor can we envision the defeat of racism if our movement continues to be beheaded and decimated by a ruling clique intent on protecting the booty of a small minority of corporate capitalists by all means available to them. Our revolution cannot proceed apace until we can create a strong, mass based defense movement which can serve as a shield for those who carry out the herculean task of gathering together and leading the potential revolutionary elements in this country—working class Blacks, Chicanos, Puerto Ricans, Asians and Native Americans; working men and women, students, conscious of the threads which tie their exploitation to the racist oppression of people of color all over the world; prisoners who recognize the need to transform their ineffective individual responses to a society which deprives them of basic necessities into a cohesive, collective onslaught in the direction of liberation.

The most important prerequisite of constructing this shield is the firm resolve to lay aside sectarian differences. An effective defense movement cannot be an arena for ideological struggle, whose appropriate place is elsewhere. We must be careful to avoid the tendency of building personality cults around specific individuals; this detracts from our ability to defend all our brothers and sisters

—especially those whose names remain unknown—with a strong, vigorous and militant united front.

Let us employ all the traditional channels of protest still open and at the same time direct our creative energies in the search for new means of impelling masses of people to forcefully make their demands for the freedom of political prisoners known. If we fail to free the Soledad Brothers, if we fail to free Bobby and Ericka and all our brothers and sisters held captive because of their steadfast commitment to liberation, then we, the people, must hold ourselves accountable for a new era of uncurbed terror and official barbarism.

Free All Political Prisoners!

10

On Prison Reform

from a letter by John Clutchette*

. . . After pondering the discussion we had concerning the term
prison reform, I have concluded that more people will support our
cause and you will avoid apathy by centering your efforts around
the title that has already been established—political prisoners, the
title carries the immediate aim of prisoners for humanity and justice. I also think that all letters, articles, pamphlets, etc., etc.,
should fall under this title. The word justice should be emphasized
and must be recognized by the people. Justice is the word that
indicates our goal. But you know more about these things than I.
What I want to get across is that it would be reactionary to our
position here to support the rambunctious call for prison reform,
and I think this term should be defined to the people—all people.
You can even go as far as to call it a dirty word. In order to resolve
this issue and move forward to further progress, we must analyze
the term reform (prison reform) and its fundamental objective.
There is but one imperative—overhaul! Which means changing the
frame on the wall—but not the picture itself. On the one hand it
brings into existence a new policy of administrative control, the
order of old rules and regulations are re-organized and formulated
to fit a new pacification program, this program is designed and
regulated to pacify inmates by offering them a movie, a new radio
station, a new and freshly painted cell, bars included. But no
immediate parole, in short the objective is to keep the inmate
happy and the assembly lines rolling. On the other hand it main-
tains the use of weapon control (changing the frame but not the

* This letter was written to a woman active in Clutchette's behalf who
asked his views on the issue of prison reform.

136

picture); it carries out the use of tear gas, billy clubs, pick handles, the sweat box, solitary lock-up (a prison within a prison), and the use of 30/30 automatic rifles.

This process of dehumanization, this method of psychological repression, the open physical attacks against inmates by sadistic guards all take on a moderate tone, and inmates are taken behind closed doors, for inmates who have and over a period of years attempted to expose the blatant atrocities of U.S. concentration camps, are inmates who are classified a threat to the system based on (their) political ideology. These inmates are forced to live in the sediment and filth of solitary lock-up for protesting prison conditions—they are forgotten and castigated. So parole manipulation and the wheels of vengeance, retaliation, and injustice run full speed ahead. . . . Beyond this, prison reform obstructs, falsifies, mis-leads, attacks and oppresses the call for abolishing U.S. neo-concentration camps.

However, this does not mean that conditions should be forgotten, that work should stop in this area; on the contrary all efforts should be made in helping to eliminate all conditions affecting our welfare and at the same time all efforts should be made in gaining the release of inmates who are penalized by the California Adult Authority as a result and direct penalization for trying to make the people aware of the type of activities existing behind the stone walls of U.S. prisons—who operate under the guise of prison reform. . . . my friend, there are many people who hold misconceptions about prisons and the type of people inside them, and many have asked more than twice, "Why are prisons called concentration camps?", "Why should prisons be abolished?". But these are questions that evade answers. But this is not new; the existing prison system has a long antagonizing and rampant history of falsifying, evading, covering-up and hiding their unlawful activities from the eyes and ears of the people. This, however, results from a pathological prison administration which consistently lies. The aftermath being the catalyst motivating the unaware to take sides with the system, rather than the victims of the system.

Today's prison camps are called neo-concentration camps because they are regulated and controlled by neo-nazi, pro-fascist type attitudes. In prison we are governed and controlled by the

same attitudes that govern and control the lives of the people outside of prison, the attitudes of incompetent public officials, off-
springs of the establishment . . . the system that excludes and
debases the human rights of the people, the system that has no
concern for the people's welfare or their lives; the attitudes of control by force—there is force all around us, above us. Force is the
weapon used against the people's will . . . Here inside the concentration camp these attitudes are more to the extreme, we
are, like the people outside of the prison walls . . . forced . . .
into . . . resisting . . . force!

Today's prison system should be abolished because it is a system
pre-designed and constructed to ware-house the people of un-
developed and lower economical communities. Under the existing
social order men and women are sent to prison for labor (free
labor) and further economical gain (money) by the state. Where
else can you get a full day's work for two to sixteen cents an hour,
and these hours become an indeterminate period of years. This
is slave labor in 20th century America. Repeat! Men and women
are sent prison for free labor, not for what contributions they
might make to their communities, under the guise of rehabilitation.
Ninety-eight per cent of (all) people held in U.S. concentration
camps are people of oppression, we are the people who come from
the under class of the system, we are the people castigated and
barred from the productive arenas of social employment, decent
housing, correct education, correct medical care, etc., etc., a war of
survival . . . Bear with me I don't intend to sound bitter, but only
to relate the truth; we must come to know the truth, we are the
people left to the crumbs of the system . . . we are the people
who lay prey to the criminal elements of the system. The choice
—survive or perish??? The first always being to survive. It is a
fact that man is a product of his environment; that the character
and state of mind of a people, a race, a nation, the world, depends
essentially and decisively on being able to control their economical
environment in relation to controlling the fruits of their labor (production) in essence this is the determining factor of one's social,
political and economical power. Again ninety-eight per cent of all
the people in concentration camps are members of the oppressed
class. You won't find members of the ruling-clique in places like

this, but you will find their victims. I along with others who are locked up here acknowledge the fact that there are many sincere people with good intentions who have rendered their time and efforts in trying to reveal the foul conditions existing here in San Quentin, as well as in other prisons in this state, Soledad, Folsom, etc. They have shown us their position by way of actions and deeds for the number of people who fail to see the techniques used to propagandize the people—entire families, our friends, loved ones— into taking counter stands against the tens of thousands of people held in U.S. concentration camps . . . we must attempt to reach these people . . . the unaware.

In leading the people into a struggle against unjust conditions we must consider the situation as a whole. We must think in terms of the majority of the people (even though some of these suckers won't pick up a tooth pick, let alone a gun in their own behalf) and work together with them; those who are sincere and have constructive ideas which will benefit the majority rather than one individual group or another. We must grasp the principles and methods of subordinating the needs of the part to the whole. This is what is meant by considering the situation as a whole. Our only hope lies in the people's endeavor to hear our protest and support our cause. Building more and better prisons is not the solution— build a thousand prisons, arrest and lock-up tens of thousands of people; all will be to no avail. This will not arrest poverty, oppression and the other ills of this unjust social order. But the people, working in united effort, can eliminate these conditions by removing the source that produces them. We need people who will stand up and speak out when it is a matter of right or wrong, of justice or injustice, of struggling or not struggling to help correct and remove conditions affecting the people, all I ask is that the people support us, I will break my back in helping bring peace and justice upon the face of the earth.

I've seen too much injustice to remain mute or still. The struggle against injustice cannot be muffled by prison walls. I know you are a busy woman but I felt these things are essential in understanding me a little better and the conditions surrounding me. Actually I had intended on writing you a love letter, but since that last statement, I see that I am going to have to be a little more articulate in my approach, which will be very difficult for two reasons; first being I don't have the time—no telling what the outcome will be and I would prefer death to life in prison, or walking into a gas chamber like a senile dog—second, because I don't know how, I've always said things however they come thinking that was and is the right way—but if I must learn to play with words in order to accomplish my objective (you) so be it. But I'll tell you now I am not going to like putting on airs, I would rather be the same old funky speedy I've always liked and I'm sure you would like him too if you gave him a chance instead of hindering his efforts with madness.

I'm in hopes that after reading my last letter, that you will sit down and try to understand what I am saying—not just with words but with all of me; I realize that I may never come out of this alive, and that I may not be able to be to you all that a woman seeks in a man being that I'm behind bars, but my heart is out there constantly—my way of escaping from this madness. I think at times I may never be able to have the simple things in life; a woman, a son which I want badly—I have a daughter she will be five this month . . .

11

Towards
The United Front
by George Jackson

There exists already a new unitarian and progressive current in the movement centering around political prisoners. The question at this point, I feel, is how to develop unitarian conduct further— against the natural resistance of establishment machinations— through the creation of new initiatives and a dialectic so clear in its argumentation, presentation and implementation that it will of its own weight force the isolation of reactionary elements. Both individual-attitudinized and organized reaction must be isolated.

Unitary conduct implies a *"search"* for that something in common, a conscious reaching for the relevant, the entente, and in our case especially the reconcilable. Throughout the centralizing-authoritarian process of American history, the ruling classes have found it expedient, actually necessary to insinuate upon the people instrumentalities designed to discourage and punish any genuine opposition to hierarchy. There have always been individuals and groups who rejected the ideal of society above society. The men who placed themselves above society through guile, fortuitous outcome of circumstance and sheer brutality have developed two principal institutions to deal with any and all serious disobedience —the prison and institutionalized racism. There are more prisons of all categories in the United States than in all other countries of the world combined. There are at all times two-thirds of a million people or more confined to these prisons. Hundreds are destined to be executed outright legally and thousands quasi-legally. Other thousands will never again have any freedom of movement barring a revolutionary change in all the institutions that combine to make up the order of things. Two thirds of a million people may not seem like a great number compared against the total population of nearly two hundred and five million. However compared to the one million who are responsible for all the affairs of men within the extended state, it constitutes a striking contrast not at all coincidental, and perhaps deserving of careful analysis. What I want to explore now are a few of the subtle elements that I have observed to be standing in the path of a much needed united front (nonsectarian) to effectively reverse the legitimatized rip-off.

I will emphasize again that prisons were not institutionalized on so massive a scale by the people. Though all crime can be considered a manifestation of antithesis, some crime does work out to the well understood detriment of the people. Most crime, however, is clearly the simple effect of a grossly disproportionate distribution of wealth and privilege, a reflection of the state of present property relations. There are no wealthy men on death row, and so very few in the general prison population that we can discount them altogether—imprisonment is an aspect of class struggle from the outset. A closed society intended to isolate those who quite healthfully disregard the structures of a hypocritical establishment with their individual actions, and those who would organize a mass basis for such action. U.S. history is replete with examples of both types, the latter extending from the early Working Men's Benevolent Association through the events surrounding the Ancient Order of Hibernians, The Working Men's Party who organized against the excesses of the 1877 depression, all the way to the present era when the Communist Party was banned (during this country's fascist takeover), and the Black Panther Party in the practical sense assaulted and banned.

The hypocrisy of Amerikan fascism will not allow it to openly declare that it does hold political offenders—thus the hundreds of versions of conspiracy laws and the highly sophisticated frame-up. This is the first point of attack in the educational sense. Why do prisons exist in such numbers, what is the real underlying economic motive of crime, and the diacritical breakdown of types of offenders or victims? If offenders is the better term it must be clearly presented that the language of the law is definitely weighted and deceptive, it should be clear that when one "offends" the totalitarian state it is patently not an offense against the people of that state, offending the state translates into an assault upon the privilege of the privileged few.

Could anything be more ridiculous than the officious titles to indictments reading: "The People of the State . . . vs. Bobby Seale and Ericka Huggins" or "The People of the State . . . vs. Angela Davis and Ruchell Magee." What people are referred to?— clearly the hierarchy, the armed minority.

Then in the John Doe cases where an actual robbery or theft was committed, we must elucidate the real causes of economic crimes; or any crime, of passion against repression, the thrill crime, we must be all inclusive. All crime is motivated by simple economic oppression, or the psycho-social effects of an economic order that was decadent 100 years ago. Objective socio-economic conditions equals social productive or counter-productive activity, in *all* cases determined by the economic system, the method of economic organization, the maintainance of that organization against the forces of progress that would change it. Even the psychology of the sick individual, perpetrator of a "thrill crime" must ultimately be traced to a sick society.

Prisoners must be reached and made to understand that they are victims of social injustice. This is my task working from within (while I'm here—my persuasion is that the war goes on no matter where one may find himself on bourgeois dominated soil). The sheer numbers of the prisoner class and their terms of existence make them a mighty reservoir of revolutionary potential. Working alone and from within a steel enclosed society there is very little that people like myself can do to free the retrained potential revolutionary. That is part of the task of the "Prison Movement." "The People of the State . . . vs. John Doe" is as tenuous as the clearly political frame-ups. It's like stating "The People vs. The People." Man against himself.

The "Prison Movement" serves another important political end. It makes the ruling class conscious of our determination to never surrender our economic right to hold the implements of production in our own hands short of physical death. Detention will not check our movement. The August 7th movement and all actual acts of, and attempts to, put the keeper to death serve this notice best. They also hint at the ultimate goal of revolutionary consciousness at every level of struggle, the major level at the point of production, and all the substructural levels. The goal is always the same: the creation of an infrastructure capable of fielding a people's army.

There should be no one among us who still doesn't understand that revolution is aggressive, and that the making of demands on the manipulators of the system, that they cannot or will not meet must eventually move us all into a violent encounter with that system one day. These are the terminal years of capitalism and as we move into significant areas of antiestablishment activities, history clearly forewarns us that when the prestige of power fails a violent episode precedes its transformation.

We can attempt to limit the scope and range of violence in revolution by mobilizing as many partisans as possible at every level of socio-economic life, but considering the hold that the ruling class of this country has on the apolitical in general and its history of violence, nothing could be more predictable than civil disorders, perhaps even civil war. I don't dread either, for there are no good aspects of monopoly capital, no good or beneficial guarantees, so no reservations need be recognized in its destruction. No interpretation of what revolution will be is required really, not in the U.S., not in the face of monopoly capital. As it stands above us monopoly capital is an obstruction that leaves us in the shade and has made us its servant. It must be completely destroyed, not rejected, not simply transformed, but destroyed utterly, totally, ruthlessly, relentlessly—as immediately as possible terminated!

With this as a common major goal it would seem that unitarian conduct of all parties concerned in active antiestablishment struggle on various levels should find little difficulty in developing initiatives and new methods consistent with the goals of mass society.

Regretfully this has not been the case, although as I stated there can be detected in the prison movement the beginnings of a unitary current cutting across the ideological, racial and cultural barricades that have in all times past blocked the natural coalition of left wing forces: This brings us to another vital aspect of the activity surrounding political prisoners. Perhaps on our substructural level with steadily attentive efforts at building the united front we can provide an example for the partisans engaged at other levels of struggle. The issues involved and the dialectic which flows from the clear objective existence of overt oppression could be the basis of, or a spring board for our genuine entrance into the tide of increasing world wide socialist consciousness. In clearing away the obstacles that preclude a united left for the defense of political prisoners and prisoners in general there must first be a renunciation of the idea that all participants must be of one mind and should work at the problem from a single party line or methodical singularity. The reverse of this is actually desirable. "From all according to ability." Each partisan, outside the vanguard elements, should proceed in a popularization strategy in the area of their natural environment, the places where they pursue their normal lives when not attending the rallies and demonstrations. The vanguard elements (organized party workers of all ideological persuasion) go among the people concentrated at the rallying point with elevation strategy, promoting commitment and providing concrete, clearly defined activity for them to popularize. The vanguard elements are first searching out people who can and will contribute to the building of the commune, the infrastructure—(with pen and clipboard in hand)—for those who cannot yet take that step a "packet" of pamphlets is provided for use in their individual pursuits.

Unity of the left factions in this substructural aspect of the movement, that centers around political prisoners and prisons in general is significant then in several ways. With our example we can begin to break the old behavioral patterns that have repeatedly won bourgeois capitalism, its imperialism and fascism, life after death over the last several decades. We free a massive potential reservoir of partisans for cadre work, and finally we begin to address one of the most complex psycho-social by-products that economic man with his private enterprise has manufactured—Racism.

I've saved this most critical barrier to our needs of unity for last. Racism is a question of ingrained traditional attitudes conditioned through institutions—for some, it is as natural a reflex as breathing. The psychosocial effects of the dichotomous habitudes set up by a particularly sensitized racism compounded with the bitterest of class repression has served in the past to render us all practically inactive, and where we attempt progressive action, particularly impotent.

If a united left is possible in this country the major obstacle must be considered racism, white racism to be blunt. The categories can be best simplified by reducing them to three, the overt self-satisfied racist who doesn't deign to hide his antipathy, the self-interdicting racist who harbors and nurtures racism in spite of their best efforts, and the unconscious racist, product of preconceived notions that must be blamed on history.

I deny the existence of Black racism outright, by fiat I deny it. Too much Black blood has flowed between the chasm that separates the races, it's fundamentally unfair to expect the Black man to differentiate at a glance the self-accepting racist, the self-interdicting racist and the unconscious racist. The apologist's term 'Black racism' is either a healthy defense reflex on the part of the sincere Black partisan attempting to deal with the realistic problems of survival and elevation, or the racism of the government stooge organs.

As Black partisans we must recognize and allow for the existence of all three types of racists, as we accept ourselves in relation thereto, but all must still be viewed as the effect of the system. It is a system that must be crushed first, for it continues to manufacture new and deeper contradictions of both class and race. Once it is gone we may be able to address in depth the effects of its presence but to a great extent, we must combat racism while we are in the process of destroying it. The psycho-social effects of hundreds of years of mutually exclusive attitudinal positions on race and class and symbols, hierarchy in general must be isolated.

The self-interdicting racist, no matter what his acquired conviction or ideology, will seldom be able to contribute with his actions in any really concrete way. Their role in revolution, barring a change of basic character, will be minimal throughout. Whether the basic character of a man can be changed at all is still a question. But . . . we have in the immediacy of the *"issues in question"* the perfect opportunity to test the validity of materialist philosophy again.

The need for unitarian conduct goes much deeper than the liberation of Angela, Bobby, Ericka, Magee, Los Siete, Tijerina, white draft resisters and now the indomitable and faithful James Carr. We have fundamental strategy to be proved—tested and proved. The activity surrounding the protection and liberation of people who fight for us is an important aspect of the struggle, but it is important only if it provides new initiatives that redirect and advance the revolution under new progressive methods. There must be a collective redirection of the old guard, the factory and union agitator, with pamphlet and silenced pistol, the campus activist who can counter the ill-effects of fascism at its training site, the *lumpen-proletarian* intellectuals with revolutionary scientific socialist attitudes to deal with the masses of street people living outside the system already. Black, Brown, White are victims, fight! At the end of this massive collective struggle we will uncover our new man; he is a creation of the process, the future, he will be better equipped to wage the real struggle, the permanent struggle after the revolution—the one for new relationships between man.

12

Letters
to Jonathan Jackson

To the Man-Child,
Tall, evil, graceful, brighteyed, Black man-child—Jonathan
Peter Jackson—who died on August 7, 1970, courage in
one hand, assault rifle in the other; my brother, comrade,
friend—the true revolutionary, *the Black communist guer-*
rilla in the highest state of development, he died on the
trigger, scourge of the unrighteous, soldier of the people. . . ,

George Jackson

September 25, 1969

Dear Jon,

Robert told me that you were driving the new automobile to
school. If that's right, you're not doing too bad. Do you use it at
school and drive home too? But he also mentioned that if you
didn't show improvements in things of a scholastic nature, he
would be very disappointed.

I am thinking that he feels a lot for you. He really does, I know.
He simply doesn't know how to relate to you. When I was young,
I felt that Robert didn't care for me very much because he wouldn't
take me anywhere or ever talk to me in anything less than a
shout. Mama used to talk him into beating me up just for leaving
the house to play ball or talk with my peers. I mean real beating,
belts, table legs, fists, etc. But what I didn't notice was that he

148

was feeding me and that whenever I got into a bind with the local representatives of the oppressors (police), he would always be there to help me. *Always,* no matter what I had done or how much he hated what I'd done.

Life has been one long string of disappointments for Robert. It wouldn't be too good to just take lightly his wishes to see you become more aggressive in your development. It isn't necessary to disappoint him. You can satisfy him, help yourself, and serve the cause of Black self-determination by picking yourself up and taking Chairman Mao's Great Leap Forward.

I hope you are involved in the academic program at your school, but knowing what I know about this country's schooling methods, they are not really directing you to any specialized line of study. They have not tried to ascertain what fits your character and disposition and to direct you accordingly. So you must do this *yourself*. Decide now what you would like to specialize in, *one thing* that you will drive at. Do you get it? *Decide now.* There are several things that we as a group, a revolutionary group, need badly: chemists, electronic engineers, surgeons, etc. Choose one and give it special attention at a certain time each day. Establish a certain time to give over to your specialty and let Robert know indirectly what you are doing. Then it only remains for you to get your A's on the little simple unnecessary subject that the school requires. This is no real problem. It can be accomplished with just a little attention and study. But you must now start on your specialty, the thing that you plan to carry through this war of life. You must specialize in something. Just let it be something that will help the war effort.

GEORGE

December 28, 1969

Dear Jon,

. . . Forget that Westernized backward stuff about god. I curse god, the whole idea of a benevolent supreme being is the product of a tortured, demented mind. It is a labored, mindless attempt to explain away ignorance, a tool to keep people of low mentality and no means of production in line. How could there be a *benevolent* superman controlling a world like this? He would have to be malevolent, not benevolent. Look around you, evil rules supreme. God would be my enemy. The theory of a good, just god is a false idea, a thing for imbeciles and old women, and, of course, Negroes. It's a relic of the past when men made words and mindless defenses for such things as sea serpents, magic and flat earths.

Strength comes from knowledge, knowing who you are, where you want to go, what you want, knowing and accepting that you are alone on this spinning, tumbling world. No one can crawl into your mind and help you out. I'm your brother and I'm with you, come what may, and against anything or anybody in the universe that is against you, but you'll still be alone, with your pain, discomfort, illness, elation, courage, pride, death. You don't want anyone to crawl into your head with you, do you? If there were a god or anyone else reading some of my thoughts I would be uncomfortable in the extreme.

Strength is being able to control yourself and your total environment, yourself first, however.

Take care of yourself.

GEORGE

August 9, 1970
Real Date, 2 days A.D.

Dear Joan,

We reckon all time in the future from the day of the man-child's death.

Man-child, Black man-child with submachine gun in hand, he was free for a while. I guess that's more than most of us can expect.

I want people to wonder at what forces created him, terrible, vindictive, cold, calm man-child, courage in one hand, the machine gun in the other, scourge of the unrighteous—"an ox for the people to ride"! ! !

Go over all the letters I've sent you,* any reference to Georgia being less than a perfect revolutionary's mama must be removed. Do it now! I want no possibility of anyone misunderstanding her as I did. She didn't cry a tear. She is, as I am, very proud. She read two things into his rage, love and loyalty.

I can't go any further, it would just be a love story about the baddest brother this world has had the privilege to meet, and it's just not popular or safe—to say I love him.

Cold and calm though. "All right, gentlemen, I'm taking over now." **

Revolution,

GEORGE

* George Jackson is referring to the letters in his book *Soledad Brother*.
** He quotes his brother's words from the San Rafael courthouse.

V

Ruchell Magee

13

Ruchell Magee

by Robert Kaufman

Ruchell Magee was the one survivor of the four Black men, one, the seventeen year old brother of a prisoner, the other three, prisoners themselves, who made a bid for freedom at the Marin Civic Center, San Rafael, California on August 7, 1970.

In the racist atmosphere of the United States, that alone makes the affirmation of his humanity a difficult idea to get across to millions of white people. He is categorized into a less than human stereotype—criminal, inmate, con, and, as of August 7, brutish killer.

The Establishment media has had a field day wallowing in their own vision of the contrast between Angela Davis, the bright, educated, cultivated philosopher-revolutionary; and Magee the crazed brute, the moron. How often did you see that number attached to Magee's name, like a slaver's brand—78: "Prison authorities revealed his IQ, tested at Angola State Penitentiary in Louisiana, at a low 78." The mentality of the press was the mentality of the slave buyer around the auction block.

The only contrast between Ruchell Magee and Angela Davis beyond the contrasting uniqueness of each human being, was that while Ruchell was forced to taste prison life by a system of racist oppression before his thirteenth birthday, Angela Davis was not finally trapped until she was 26.

Thirteen. For a Black child in Franklin, Louisiana in 1952 it was not an unusual apprenticeship in a state among many that relies to this day on Black slave labor from its crowded prisons. Ruchell was arrested again at age sixteen, and again was sent to prison. The charge: attempted rape of a white woman. For a Black child to

155

look at a white woman such a charge could easily result. A few years later in neighboring Mississippi a Black child named Emmett Till—a child younger than Magee—was murdered for looking at a white woman. The locals called it rape then also.

Magee was imprisoned in Louisiana State Penitentiary at Angola, whose horrors have made it notorious beyond most prisons in the United States. Here Ruchell Magee managed to survive until his release in 1963. He was twenty-three years old, illiterate and unskilled, but he was not broken.

On parole to the custody of his aunt in Los Angeles, California, he managed to eke out a living working as a car washer and house painter for seven short months before he was arrested again. This time the incident involved only a $10 purchase of marijuana, a commonplace enough act, even in 1963. But that was a period of intense brutality against the Black community in Los Angeles by the police—a brutality that continued and grew worse and finally resulted in the first ghetto uprising of the 1960's—the Watts Uprising—of August 1965.

For that incident Magee was sentenced to life imprisonment. How that happened is a case study in what due process of law means in the ghettos of the United States. The story, as Magee tells it, is this: On March 23, 1963 he paid a Ben Brown $10 for marijuana, and then had Brown drive him, his cousin Stewart and a young woman to 68th and Central avenues in Los Angeles. There he got into a "brief scuffle" with Brown over an earlier argument. Brown ran, leaving his car, and called the sheriff. Magee was arrested, charged with kidnapping, and when he told the sheriff he didn't have the car keys, he was beaten so badly he was later taken from his cell coughing blood. He spent five days in Los Angeles County General Hospital.

Magee charges his cousin Stewart was beaten into confessing to the kidnap charge. At the trial, after Brown's testimony was thrown out, the prosecution played a tape of Stewart's confession, and asked that, since Stewart had pleaded guilty (on advice from the Public Defender) the jury find Magee guilty too.

It did. And Magee was given a life sentence. That is, under California's indeterminate sentencing procedure Magee was sentenced to from one year to life.

Magee knew he was guilty of nothing but being Black. He had survived Angola and he resolved to get himself out of the California prisons. With the help of a friend he met in the Los Angeles County jail he taught himself to read, using a legal dictionary and the Constitution of the United States. As his friend remembered later: "We started to learn legal terminology so we could understand what was going on in court. We convinced ourselves that since we were innocent we could fight our cases and even win them. The first thing we found we had to do in order to practice law was to learn the Constitution, especially the first Ten Amendments, the Bill of Rights. We got very down with the Constitution."

Thus equipped, and without any outside legal aid, but through his own writs and appeals his conviction was set aside and a new trial ordered in December 1964.

Magee was sent back to Los Angeles for the retrial sitting up and shackled for five days on a prison bus while it travelled around the state picking up convicts.

At this retrial a lawyer Magee had never seen before was appointed by the Court to represent him. Without consulting his client, the lawyer entered a plea of not guilty by reason of insanity. When Magee rose to object, the judge, Herbert V. Walker, ordered him gagged. He was then beaten by guards and dragged from the courtroom. Witnesses in the corridor who saw him being dragged out said his eye was already swollen and the guards were still kicking him. He was taken to the county jail hospital.

With altered testimony from the same drug dealer whose testimony was thrown out in the first trial and Judge Walker's instructions to the jury to find Magee either guilty or insane, Magee was convicted again. Sentence: life imprisonment without the possibility of parole.

It is not unfair to Magee to say that he became obsessed with winning justice through his own efforts in the courts as he increasingly lost faith in the courts and in the competence, good intentions and sincerity, of the lawyers arbitrarily picked to represent him.

The men who knew Ruchell Magee in San Quentin remember him as a man of slight build and intensity of manner, always carrying law books and legal papers. Through his encouragement he infused the spirit of unity into his fellow brothers which resulted in self-help education and in the setting up of Black organizations in the prison. One friend remembered "him and I walking in the yard, talking to the brothers, trying to encourage them to stop playing dominoes, stop pitching horseshoes and come up to the tutoring programs."

Magee spent much of his time in the meager law library won by the inmates in San Quentin, and the rest of his time writing briefs, and filing legal papers for other convicts. "He was not on a capitalist trip" his friend remembers. Some "writ writers" charge for their legal assistance; but not Magee.

Out of his work providing legal aid to his brothers, Magee saw the necessity of organizing their families on the outside to provide the kind oof assistance impossible for a man on the inside without money or contacts. Prisoner friends carried the idea out when they were released; and it soon blossomed into Connections—a thriving organization of prisoners' families and ex-prisoners that has contributed much to building the struggle against the oppressive prison system in California. Many in Connections don't know that the survivor of August 7 is one of its founders.

Ruchell Magee was a quiet man, rarely getting into arguments with his brothers. But with the guards it was another story. He was constantly being harassed by the guards because of his law work. They would accuse him of having a typewriter without permission, or over almost anything he did, such as carrying the legal papers of another prisoner, or carrying legal papers into the dining hall. And for this or that he would be thrown into solitary confinement—the Adjustment Center to the prison authorities, 'the hole' to the prisoners.

Many men benefited from Magee's legal help; but for him the years were ones of bitter frustration. He wrote brief after brief in his own behalf, only to see them either blocked by the prison authorities or ignored by the courts. Even his right to correspond with the outside was invariably denied, apparently for fear of exposure of the realities of the prison system. It is not surprising therefore that his belief that if only an unbiased court could hear him the injustice done to him would be undone, was fast waning.

The turning point came on the night of February 26, 1970 when a young Black prisoner, Fred Billingslea, was killed by prison guards inside San Quentin. The men knew that Billingslea was emotionally disturbed, and they believed that the authorities had no business putting him in a prison, much less in its "adjustment center." The authorities said he had set fire to his mattress, and that as a result he had suffocated to death. But it was soon discovered that this was a lie.

What apparently happened was that Billingslea had set fire to his mattress; and when the guards came he had refused to come out of his cell. As he resisted the guards they threw tear gas canisters into his cell and locked the door. After a while the guards entered his cell, and dragged the now unconscious prisoner from his cell and down three flights of stairs. Other prisoners who witnessed this, swore in legal affidavits that Billingslea was beaten by the guards as he was dragged away. By morning the young Black prisoner was dead.

Ruchell Magee was among those prisoners who vowed to get word of what had happened to the outside world, and bring the people responsible for the murder to justice. Many of the prisoners were harassed, beaten, thrown in "the hole" or worse for collecting statements of witnesses, writing letters to friends and family and attorneys about the murder, and filing legal papers on the case.

Ruchell Magee's letters and briefs on the Billingslea case were blocked at every point. He came to believe, with every justification, that the prison officials would kill him and the other prisoners rather than allow the truth of the Billingslea murder to reach the outside world.

This was the situation on August 7, 1970 when Ruchell Magee was brought to the Marin County Court House to be a witness for another prisoner, James McClain, who was charged with stabbing a guard. James McClain who was then facing his second trial had defended himself in his first trial and had been so effective and eloquent in his pleadings that an all-white jury was hopelessly deadlocked and reached no verdict.

On August 7, 1970 McClain was on trial again before the same judge who had presided in his first trial, and the same prosecutor who, incidentally was the husband of the judge's niece. In such ways do these authorities teach respect for the law!

When young Jonathan Jackson rose in the courtroom, raised his

rifle and said: "All right gentlemen, this is it," McClain, Magee
and another witness in McClain's case, William Christmas, joined
with Jonathan in a bid for freedom. With them they took the
judge, his kinsman the prosecutor and three women jurors as
hostages.

But it was not to be. The prison guards have a rule. Hostages
are not to be protected. Disregarding the lives of the judge, the
prosecutor and the women jurors, prison guards and sheriff's dep-
uties opened fire on the men and their hostages. Inside the escape
van prosecutor Gary Thomas claims he grabbed a gun and started
shooting the prisoners. Christmas, McClain, Jackson and the judge
were killed; Magee was severely wounded and the prosecutor was
paralyzed. The jurors escaped with minor injuries.

Ruchell Magee has charged that almost at once the state went
to work trying to get him to implicate Angela Davis in the escape
attempt. They thought they had a man who would make a bargain
for his life. They did not know Ruchell Magee.

From his very first appearance in court on the charges arising
from the escape-attempt Magee has legally challenged the right of
the State courts to try him, arguing that the State has denied him
his civil rights and obstructed the due process of law since his
1963 conviction. He thus petitioned to have his case removed to
the jurisdiction of the Federal courts. Thus far his efforts have
not been successful. Magee also continues to fight for his right to
serve as his own attorney.

The authorities have chained and shackled Magee at every one of
his court appearances. Picture a man trying to defend himself,
trying to leaf through his legal papers, with his wrists handcuffed
and linked to a chain cinched tightly around his waist.

They have tried to humiliate him, to force him back into the
mold of "Magee the Moron."

But Ruchell Magee has persevered. He had already forced one
judge to admit to his own prejudice and disqualify himself from
the proceedings. He has remained steadfast in his refusal to allow
any court-appointed lawyer to conduct his defense, and he has
remained steadfast in his solidarity with Angela Davis.

14

Letters
to Angela Davis

December 16, 1970

Respectfully Soul Sister:

Your letter was received and read anxiously. My mind was greatly relieved to know you have faith in me. However it depresses me for you to be imprisoned even though it's only temporarily—when your innocence is known not only by me, but by Reagan, Rockefeller, Nixon, and California Judges McGuire, Wilson and Zirpoli (Federal Judge) and Bruce Bales the Marin County District Attorney.

I have sought diligently to get in touch with you, but the "pigs" are doing and have done all in their power to hold me incommunicado.

The first thing I must tell you is, we, you and I, threaten the entire establishment (not because we are guilty, but because we are innocent—and the establishment has knowingly and falsely accused us to further their oppressive tactics). And when we expose these pigs the final destiny may be death—but I'm going to get you freed.

Your lawyers should let the world know that the indictment against you is a fraud! That's why the State of California won't give up the transcript.

The truth is that they thought you had left the country, so the politicians verbalized a warrant for your arrest, when in fact they had no charge against you. (They have slandered your name, and you can and should sue.) When they discovered their error they attempted to add you to the indictment against me. But this they could not legally do, because I had petitioned the Federal Court for Removal, and that put the State of California in a position where they could not dismiss the indictment or alter it in any way —this is the law.

Seek to Kill You

Because they had lied and politically slandered your name so vociferously, they entered into a conspiracy and brought about a fraud indictment against you. (They tried to have me lie to help frame you—but I refused). I'm not just talking—I have proof that Richard Nixon on down to the lowest pig—they have all conspired to kill you.

When I tried to tell the world about this I was silenced. I have refused to talk to anybody but your mother. Because I know mothers won't sell out.

Slavery

For seven (7) years I have been forced into slavery on a flagrant, racist slave conviction, where the pigs have used any and all types of falsehood to avoid releasing me and to hide their Klan acts in this case.

In my conviction is to be found the history of indisputable vicious police brutality, and the use of known false and fraud evidence (known by the court) instigated by the District Attorney at my trial.

The same Klansman, California Attorney General Thomas G. Lynch, has conspired with other cowards to murder me and you through the use of their best game "false and fraud evidence," while simultaneously hiding the real issues surrounding this case.

Your name is being used as propaganda to exploit Blacks and make a bunch of "Toms," lackeys and Klans rich.

During this period of over 7 years I have been in prison-slavery, on known fraud and false evidence, I have filed numerous petitions, documents, etc. in State and Federal courts—only to receive flagrant racist court orders, delays and denials.

When I appealed to the appellate courts trying to obtain justice

Klan-pig Attorney General Lynch, the judges and court-appointed attorney willfully suppressed records (evidence) and fraudulently prepared some transcripts to use on appeal.

Based on those fraudulent records my case was reversed (and I should have gone free). But it went back to the Superior Court for the second trial, where I was viciously beaten in the courtroom in presence of the trial judge and spectators of the court for merely attempting to represent myself, and then I was beaten, tied and gagged and again convicted on false and fraud evidence.

In this Marin County court case they should have done the same thing except too many people were watching. I have Thomas G. Lynch now on appeal—he has been caught red handed in the U.S. 9th Circuit Court with fraud transcripts. Not only is Lynch using fraud, but also they are suppressing records (evidence) to continue to illegally enslave me.

Now after putting and forcing me to remain in slavery, the prison (klan) officials entered into the overall conspiracy to illegally and criminally enslave me. They stopped my mail, suppressed and destroyed legal documents and were able to hold me in slavery by force, fraud, trickery and deception for over 7 years secretly.

There Is No Legal Cause to Show for My Imprisonment

Nobody dares deny the fact that I have been illegally held in slavery for 7 years; but they don't have to, because the courts are all full of coward Klan judges "practicing slavery under color of law—without authority"—then with their witty play on words to avoid confrontation with the true issue.

Thinking there may be some justice somewhere, I appealed to Governor Reagan, showing him my illegal conviction on part of the judicial racism—all Reagan did was to condone the slavery and the Klan acts, even after I showed him the attempts to murder me, for attempting to expose the many violations of my civil and constitutional rights.

I have relatives, but their ignorance (individualism) coupled with their fear, made my induction into flagrant racist slavery all the easier for the pigs.

I wrote to all Black and other representatives for more than seven years. I even smuggled mail out of prison but received no help, or way out of prison-slavery until August 7, when Jonathan came to my succor.

As you can see from the little I've stated here, Reagan's gang (while prosecuting us) seeks to avoid answering questions such as:

(1) Didn't Magee have a right to rebel against flagrant racist slavery in such a criminal case?

(2) Were Magee and others in a conspiracy to take justice, with or without criminal intent when the police killed those people?

(3) Why does the news media refuse to tell what Magee and McClain left with those twelve jurors to tell the people about Magee being secretly kept 7 years in illegal slavery confinement?

Sister, what the hell do the California pigs look like prosecuting you or me, while they are at this moment suppressing evidence (trial records) violating the law to enforce their law?

Is not this the same law about which you are trying to inform the masses, for which our men are dying in Vietnam? If the people recognize what's destroying this country they'll immediately take action and this is why they are scared that somebody other than Nixon, Hoover, etc. is going to investigate this flagrant racism, slave and murder case.

We are going to win, because they cannot stand an investigation by the people—Black people—because pigs are the law breakers, not us.

We are going to bring out the real reason the pigs suppressed Grand Jury transcripts following the fraud indictment against you.

In an attempt to hide the truth and silence me, they have tried and tried to force on me a sell-out lawyer. . . . They don't want me to represent myself because I am going to tell the truth of the frame-up against you, and the facts that innocent persons were murdered to hide flagrant racism and slavery in this case. I will not use verbal trickery to fool the people and hide the pigs' acts.

The Marin County judges ran out of the case the moment I started to expose the slavery and murder, but Lynch doesn't have anything to lose, he has already committed enough crimes against the people to be put in the gas chamber—both he and Reagan.

Sister, all that is needed now is someone to trust, who will follow instructions, to present vital evidence to the people, and we'll run Reagan and his Klan-gang into the sea.

My best advice to you is watch everybody. The pig is trying to hide the truth, they're scared. And that's when they are most dangerous. This is not to scare you, but to make you more aware because the pig coward dog is playing with your life to make a dollar.

All comrades send their regards, and Right-On!

You will be freed!

All Power to the People!

RUCHELL MAGEE

P.S. Give all of my revolutionary regards to all my revolutionary sisters.

April 23, 1971
San Quentin Prison

Sister,

. . . Angela, the reason I am being "yoked" with lawyers is because I have evidence of the murder of Fred Billingslea, who was a witness in my case. Other witnesses to my case have been beaten, [maimed] and some killed—murdered by State agents, so there will be no witnesses to their acts.

No *"lawyer"* will touch this case exposing these above-mentioned and other *"facts,"* but even if anything is [ever] mentioned by them, it will be so watered down [that] it will sound untrue.

Angela, Governor Ronald Reagan conspired with other known pigs to murder me long before you ever came into this case. And [there are] murders in this case you know nothing about.

In the month of July 1970, Governor Reagan ordered prison warden Louis S. Nelson to confine and keep me in the prison "hole" cell, alleging that I threatened him as a result of Reagan concealing documentary evidence . . . After being put in the hole, they had a white nazi inmate take a swing at me with his fist, and [then he] moved swiftly back out of the way, while a Guard shot at me but other Blacks jumped in front of me and exposed the plot by shouting, "You are all trying to murder the brother, to hide murder [while] illegally enslaving this man . . . We all know what's happening."

That same day the same brothers fought and beat the inmate nazis on the yard, because of Reagan's set up to murder me.

August 7, 1970, while I was still in the prison hole, held incommunicado, James McClain called me as a witness to save my life and lost his.

But this, among other things, is why the pigs kept secret what was given [to] those 12 jurors during the conference on August 7 in Judge Harold Haley's Courtroom, when we explained what we [sought] to expose.

Angela, you're being framed for something you know nothing about. Only those guns are being used as a trick way to tie you into this slave case, and to deceive the people to believe that the case is something other than what it's all about: "murder and flagrant racism slavery."

. . . I can and will prove your innocence and expose the frame-up charges against us. I will prove and show that nobody made any escape attempts, etc. trying to free the three Soledad Brothers as the Klan news media and fraud indictment allege. I will prove and show that the only statement which was made concerning the Soledad Brothers was that relating to Jonathan Jackson (one of the Soledad Brothers—brother) who McClain stated that we wanted Free to Speak. Yes, Jonathan was going to tell why he brought those guns into Court—but he was killed before we reached the radio news station. We—me, McClain and Christmas [were] going to tell that which we told those 12 jurors, and expose some more to the world—the conspiracy between the California judicial and prison system murdering and enslaving innocent people under color of law, without legal power or authority.

I can and will prove that I had a right (human right) to rebel against slavery after receiving 7 years of flagrant racist courts, insults, delays and denials. I can and will prove the conspiracy that exists from the U.S. Supreme Court, President Nixon [on down] to the prison guards in this case. It was Nixon who used the news media to deceive the people to believe that we [were] guilty as charged before a trial . . .

. . . Yes, the people have heard the District Attorney Gary Thomas and other pigs accuse me of killing Judge Haley . . . But truth is, Gary Thomas is lying and in a direct conspiracy with the Los Angeles County pigs and others to have me murdered to hide their klan bestial acts. *All they are doing is strengthening fraud to hide fraud.* Why do you think that I am being denied freedom of press and of speech? The klan Judges have it so that I cannot see or speak to members of the press whom I choose to see . . .

All Power to the People

RUCHELL MAGEE

VI

Angela Davis

15

A
Political Biography

In these times, when the fight to uphold one's humanity is a revolutionary act, the false difference between "personality" and "politics" can no longer be maintained. It is in this light that we must understand the life of Angela Davis, for, as she said, the struggle of a true revolutionary is *"to merge the personal with the political to the point where they can no longer be separate."* In the profoundest of ways, it is only when *"you don't see your life, your individual life, as being so important"* that it begins to become important, politically, for others in the common fight for freedom. *"I have given my life for the struggle,"* Angela declared. *"My life belongs to the struggle."* In order, then, to understand this life, we must understand that struggle.

It is a struggle that Angela Davis, raised in the deep South of Birmingham, Alabama, was born into 27 years ago. She grew up among a whole generation of Black people who had seen their men risk their lives overseas in a fight against foreign fascism only to return home and find that same mentality still directed against themselves. They returned to a South where racism was "God's own truth" and segregation "the American way of life." It was in this South that Angela, like so many other Blacks, grew into awareness. She saw the symbols of law and order represented by the likes of George Wallace and Bull Connor, the burning cross of the old South, the electric cattle prods of the new. Yet she also saw, among her generation, the first glimmerings of a renewed resistance, and she joined that resistance, picketing segregated facilities, canvassing in voter registration, participating in integrated study groups. These early years were years of young hopes, old, abiding fears. She lived on "Dynamite Hill," where Black families lived in constant fear of racist reprisals. *"Every night now,"* she wrote, *"I'll hear white crackers planting bombs around the house. We are supposed to be next anyway."* It was this same Birmingham of her youth that brutally returned to her in those nightmare days of 1963 when four Black children were killed in the bombing of a Birmingham church. Angela knew these four girls and their families and, like others in Birmingham, she knew who their killers were. But of course no arrests were made. No wonder she could write to a friend up North several years later, *"Policemen are watching our house all the time. Perhaps I won't leave Birmingham alive."*

When she was 15, Angela did leave Birmingham. She received a Quaker scholarship to a New York City high school. There, despite her obvious intelligence, she had to study harder than most of the students to compensate for the inferior, segregated education she had received in the South. But she made rapid progress and at the end of her senior year Angela was awarded a scholarship to Brandeis University, where she chose French literature as her major field.

In her junior year, she studied at the Sorbonne in Paris, where she met Algerian students who told of their country's struggle for liberation from French colonialism. And she watched the French police constantly stop, search and harass the Algerian students or any "dark-complexioned person" suspected of being Algerian, because their nation wanted independence. In her final year at Brandeis, Angela began philosophical studies with Professor Herbert Marcuse and devoted herself to her studies, graduating magna cum laude with honors in French literature.

She changed to philosophy for her graduate work, continuing her studies on a German State Scholarship at Goethe University in Frankfurt, West Germany. There, Angela became active in German SDS, a socialist student group which organized demonstrations against the Vietnam War. After two years of study, however, she decided to leave Germany. She returned home to join the struggle.

She enrolled at the University of California at San Diego to complete her doctoral program under Professor Marcuse. While at UCSD, Angela became intensely involved in the Southern California Black community, organizing around community issues, unemployment, police brutality, and, on her own campus, fighting for a Third World people's college—Lumumba-Zapata College. At this time, she also saw that such activities do not go long unpunished in an oppressive, racist society. The murder of 18 year old Gregory Clark by the LA police signalled to her the fascist, police state tactics that would become commonplace in countering any genuine, social advance in the struggle for equality and freedom. Joining the struggle was no mere "intellectual" commitment, for it meant putting one's life on the line. Soon thereafter, Angela joined the Communist Party and became an active member of the Che-Lumumba Club, an all-Black collective of the Communist Party in Los Angeles.

Later she worked closely with the Black Panther Party. During that period she saw two of her friends, Los Angeles Panther leaders John Huggins and Alprentice (Bunchy) Carter, gunned down on the U.C.L.A. Campus. These were days of personal peril as well as commitment.

Some professors maintain the luxury of merely "entertaining," playing with ideas; others, who take their task more seriously, refuse to *profess* what they do not believe. Angela was one of the latter group; she stood by and was committed to her professed ideals. Therefore, after being appointed as a UCLA philosophy professor in the Fall of 1969, when she was fingered by an FBI undercover agent as a Communist, she replied to the University of California Board of Regents, *"Yes, I am a Communist. And I will not take the fifth amendment against self-incrimination, because my political beliefs do not incriminate me; they incriminate the Nixons, Agnews, and Reagans."* These men, she insisted, are the real criminals of this society, capitalist yes-men who have stolen the wealth of the world from the people by exploitation and oppression.

Angela was aware of the fact that, as masses of people here and abroad are radically challenging this state of affairs, so the oppressors would respond with ever higher levels of repression and go to any lengths to silence and, if necessary, murder any individual who spoke out and organized against their system. And yet she dared to speak out. This example of a Black woman proudly admitting to being a revolutionary, a Communist, and openly challenging capitalism gave inspiration and pride to those who had been too long silent. She was becoming a symbol of free speech and open resistance that Governor Reagan and his co-conspirators could no longer tolerate. And so began the conspiracy to silence her, the legal schemes, the lynch mob atmosphere, the open use of force. First, they attempted to fire her from UCLA because she was a Communist, but when the Courts ruled this move unconstitutional, they were forced to look for other ways.

Meanwhile, Angela continued to teach at UCLA. Her classes in recurring philosophical themes in Black literature were the most widely attended in the history of the school. She prepared her lectures scrupulously, gave freely of her time and knowledge, and at the class evaluation, was given "excellent" ratings by all but one of her several hundred students.

In early 1970, Angela became active in the defense of the Soledad Brothers, three Black prisoners unjustly accused of killing a prison guard. In her speeches, she constantly pointed out the fact that 30% of the national prison population was Black, while Blacks were only 15% of the population at large. This, she said, was indicative of the inherent racism of the American judiciary system. She protested against the growing number of political activists, especially Black Panther Party members, killed and jailed under the guise of law and order. Wherever she appeared, she emphasized the rise of police terror and repression and she continually explained that the loss of her job was small compared to the growing loss of Black and Brown lives.

In the course of the struggle around the Soledad Brothers' case, Angela became good friends with Jonathan Jackson, the younger brother of one of the Soledad defendants. Her own life was placed in constant jeopardy from a barrage of vigilante threats. Jonathan Jackson, as well as members of the Che-Lumumba Club, acted as security for Angela in order to prevent those threats from becoming reality.

Because of Angela's refusal to be silenced, because she continued to speak out against the growing repression of the state, because she organized people against the coming reign of police terror, Reagan once more tried to take away her job. In June, Angela was again fired by Reagan's Board of Regents. This time, the reason given was her speeches and active opposition to the genocidal policies of this government. Those people who had earlier accepted her being fired for Communist Party membership now began to have second thoughts. Could a person lose her livelihood only because she exercised her constitutional right to free speech? If this were the case, who might be next?

Reagan's firing of Angela came too late to stop the mass upsurge in her defense. Angela Davis had become a symbol of open and courageous resistance. She articulated a broad sentiment of defiance against oppression and the abridgement of civil and human rights. Her expulsion from the university only served to make those issues all the more clear. The Constitution, it seemed, was an expendable document to be bent to the wishes of those who rule us. Since taking Angela's job had not proven sufficient, Reagan now sought a new way to destroy her. He seized upon the August event at San Rafael courthouse as the perfect excuse. Using the most vague and unsubstantiated of charges, not of direct involvement but of "conspiracy," he is attempting to take Angela's life.

Thus ensued what was perhaps the most vicious and intensive manhunt in the history of this country. A young Black woman without any prior record of arrest, not directly accused of the commission of a crime, became the third woman in history to be placed on the FBI "Ten Most Wanted" list. Placing Angela on this list, where she was described as being "armed and dangerous," was equivalent to giving any crazed racist the right to shoot her on sight. The manhunt was also used as a pretext to raid private homes and movement offices across the country in an attempt to intimidate and harass all those who shared Angela's political views. She was finally arrested by FBI agents in New York on October 13, 1970.

While held in the Women's House of Detention in New York City, fighting extradition to California where she had been charged with kidnap for ransom, murder, and conspiracy, Angela was placed in solitary confinement. She had been isolated in a "psychological ward," away from her fellow prisoners, placed under 24 hour surveillance and harassment. In the tradition of all political prisoners, her captors had separated her from contact with others, for they fear, even here, her right of free speech, the power of her ideas. And while she was bound in solitary, outside, her accusers have continually attempted to try and convict her in the mass media. Richard Nixon congratulated J. Edgar Hoover over nationwide television upon her "capture," saying that her arrest would serve as an example to "all other terrorists." A lawsuit by the National Conference of Black Lawyers, mass demonstrations, thousands of letters and telegrams, achieved a victory by Judge Lasker's ruling to have Angela Davis released from solitary confinement.

Angela Davis was extradited to California three days before Christmas.

And so we stand, once more, in Angela's words, *"at the crossroads on the path of liberation."* Some would have us believe that Angela's political activities stem from a misguided or purely intellectual curiosity. But Angela's involvement in the struggle, as we have seen, grew out of the deep roots cast in the bloodstained earth of her Southern childhood, her experience of alienation as a token Black in an all-white university, the small, everyday indignities of being a Black woman in racist America; they are the result of her constant and continual resistance to injustice and inequality; her search for solutions to our problems of racism, exploitation, repression; her refusal to be silenced in that search by force or intimidation.

Of what, then, is Angela Davis guilty? Of being the natural product of a society based upon racism, exploitation, and dehumanization? Of her struggle for a socialist society? Her accusers have locked her into their cells of silence for they fear what she professes, what she freely and courageously declares. But when they cannot silence her even here, when her words echo far beyond these closed and soundproofed walls, then they seek to take her life. The final solution—Death.

So, for her, the life—the struggle, are one. Not merely in conjecture, in abstract theory, but in brutal fact. For her beliefs, for her life, Angela Davis stands accused. Her life is at stake. And yet she is innocent. Innocent of the charges of murder and kidnap. She stands guilty only of loving humanity and fighting with her life for the freedom of all of us.

FREE ANGELA! FREE OUR SISTER!
FREE ALL POLITICAL PRISONERS!

The National United Committee
to free Angela Davis, Nov. 1970

16

Prison Interviews*

Q. *Are you hopeful of winning justice in the courts, or not?*

A. The court system in this country is increasingly becoming a powerful instrument of repression. It is being used to crush the struggle for the liberation of oppressed people and not only to crush the conscious revolutionary but to break the rebellious spirit of black people, Chicanos and Puerto Ricans in general. And I think that one of the best methods of radicalizing an individual today is to have him spend a day in court witnessing the way we are unceasingly railroaded into the jails and prisons. Now even the facade of democracy is beginning to fall. Therefore we can't expect justice from a repressive judicial system and I'm sure that an exclusively legalistic approach to my defense would be fatal. So what we have to do is to talk about placing the courts on trial. Oppressed people must demonstrate in an organized fashion to the ruling class that we are prepared to use every means at our disposal to gain freedom and justice for our people.

I understand that you have been getting mail from all over the world. Could you give us some idea of your thoughts on the worldwide support that you're getting and what the nature of your mail has been?

Well, the support from abroad has been overwhelming. All the socialist countries have lodged protests in some way or form. I was particularly pleased to hear of the activity that has been going on in Cuba and in Europe, especially in Germany, Italy and France. Demonstrations have been organized. Petition campaigns, poster

---

* Portions of these interviews appeared in the *Guardian,* and *Muhammed Speaks.*

and button campaigns have been initiated and funds are being raised. Right now I receive from 100 to 400 letters a day, at least half of them originating from abroad, including many countries in Latin America, Asia and Africa. The thousands of letters from school children in the GDR have been tremendously moving. Just recently the World Council of Peace met at Stockholm and decided to wage an international campaign in my defense. The international support I've been receiving is extremely important but I think it is all the more important that this campaign be extended, that its limits be extended to become a fight to release all political prisoners within this country.

In your own formation as a revolutionary you spent a good deal of time in countries like France, West Germany and Cuba. Can you compare your experiences abroad in this regard?

One can't really be a true revolutionary without being cognizant of the need to link up with forces all over the world battling with imperialism. My trips abroad, most of which were undertaken for purposes involving my university studies, contributed a great deal to my own political development. In Paris in 1962 experiences which were transmitted to me by partisans of the Algerian struggle provided a stark contrast to our civil rights struggle in the United States. The increasingly aggressive posture being assumed by the Algerians gave me a concrete idea of the general direction in which our own movement should be heading; that is, if we were really serious about total change. As for the French themselves, they conveyed to me the idea, free from abstraction, that repression was a universal phenomenon wherever there were people struggling for freedom and justice. In a number of demonstrations, I personally felt the cutting streams of water from the firehoses manned by French police. And of course my Algerian acquaintances were incessantly subjected to police harassment.

My trip to Germany, inspired by a desire to learn more about the philosophical tradition out of which Marxism arose, taught me one basic fact. Marx was right when he said in the 11th of the Feurbach theses that philosophers as philosophers have simply interpreted the world and that the point, however, is to change it. This I experienced by witnessing and participating in the student movement growing conscious of itself, growing conscious of the need to break away from the mentors—the very philosophers who had stimulated the students to comprehend the nature of Marxism—and begin to act, to act directly. This action took the form of increasingly militant demonstrations against U.S. imperialism, its aggression in Vietnam, its flunkies in West Germany and also the form of moving to organize the dispossessed at a grassroots level and the attempt to involve labor. It was my involvement in the demonstrative political activity led by German SDS (Socialist Students League) which made me realize that I had to come home to wage the fight among my own people, black people.

The Cuban experience was immensely enlightening. My first prolonged contact with a socialist country through my own eyes and limbs too, I might add, since I cut cane for a while. Through discussions with Cubans throughout the country—workers, students, Communist party leaders—I became aware of the tremendous commitment, sacrifice and knowledge that is required in order to make a revolution work. We saw the problems as well as the achievements and I think that the brother in The Battle of Algiers was unquestionably correct when he contended that although a revolution is hard to initiate and although it is even harder to sustain to the point of seizing power, the most difficult period of all is the building of the revolutionary society after the seizure of power.

I was most concerned with the transformations that had occurred with respect to the position of black people. The total picture was overwhelmingly positive, but we detected vestiges of cultural racism which have to be combated, of course, in order to insure the continued success of the revolution. Cubans, both black and white, were very receptive to our comments which were often critical in this regard. Learning from the Cuban variety of pre-revolutionary racism which was certainly much less ingrained in the institutional and psychological makeup of Cuba under the puppet regimes of North American imperialism than is the U.S. variety, it became obvious that we would have to wage a relentless battle against racism at all times and on all levels. The Cuban experience was very invigorating. The people's day-to-day achievements as well as the problems they confronted in constructing socialism in their country through identification with all struggles against U.S. imperialism, particularly with the militant fights of Africans in America, all this infused me with more determination to return home and help to advance our struggle to higher planes.

Could you tell us, Angela, what led you to join the Communist party here in the United States?

My decision to join the Communist party emanated from my belief that the only true path of liberation for Black people is the one that leads towards a complete and total overthrow of the capitalist class in this country and all its manifold institutional appendages which insure its ability to exploit the masses and enslave Black people. Convinced of the need to employ Marxist-Leninist principles in the struggle for liberation, I joined the Che-Lumumba Club, which is a militant, all-black collective of the Communist party in Los Angeles committed to the task of rendering Marxism-Leninism relevant to Black people. But mindful of the fact that once we as Black people set out to destroy the capitalist system we would be heading in a suicidal direction if we attempted to go at it alone. The whole question of allies was crucial. And furthermore aside from students, we need important allies at the point of production. I do not feel that all white workers are going to be inveterate conservatives. Black leadership in working class struggles is needed to radicalize necessary sectors of the working class.

The practical perspective of the Che-Lumumba Club is based on an awareness of the need to emphasize the national character of our people's struggle and to struggle around the specific forms of oppression which have kept us at the very lowest levels of American society for hundreds of years, but at the same time to place ourselves as black people in the forefront of a revolution involving masses of people to destroy capitalism, to eventually build a socialist society and thus to liberate not only our own people but all the downtrodden in this country. And further, recognizing the international character of the revolution especially in this period when the battle against our homegrown capitalists is being carried out all over the world, in Indochina, Africa and Latin America. My decision to join the Communist party was predicated in part on the ties the party has established with revolutionary movements throughout the world.

How do you see the relationship of Blacks and whites in terms of united struggle here in this country? Do you think that black-white unity is possible and if so, on what grounds?

Well, the point has been made often that the Black people acting alone are capable of overthrowing the capitalist system in this country. If we organize ourselves correctly, this position continues, we can unleash enough violence to bring the country to its knees; we can destroy it entirely. Perhaps this is true, I don't know—but nonetheless, I think there is a fundamental fallacy in the notion of revolution that's implied in this position, for the essence of a successful revolution in this country will not be the destruction of the country but rather the destruction of the institutions which deter the people from having access to their own creations. And no one can deny that the genesis of U.S. capitalism was inextricably bound up with the exploitation of slave labor. Black people created the basis for all the wealth and riches accumulated in the hands of a few, powerful families in this country today. We therefore have a right to this wealth. Therefore, our fundamental strategy ought to consist not in destroying this wealth, but rather in abolishing the property relations which allow those few to hoard wealth while the masses of Black people eke out their existence at an extremely low economic level. We must destroy the institutions in which racism and exploitation are crystallized and project at the same time new institutions which will allow us to be free.

But while the former position—the one that says Black people can destroy the country acting alone—bases its activity on military strategy alone, the latter position of course will have to call for political strategy in the context of which perhaps military tactics will play a subordinate role together with all the varying tactical considerations we decide will best carry us to victory. Now starting with the assumption that we African men and women, super-exploited over the centuries in all and sundry forms, want total liberation from capitalism, we must inevitably draw the conclusion that our thrust towards liberation must be organically bound up with the movement involving large numbers of white people who through a socialist revolution will liberate themselves. And particulary whites at the point of production, for after all we want to take over, not destroy, the production apparatus in order to revolutionize the relations of production so that the people who work that apparatus collectively receive the fruits of their labor. This is the only way we as black people can come into our own and this is the only way the masses of white people can cease to be puppets for the ruling class. But we can never lose sight of the fact that insofar as the oppression of Black people is concerned, the majority of whites in this country has been deluded not only in the sense of accepting the racist policies of the capitalist class and its government but they've also actively perpetuated racism to the degree that it has become absolutely imbedded in the social fabric of this country. Therefore, the whole problem of black-white unity is a very tenuous one under these circumstances and precisely because of the all-pervasive nature of racism, the issue of black-white unity can be resolved only by recognizing the necessity for black people to provide the leadership for the total struggle.

Black-white unity with black people in the forefront—because the phenomenon of racism and super-exploitation under capitalism has not only placed black people at the very lowest plane of the social order but it has also paralyzed the ability of whites to struggle in a radical fashion. The reactionary tendencies of many trade unions are directly proportional to their inability to transcend their own racist policies. Black people, on the other hand, have unfolded in response to our oppression an increasingly revolutionary understanding as well as an increasingly militant practice to rid ourselves of our oppressors. In order for black-white unity to become a reality it will be imperative for whites to acknowledge the central necessity of combating racism on all levels. It will be imperative for whites to accept the leadership of Black people.

Do you think it is possible to beat back and defeat the Nixon administration's attempt to drive the country to the right?

First of all, if we attempt an objective appraisal of conditions in this country, I'm convinced that we will not infer that fascism in its full maturity has descended upon us. This evaluation, however, does not indicate that we now live within the confines of a perfect bourgeois democracy—by no means. This country is galloping at high speed down the path leading to South African-type fascism. The very fact that political prisoners are rapidly increasing in number and are emerging as a central focus around which masses of people are mobilizing is indicative of the fascist tendency of the time. And we should never forget that fascist tactics have been employed against Black people, Black communities, for centuries. Fascist tactics of repression should, however, not be confused with fascism. To do so would be to obfuscate the nature of our struggle today—for once we have acknowledged the existence of a mature fascism our struggle takes on a purely defensive character and virtually all of our energies are concentrated on the task of defending ourselves from the onslaught of oppression, for the circumstances surrounding our existence have so degenerated that we have lost all possibility of movement; that the only alternative for organizing is the clandestine type. Conditions in this country have not yet deteriorated to that level. We still retain a slight degree of flexibility. Therefore, we must continue to make use of the legal channels to which we have access which of course does not mean that we operate exclusively on the legal plane. At this point, the underground movement has its role to play also. The important thing is to realize that we must do everything in our power to consolidate and solidify a mass movement devoted to struggling not only against repression but with the positive idea of socialism as its goal. This means, of course, that we assume an offensive rather than a defensive posture.

As an active campaigner for the freedom of political prisoners before your own arrest and now as a political prisoner yourself, how do you see this fight in its relation to the movement as a whole?

The movement which is beginning to crystallize around political prisoners is extremely important on a number of different levels. Under fascism such a movement would be virtually impossible, relating to what I said before. At this juncture the success of that movement will be determined not only by its ability to secure the release of political prisoners, but perhaps more important by its ability to expand into a movement geared to overthrow the system itself.

It is important in this connection to realize the Black political prisoner is very often a communist, whether she or he be a member of the Communist party, as I am, or an independent communist such as George Jackson [brother of the slain Jonathan Jackson and a prisoner in Soledad]. The meaning of scientific socialism and therefore the underlying reason for many of the frameups of Black revolutionaries must be revealed to the masses of people, particularly Black people. And eventually the fight around political prisoners will become one of the many components out of which a mass, socialist-inspired movement for liberation of black and white will emerge.

This means people must begin to understand not only that George Jackson and the other Soledad Brothers have been falsely accused of killing a prison guard of that "correctional facility" as it's called, but that George was singled out because he is a Black communist and in fact, he had been previously compelled to do 10 years for a crime which ordinarily entails no more than two years by the oppressive California parole board precisely because of his politics and his efforts to persuade his fellow captives to enlist in the struggle for Black liberation, to enlist in the struggle for the destruction of capitalism.

To move to another level on which the fight around political prisoners must be waged, we must also link up the circumstances leading to the frameup of so many Black revolutionaries with the generalized genocidal attack on our people and thereby relate the issue of the political prisoner to the concrete needs and interests of Black people.

For it is not often that one encounters in any Black ghetto in this country a family that has not experienced some immediate contact with the corrupt judicial system and a repressive prison apparatus. It is not only impossible for a Black revolutionary to get justice in the courts, but Black people in general have been the victims rather than the recipients of bourgeois justice.

Therefore, a major focus of the struggle around political prisoners ought to be offensive rather than defensive in character and should consist in placing the bankrupt judicial system and its appendages, the jails and prisons, on trial. We must lay bare the whole system and concretely associate the movement to liberate political prisoners with the grassroots movements that are exploding in the dungeons all over this country.

The press, as you know, has vilified David Poindexter and some of this feeling has been picked up by sections of the left. Can you say something about David Poindexter?

The bourgeois press will always resort to the most devious means of discrediting those who rebel against the establishment. They consciously contrived an image of David Poindexter as the "mysterious companion" implying often that in fact, it might have been this man about whom nothing was known who turned me in.

Those individuals on the left who drew such conclusions allowed themselves to be led into a trap set by agents of our enemy. I insist that David Poindexter should be admired for his acts, for he put his life on the line in order to assist me to escape my executioners. And I ask this question, how many of those who have criticized him would have been willing to go so far?

How do you see the women's movement? Also, do you consider it to have a special role for Black women?

Let me begin by saying this: no revolutionary should fail to understand the underlying significance of the dictum that the success or failure of a revolution can almost always be gauged by the degree to which the status of women is altered in a radical, progressive direction. After all, Marx and Engels contended that there are two basic facts around which the history of mankind revolves: production and reproduction. The way in which people obtain their means of subsistence on one hand and in which the family is organized on the other hand.

Further, if it is true the outcome of a revolution will reflect the manner in which it is waged, we must unremittingly challenge anachronistic bourgeois family structures and also the oppressive character of women's role in American society in general. Of course, this struggle is part and parcel of a total revolution. Led by women, the fight for the liberation of women must be embraced by men as well. The battle for women's liberation is especially critical with respect to the effort to build an effective Black liberation movement. For there is no question about the fact that as a group, Black women constitute the most oppressed sector of society.

Historically we were constrained not only to survive on an economic level as slaves, but our sexual status was that of a breeder of property for the white slave master as well as being the object of his perverse sexual desires. Our enemies have attempted to mesmerize us, to mesmerize Black people, by propounding a whole assortment of myths with respect to the Black woman. We are inveterate matriarchs, implying we have worked in collusion with the white oppressor to insure the emasculation of our men. Unfortunately, some Black women have accepted these myths without questioning their origin and without being aware of the counter-revolutionary content and effect. They're consequently falling into behind-the-scenes positions in the movement and refuse to be aggressive and take leadership in our struggle for fear of contributing to the oppression of the Black male.

As Black women, we must liberate ourselves and provide the impetus for the liberation of Black men from this whole network of lies around the oppression of Black women which serve only to divide us, thus impeding the advance of our total liberation struggle.

There is must to be learned from the progression of George Jackson's ideas around the issue of Black women. His book ["Soledad Brother"] ought to be read from that perspective. Unfortunately a letter to me that dealt extensively with the transformation he had experienced himself with respect to Black women was not among the few that were published in the book. Perhaps it can be published at a later date.

Can you describe how you are being treated in the women's house of detention?

This is a prison and the atrocious conditions that characterize virtually every American prison are present in this place. Rather than start with the specific treatment I have been receiving, I would like to delineate the circumstances under which all of us are compelled to exist.

First of all, the prison is filthy. It is infested with roaches and mice. Often we discover roaches cooked into our food. Not too long ago, a sister found a mousetail in her soup. A few days ago I was drinking a cup of coffee and I was forced to spit out a roach.

Roaches literally cover the walls of our cells at night, crawling across our bodies while we sleep. Every night we hear the screams of inmates who wake up to find mice scurrying across their bodies. I discovered one in bed with me last night in fact.

The medical conditions here are abominable. The doctors are racists and entirely insensitive to the needs of the women here. One sister who is housed in my corridor complained to the doctor not too long ago that she had terrible pains in her chest.

After which the doctor suggested to her that she get a job without once examining her. It was later discovered that the sister had tumors in her breast and needed immediate hospital attention. This is indicative of the way we are treated here.

We spend most of our time in either 5 x 9 cells with filth and concrete floors or outside on the bare corridors. We are not even allowed to place blankets on the floor where we must sit to protect ourselves from the filth and the cold.

To talk a little about the library, they have a collection of adventure stories and romances which they have designated the library. It is important to realize that although the prison population is 95 per cent Black and Puerto Rican, I found only five or six books about Black people and literature in Spanish is extremely scarce.

I could go on and on but perhaps now I will turn to the specific kinds of treatment I have been receiving myself. I am convinced that the authorities in this place have been instructed to make life as difficult as possible for me, probably in order to convince me to stop fighting extradition.

Of course after the courts overruled them and they were compelled to release me from solitary confinement and 24-hour guard, they had to seek other ways to assert their dominance.

Unlike the other women who are being held for trial. I am forced to wear institutional clothing. They say I am a high security risk and they want to make it difficult for me to escape.

They refuse to permit my attorneys to give me legal material unless they first read it over, demonstrating that they have no respect whatsoever for the confidentiality which is supposed to exist between lawyer and client.

I could continue to enumerate a hundred little things that have been done in the hope of breaking me but I continue to give notice to them that there is absolutely nothing they can do to break my determination to keep struggling.

The only way they can accomplish this is by taking my life and then they would have to face the wrath of the people. The same holds true for Ericka, Bobby, George, the Soledad Brothers, etc.

What is your relationship with the other prisoners?

I have never encountered such an overwhelmingly warm and cordial welcome. Obviously the reason why the prison authorities isolated me was the enthusiastic welcome I received. Each time I go from one area of the jail to another, the sisters hold up their clenched fists and convey expressions of solidarity.

While I was in solitary confinement, the sisters on the floor conducted demonstrations in my behalf. When I embarked upon a hunger strike, many of them joined.

After I was transferred into population, some of the sisters on my corridor, with whom I had spent a great deal of time, were helping me answer letters from the outside. They were all immediately transferred to another floor but we still find ways to communicate with one another.

I have already mentioned the state of the so-called library. After many requests and arguments, I was told that if books were sent directly from the publishing company I could receive them.

Now the authorities allow me to bring up five of these books at a time per week. The sisters are immensely interested in the reading material I receive—everything from George Jackson's prison letters to works by Lenin.

The books circulate all over the floor and are the occasion for many a discussion. Since the authorities have indicated that they are totally insensitive to the desires of the inmates, I would hope that brothers and sisters in the streets take it upon themselves to donate relevant literature to the library here.

VII

Angela Davis and
Ruchell Magee on Trial

17

Angela—
Symbol of Resistance
by Howard Moore, Jr.*

Angela Davis had nothing whatsoever to do with the Slave Insurrection of August 7, 1970, the so-called shootout at the Courthouse in Marin County, California. Yet, Angela is locked in a barren, sunless cell on the second floor of the Marin County Civic Center Annex soon to stand trial for her life on charges that she kidnapped, murdered and conspired with seventeen year old Jonathan Jackson to commit those crimes and to secure the rescue and escape of other Black prisoners. It sounds incredible that, though Angela neither instigated, encouraged, aided or abetted those who participated in that Slave Insurrection, she must nonetheless defend her life against these charges.

Upon Angela's appointment as Assistant Professor of Philosophy at the University of California at Los Angeles, she did not give in to the pressure of Ronald Reagan, reactionary Republican Governor of California, and his Board of Regents when she was accused in the fall of 1969 of being a member of the Communist Party. "Yes, I am a Communist," she boldly admitted and seized the offensive.

Her lectures drew record attendance of 1500 students. Most of the faculty and student body at the University defended her right to teach and to belong to the Communist Party, to them a basic issue of academic freedom. In her first lecture on Frederick Douglass, Angela said for a people in slavery, "the first condition

* Mr. Moore is chief counsel for Miss Davis.

of freedom is an open act of resistance—physical resistance, violent resistance."

Angela quickly became a much sought after public speaker, and as her views and courage became more widely known, she became a public figure. The power and clarity of her ideas drew the attention of other sectors of the American people. Her ideas were relevant and compelling. Angela's thoughts about education were that, "education itself is inherently political. Its goal ought to be political." She called academic freedom "a concept which many professors seek to use to guarantee their right to work undisturbed by the real world, undisturbed by the real problems of this society."

All the time, the Regents of the University of California were monitoring her speeches. Upon discharging Angela in June 1970, despite her two-year teaching appointment, the Regents cited as proof of her unsuitability to continue teaching a speech in which she declared it was necessary "to unveil the predominant, oppressive ideas and acts of this country" and "to begin to develop not only criticism but positive solutions and to carry out these paths in the universities. Otherwise academic freedom is a real farce."

These words were not idle rhetoric, only intended to draw excited "Right Ons" from captive audiences, but rather serious statements of conviction which soon led to Angela's involvement in the mass movement to "Save the Soledad Brothers from Legal Lynching." The lives of the Soledad Brothers rested on the formation of a mass movement, which would use every legal avenue of struggle to save them from lynching early one morning in the green room of California's San Quentin Prison.

Angela joined that movement and inspired it to reach new heights of struggle and the rallying cry to save the Soledad Brothers became a popular slogan, signalling broad-based resistance to that special kind of oppression that is the lot of Blacks, Chicanos, and the poor. Angela's involvement in the fight to save the Soledad Brothers resulted in her becoming a living symbol of intelligent, creative, and resolute resistance to racism in California's prisons. However, these qualities standing alone would not have so readily marked Angela as the target for political repression, but Angela exemplified a dangerous quality. From her repeated statements, it was at once apparent that Angela's life had been given over to the struggles of her people—Black people—and was "organically bound up with the lives of all the millions who struggle for freedom and justice." She exemplified and exemplifies the potential for binding the wick to the keg, and, as Malcolm X taught, the wick is more dangerous than the keg.

The terror and racism which had brought death to three Black inmates and confronted the Soledad Brothers with sudden death was not localized to Soledad Prison, but had also exposed its ugly head in San Quentin Prison. On February 26, 1970, a Black inmate, Fred Billingslea, was gassed in his cell and beaten to death. The prison administration succeeded for a good while in preventing any news of the summary execution of Billingslea and of the resistance which his death generated from leaking out.

The resistance movement inside San Quentin which took the form of work refusals and hunger strikes was led by three Black inmates, James McClain, Ruchell Magee and William Christmas. They too, as were the Soledad Brothers and most prison inmates, were serving inordinately long sentences for alleged "crimes against property." Magee was serving the most cruel of all possible sentences—life without possibility of parole—for the commission of first degree robbery and kidnapping for the purpose of robbery. Ten dollars ($10) was involved in his alleged robbery, in which no one was physically harmed or injured.

Magee could not gain his freedom from prison by rehabilitation or even "Toming," which he would never do. Life in prison without possibility of parole means Magee's mere act of living from day to day is an involuntary contribution to his punishment; for the longer he lives the longer he will be unjustly punished. The only way out of prison for Magee is through death or success in court by a collateral attack on his conviction.

In his quest for freedom, Magee became a student of the law and aided others to file over a thousand legal pleadings. Many of the inmates Magee helped secured their release from prison, but ironically over a seven year span of time from August 1965 to the present Magee has not even won the right to a hearing on any of the petitions, complaints, and briefs which he has filed in his own behalf. Magee's skill as a self-taught prison lawyer has now been grudgingly admitted by at least one judge.

On August 7, 1970, Magee finally got to court as a witness in the re-trial of James McClain. The previous trial of McClain in June 1970 for the alleged assault on a San Quentin Prison Guard during the rebellion around the Billingslea murder had ended in a mistrial. During McClain's examination of Magee, Jonathan Jackson, the seventeen year old brother of George Jackson, entered the courtroom. Jonathan armed McClain and Magee with weapons which he had brought with him. One of them quickly went to the holding cell near the courtroom and released William Christmas. The four of them then had a discussion with the jurors who were sitting in McClain's trial. The *San Francisco Chronicle* for August 12, 1970 gives the following account of what happened next as told by a woman hostage:

"The Judge was the first one picked as a hostage. They didn't use this coiled wire to tie him. They taped a gun around his neck.

"They had a court reporter but they decided to take the Deputy D.A. (District Attorney) instead. They were going to tie us around the neck with the wire but decided to tie us around the waist instead.

"They started to take an older woman juror and they changed their minds. They then picked another woman juror but she said she was sick—she told me before she was always upset about being picked as a juror. So they didn't take her.

"So they took me, and two other women jurors.

"And they brought this couple into the courtroom, and they had a baby. One of them said, 'Let's take the baby,' but the mother cried, 'No, no don't take my baby,' so they didn't.

"Well, before we left the courtroom, they made the judge call the sheriff downstairs. I didn't hear what the judge said, but now I know they told him to tell his men not to shoot."

Minutes later the four left the courtroom with Judge Haley, Deputy District Attorney Gary Thomas, and three women jurors; removed the taped gun from Judge Haley's neck; entered a yellow Hertz rented van; allowed the jurors to untie themselves and attempted to drive away into a hail of gunfire from San Quentin Guards and other law enforcement officers. When the gunfire subsided, McClain, Christmas, Jonathan, and Judge Haley were dead;

Magee and Gary Thomas seriously injured, and one of the jurors slightly injured.

Governor Reagan ordered an immediate investigation "of this vicious attack." He conferred with Chief Justice Donald R. Wright of the California Supreme Court about revisions of courtroom regulations and solicited the views of the presiding judges throughout the State regarding courtroom decorum. Reagan's concern was not just about the events in Marin County on August 7th, "but also those courtroom disruptions we have seen without violence." This was an obvious reference to the recent Chicago Conspiracy trial and it thus cast a blanket condemnation of violent as well as nonviolent resistance to white supremacy under color of law in the so-called halls of justice.

When it was learned that four of the guns young Jackson brought into the courtroom allegedly had been purchased over a two-year period by Angela, Governor Reagan frankly admitted his reason for having cast the first vote to fire Angela from her teaching position was because she was "a member of the Communist Party" (*San Francisco Chronicle,* August 13, 1970). Reagan could not conceal his vintage anti-communism. He exploited Angela's alleged connection with the guns to blast the Communist Party. Reagan said: "The Communist Party is considered to be not a political party per se but a subversive organization. . . . It is listed as a subversive organization by the Attorney General's office since its members have prior allegiance to another country."

The hunt was on for Angela, though there was no evidence that Angela had provided the guns for Jonathan for his use in the escape attempt. Albert Harris, the State Prosecutor, publicly admitted on August 13, 1970 that the State had no case against Angela. When he was asked what action would be taken against Angela, Harris replied, "Nothing, unless it can be proved she gave the guns to a minor with intent to use in the escape." (*San Diego Union,* August 13, 1970, p. A2.) Yet, on August 16, 1970, and even though no formal complaint had been obtained for her arrest by the State of California, wanted posters were issued for Angela by the F.B.I., alleging that she had crossed state lines to avoid prosecution for kidnapping and murder. Showing two recent photographs of Angela and detailing her body measurements, the poster cautioned, "Consider possibly armed and dangerous." J. Edgar Hoover, the director of the F.B.I., promptly designated Angela the most wanted criminal in America. Angela thereby became a shooting target for any law enforcement officer, stomp-down racist, or nut, had she shown her face. Any of them could have shot her down without so much as asking the time of day on the pretext they were slaying an escaping felon to prevent a failure of justice, if not on the jive time claim that she placed them in reasonable fear of bodily harm. Angela lived under the spectre of summary execution until her arrest in a mid-town motel in New York City with David Poindexter on October 13, 1970. And Nixon and Mitchell and Hoover arrogantly congratulated each other during prime time on national television that they had caught a "terrorist" such as Angela Davis as a warning to other "would be terrorists."

California sent an affidavit to New York to demand the return of Angela for prosecution, but the affidavit was so defective that California had to hastily go before the Marin County Grand Jury on November 10, 1970 and indict Angela for kidnap, murder, and conspiracy in order to overcome Angela's resistance to the extradition. The New York courts made short shrift of Angela's claim that California had no legal claim or right to extradite her and, on December 22, 1970, Mr. Justice Harlan of the United States Supreme Court refused to extend a stay of extradition so that Angela could appeal the extradition order to the Supreme Court. Justice Harlan said, "I find no legal basis for staying petitioner's extradition." The pretense that America cared for its slaves and could deal justly with them was no longer to be indulged.

The State dusted off an infrequently used 1872 law which provides, in part: "All persons concerned in the commission of a crime, whether it be felony or misdemeanor, and whether they directly commit the act constituting the offense, or aid and abet in its commission, or, not being present, have advised and encouraged its commission . . . are principals in any crime so committed." (Section 31, Penal Code.)

Section 31 of the California Penal Code is in derogation of the common law, because it abolishes the distinction between accessory before the fact and principals. The concept of accessory before the fact was developed in English law to reduce the number of executions as were the doctrines of benefit of clergy and coercion. Nevertheless, when the accused was not present at the scene, the State must show that the accused aided or abetted the commission of the crime or advised and encouraged its commission.

Neither the allegations of the indictment nor the evidence produced before the grand jury assert or show that Angela aided or abetted or advised and encouraged the commission of the crime or crimes with which she is charged. The first overt act charged in the conspiracy count of the indictment alleges that Angela advocated the lawful release of the "Soledad Brothers." The State charges that on several occasions Angela attempted to visit George Jackson at Soledad and later at San Quentin, sometimes accompanied by Jonathan, George's younger brother. The State, in its hysterical attempt to get Angela, transmutes her association with Jonathan and concern for the life of his brother into evidence of guilt of murder and kidnapping to secure George's release. Magee has publicly refuted the State's claim that the purpose of the August 7th Slave Insurrection was the release of the Soledad Brothers. In a letter to Angela, which was published in the *San Francisco Examiner* on May 12, 1971, Magee wrote that the purpose of the insurrection was to "expose to the world the conspiracy between California judicial and prison system murdering and enslaving innocent people under color of law without legal power or authority." Angela is charged with lawfully purchasing weapons on four separate occasions: January 12, 1968, a pistol, caliber .380, serial number 595071; April 7, 1969, a rifle, model, carbine .30 caliber, serial number 18514, manufactured by Plainfield; July 25, 1970, a rifle, M-1 carbine, .30 caliber, serial number 18052, manufactured by Plainfield; and August 5, 1970, a shot gun, 12 gauge, serial number 67297, manufactured by Spanish. It is claimed that each of these weapons was used on August 7th and that Angela furnished the weapons to Jonathan for that purpose. The prosecutor suppressed information before the grand jury which he had already publicly acknowledged that the automatic pistol, .380 caliber, was seized by the Los Angeles police in the course of an investigation of a robbery in May of 1968 and released on court order to someone other than Angela. The State contends that on August 6, 1970, the day before the insurrection, Angela and Jonathan were seen in the vicinity of the Marin County Courthouse in a yellow Ford van. The State next claims that Angela gave her personal check for a ticket on Pacific Southwest Airlines Flight 422 at 2 p.m., on August 7th for travel from San Francisco to Los Angeles and that she was not seen publicly again until she was arrested in New York. The trip from San Francisco to Los Angeles, notwithstanding the total absence of any evidence that Angela knew that the insurrection had taken place or that she was wanted, is incriminating, according to the State's draconian sense of criminality, because she was "terribly rushed, realizing that it was the last minute." The State ignores the explanation of Angela's haste which its own witness supplies: "She was terribly worried that she wouldn't make it because she had this check to write out."

The prosecutor is most aware of the lack of any evidence, direct or indirect, to connect Angela to the August 7th Slave Insurrection. He is quoted in the *San Francisco Chronicle & Examiner* on Sunday, February 21, 1971 as intending to "use every bit of evidence we can find between now and the time of the trial." While the legitimacy of a continuing investigation may be in order, was it fair to indict Angela on three capital charges and hold her without bail and then dig up or fabricate evidence against her? Could the prosecutor have been referring to bought or perjured testimony? There have been reports that a deal was offered to Angela's co-defendant Magee, if he would incriminate Angela. Another inmate at San Quentin, Leo Robles, wrote Judge E. Warren McGuire of the Marin County Superior Court about an alleged overture made to him to approach Magee "as one convict to another, to convince him that he would be granted immunity from prosecution and better living conditions while in prison if he would testify against Angela Davis." Judge McGuire did not conduct a hearing to test the truth of Robles' allegation, but summarily dismissed Robles' claim with the comment, "Similar accusations have been made by Mr. Magee against the undersigned and are false." What the judge is saying is not that the accusations of deals are false in fact but because I said so—*ipsa dixit*.

The charges against Angela are cunningly framed. Not only is Angela charged with aiding and abetting the August 7th Slave

Insurrection, but she is also charged as a co-conspirator. Section 182 of the California Penal Code defines conspiracy thusly: "If two or more conspire: 1. To commit any crime . . . 5. To commit any act injurious to the public health, to public morals, or to pervert or obstruct justice, or the due administration of the laws . . ."

If the purpose of the conspiracy is the commission of a felony such as kidnap or murder, the punishment for the conspiracy crime is the same as that fixed for murder or kidnap—death in the gas chamber or life imprisonment. The conspiracy charge immeasurably enhances the State's chances of securing a conviction. The addition of the conspiracy count allows the State great latitude in both the kind of evidence it may offer and the order of the proof. For example, the State can offer the alleged declaration of James McClain in the hall of the Marin Civic Center, "Free or Release the Soledad Brothers by 12:30 or all, they all die," to prove that the prime purpose of the Insurrection was the rescue of the Soledad Brothers from lawful custody, as well as to establish the existence of a conspiracy.

Therefore, it is little wonder that the modern law of conspiracy is directly traceable to the Star Chamber. 8 Holdsworth, *History of English Law,* 362, at 379. Mr. Justice Jackson, in his concurring opinion in *Krulewitch v. United States,* 336 U.S. 440, clearly pointed out the inherent viciousness of a conspiracy charge. He wrote: "Few instruments of injustice can equal that of implied or presumed or constructive crimes. The most odious of all oppressions are those which mask as justice." (336 U.S., at 457–58).

The conspiracy charge places Angela in triple jeopardy and paves the way for conviction on the basis of mental hearsay; that is, a jury may convict her, because she is Black and a Communist, because of what they think she thought, or even worse, would think.

As incredible as the charges against Angela are, they must be met at both the legal and political levels. It is not enough to meet them on just one level. That would be only a partial defense. The objective of the prosecution is not just to lynch Angela but to lynch her as a symbol of resistance. Angela, as a political prisoner soon to be tried for her life, is a tool in the hands of the reactionary white racist American ruling class. Angela is a symbol of what that ruling class would do to all Blacks if the chance presented itself. The objective of the prosecution is not merely to murder Angela, under color of law as they bomb and ravage the heroic people of Vietnam in quest of a peace only they prevent, but also to provide a ghastly example to all Blacks and people of revolutionary sentiments. The use of Angela as a symbol—a sort of latter day Harriet Tubman leading her people through the ideological thicket of decadent bourgeois democracy—is a manifestation of the long struggle in the United States between Black-led progressive forces and white-led forces of reaction. If Angela is a symbol to those forces which would willingly destroy her, she is equally a symbol to Black people and all oppressed people inside the United States.

Angela is a symbol of the People's resistance to tyranny and oppression. The people will win without a doubt, because they know that their resistance is not just in defense of a symbol, but in defense of a real live and courageous human being. They give life for life, not for death. The humanity of the people will triumph over the callous inhumanity of the ruling class. RIGHT ON KOJO! FREE ANGELA AND ALL POLITICAL PRISONERS WITHOUT A DOUBT!

18

From New York to California:
The Extradition of Angela Davis
by John Abt*

The story of the extradition of Angela Davis from New York to California provides a blatant example of "law and order," Nixon-Reagan-Rockefeller style, with heavy overtones of racism and anti-communism.

Angela was arrested by the FBI in New York on October 13, 1970, jailed in the Women's House of Detention for the night, and charged next morning before a United States commissioner with violating the Federal Interstate Fugitive Act. This law makes it a federal offense for a person to travel from one state to another for the purpose of evading prosecution by the first state. It is used primarily as a pretext for involving the FBI in what would otherwise be a local police case.

The commissioner, over the protest of Angela's attorneys, Margaret Burnham and the writer, fixed her bond at two hundred and fifty thousand dollars and adjourned the case while the federal authorities decided how to proceed. At eight o'clock that night, we were called back before the commissioner who, on motion of the United States Attorney, graciously released her from the bail he had fixed and turned her over to the tender mercies of two city detectives, to be held without bail pending state proceedings for her extradition to California.

As they took her from the courtroom, the detectives condescended to inform Miss Burnham and me that Angela would be "booked" at the Seventh Precinct police station. Arrived there,

* Mr. Abt was Miss Davis' attorney during the extradition proceedings.

the desk sergeant told us he knew nothing of Angela's where-abouts but directed us to another station house three miles away. During the next few hours, it appeared that the police department had mislaid our client, for no one in authority could tell us where to find her. I finally learned that she had been brought to night court for arraignment. I found the Criminal Courts building guarded by some two hundred policemen. Admission to the court-room was denied to all but lawyers and newsmen, all of whom were frisked, and its walls were lined with more police.

When I suggested that, given the lateness of the hour and my long search for my client, an adjournment until next day was in order, the prosecutor countered with the question, "Have you any idea how much money tonight is costing the City of New York?"

It was long after midnight when the brief arraignment formal-ities were concluded and Angela was returned to the House of Detention. There she was lodged in a cell block for psychiatric cases where she was awakened at four each morning by a white woman screaming obscenities at Blacks. Our protests resulted, after a week, in Angela's transfer to a normal cell block. Twenty-four hours later, however, she was placed in solitary confinement. Our protest to Mayor Lindsay elicited the reply from the Department of Correction that there was no such thing as solitary confinement in the Women's House of Correction. How solitary can confine-ment be? Angela was locked in her cell twenty-three hours a day, under the constant scrutiny of a guard, forbidden to communicate with other prisoners. The twenty-fourth hour was spent in solitary "recreation" on the jail roof, likewise under guard and incom-municado.

Our further protests were met by the contradictory inventions: first, that Angela would stir up rebellion if allowed to mingle with the other prisoners and, second, that isolation was essential for her safety. It was only as a result of her two week hunger strike and a lawsuit instituted by Miss Burnham and the National Conference of Black Lawyers that a federal judge finally ordered her release from solitary.

Meanwhile, the extradition proceedings continued. On October 19, Bruce Bales, Marin County district attorney, swore to a complaint and affidavit as the basis for Governor Reagan's request, on the following day, that Governor Rockefeller order Angela's extradition. Under New York law, the governor has thirty days to study such a request and to secure the opinion of his legal advisers on whether to act upon it. In Angela's case, Rockefeller issued an extradition warrant within twenty-four hours after Reagan had signed his request. And he spent those hours, not in weighing the legality of the request, but in garnering votes for reelection on the sidewalks of New York.

Had Rockefeller given the Bales affidavit the scrutiny that the law requires, he would have been forced to the conclusion that it was hopelessly defective in failing to furnish what lawyers call "probable cause" to believe Angela guilty of the crimes with which she was charged.

Bales' complaint accused her of murder and kidnapping for ransom. But neither he nor anyone else has ever pretended that she was present at the Marin County Civic Center on August 7 at the events which resulted in the deaths of Judge Harold Haley, Jonathan Jackson, James McClain and William Christmas. The basis of Bales' accusation was that she had "aided and abetted" the alleged murder of Judge Haley. In California, as in most states, an aider and abettor is a person who, knowing that a crime is about to be committed, and intending to assist in its commission, aids the principal actor in accomplishing the crime. And in California, one found guilty of aiding and abetting is liable to the same punishment as the principal actor. This, in Angela's case, means a mandatory sentence of either death in the gas chamber or life imprisonment and—in the case of kidnapping for ransom— life imprisonment without the possibility of parole.

The Bales affidavit was defective even in fixing responsibility for the death of Judge Haley. It stated merely that "one of the prisoners shot and killed" him, without identifying the kidnapper in question or even the name of the witness (if there was one) who supplied this information. Moreover, although the state must have made ballistic tests, the silence of the affidavit on this subject leaves the inference wide open that the judge was killed, not by his alleged abductors, but by the deputy sheriffs and correction officers whose guns were responsible for the deaths of Jackson, McClain and Christmas and the near-fatal wounding of Ruchell Magee, Angela's co-defendant.

The only allegation of the Bales affidavit connecting Angela with these events was the statement that the guns which Jonathan Jackson carried into the courtroom on that day had been openly purchased and publicly registered by her, as shown by registration statements which she had filled out and signed in compliance with state and federal law. The affidavit did not claim that Angela furnished Jonathan with the guns, let alone that she knew what he planned to do with them or intended to aid him in accomplishing his purpose. The affidavit thus omitted the essential ingredients of the offense of aiding and abetting. In their absence, Angela's purchase and registration of the guns is evidence, not of guilt, but of innocence, particularly in the light of the surrounding circumstances.

On November 5, 1970, Miss Burnham and I filed a petition for a writ of habeas corpus in the Supreme Court of New York (the state court of first instance) challenging Rockefeller's extradition warrant and demanding Angela's freedom on the ground that the Bales affidavit was wholly insufficient to satisfy the requirement of "probable cause" which the Fourth Amendment to the U.S. Constitution makes prerequisite to a valid arrest. A hearing on the petition was scheduled for November 20.

The petition evidently alerted the prosecution to the fact that the Bales affidavit was fatally deficient. For five days after the petition was filed, a grand jury was convened in Marin County and returned an indictment charging Angela with murder, kidnapping for ransom, and conspiracy to commit these offenses. The strategy of this move was obvious.

The law assumes that a grand jury, supposedly made up of twelve unbiased and disinterested men and women, would not vote an indictment without legally sufficient evidence. So the law presumes that every grand jury heard enough evidence to give it probable cause to believe the accused guilty of the crime for which it indicted him. On this ground, too, an indictment need not recite the evidence on which it was based. The murder count in Angela's indictment, for example, simply states that on August 7,

1970, in Marin County, she "did murder a human being, to wit: Judge Harold Joseph Haley."

This theory of grand jury objectivity is the purest fiction. As every lawyer knows, a district attorney can go before a grand jury anywhere in the country and get an indictment for the asking. Yet the presumption that grand juries act only on legally sufficient evidence is universal.

California, however, is one state which at least provides a procedure for overcoming this presumption. A California statute requires that an accused be furnished with a stenographic transcript of the grand jury proceedings within ten days after his indictment. A related statute permits an accused to secure a dismissal of the indictment upon showing, from this transcript, that the evidence adduced before the grand jury was insufficient to satisfy the probable cause requirement. It seems obvious that an accused who is apprehended outside of California should be entitled to defeat extradition on the same grounds, and there has never been a court decision to the contrary.

Accordingly, I asked a San Francisco colleague to pick up a copy of the transcript of the grand jury proceedings against Angela for use in opposing her extradition. He found that Marin County Chief Judge Wilson had entered an unprecedented order when the indictment was returned. Contrary to the explicit mandate of the California statute, the order provided that Angela should not receive the grand jury transcript until she appeared in person before the Marin County Court. The effect of this extraordinary order was to furnish her with the document she required to defeat extradition only if she gave up the extradition fight and voluntarily returned to California.

We therefore filed an amended petition for habeas corpus in the New York court challenging extradition on two related grounds. First, we urged that the unprecedented and illegal order of the California court withholding the grand jury transcript violated due process of law and denied Angela the equal protection of the laws, both guaranteed by the Fourteenth Amendment. Second, we argued that the indictment was returned in bad faith for the purpose of covering up the lack of a case against Angela, and that the grand jury transcript had been withheld because, like the

Bales affidavit, it was devoid of incriminating evidence. The petition concluded by asking, as a minimum, that extradition be deferred until the California authorities produced the transcript so that the New York court could determine whether the evidence before the grand jury satisfied the probable cause requirement of the Constitution.

At the hearing on December 3, Judge Thomas Dickens, a Negro judge chosen for the occasion, attempted to shut off argument of these constitutional points, then listened with ill-tempered impatience, and immediately ruled against us. His single concession was to stay extradition for five days to permit an appeal. The Appellate Division granted a further stay to December 16, the date it set to hear the appeal.

There followed the fastest Cook's tour of the appellate courts that I have ever been given in 45 years of practice. On the average, it takes well over a year to exhaust the appellate process in a New York extradition proceeding—and this where the defendant's points are insubstantial to the point of the frivolous. In Angela's case, our constitutional arguments received a brush-off by five courts in as many days.

The Appellate Division heard argument on December 16, decided against us an hour later, and gave us until 6 p.m. next day to seek a stay from the Court of Appeals, the highest state court. At 9:30 next morning, I appeared before Chief Judge Fuld who denied a stay at 11. At noon, we took the next step by filing a petition for a writ of habeas corpus in the United States District Court. Judge Frankel heard argument that afternoon and, next morning, handed down an opinion denying the petition but granting a stay pending an immediate application to the United States Court of Appeals. Within the hour, three judges of that court were convened, heard argument, and affirmed Judge Frankel. It being a Friday, the court stayed extradition until 4 p.m. the following Monday to permit us to apply to the Supreme Court in Washington.

I presented the application to Justice Harlan—our final recourse —at 10 a.m. Monday morning, received his denial in the early afternoon, and returned to New York too late to visit Angela that evening. I had been informed, however, that she would be taken to California by commercial air line on Tuesday afternoon.

At 3:30 Tuesday morning, I was awakened by a reporter with the news that she had just left the House of Detention and was evidently bound for the Coast. We didn't get the full story until Miss Burnham and I saw Angela in the Marin County jail next day.

She had been awakened at 3:00 on Tuesday by a prison matron who said that her lawyer was downstairs to advise her about extradition. Instead of her lawyer, she encountered two policemen and two policewomen. When she refused to accompany them, a policeman threw her to the floor, bruising her arms and legs. The four then forcibly took her to a car and, after a short ride, transferred her to another where the California authorities took over. Then, escorted by twenty police cars, she was driven through the Holland Tunnel (closed to all other traffic for the passage of this dangerous woman) to a military airport in New Jersey, whence she was flown by National Guard plane to San Francisco.

It should be added that on her appearance before the Marin County Court Wednesday morning, the grand jury transcript was delivered to us and confirmed our charge that the evidence it contained was as barren of incrimination as the Bales affidavit—a point which is being argued as this is written in support of motions to dismiss the indictment or grant bail.

Turning from the crimes of which Angela is innocent, a word should be said in conclusion about the crime of which she is guilty. For Angela's real crime is more heinous in the eyes of the Nixons, Reagans and Rockefellers than the crimes of which they have charged her. It consists in this, that she—a young Black woman —showed that she can make it in white, masculine America. And did she then bow down in humble gratitude to the Reagans and big business moguls of the California Board of Regents, and give thanks for the glorious opportunity they afforded her? Did she offer up hosannas to the free enterprise system which made it possible for her—a young Black from the deep South—to scale the heights of her chosen profession?

She did not. She trod a different path, one marked out by those giants, W.E.B. Du Bois and Paul Robeson. She rejected the false values of affluent white America. She identified herself with her own people, with the poor, the oppressed, the exploited of all colors and all lands. She joined the Communist Party and worked with ardor and militance to help bring into being an America with other values—a socialist America in a world free from war and imperialist tyranny in which all men and women can develop and utilize their talents to the full and live out their lives in peace, dignity and freedom.

It is to punish Angela for taking that path and to intimidate others from daring to follow her that Reagan is demanding her death in the gas chamber or life imprisonment without the possibility of parole. By the same token, the cause of freedom for Angela is the common cause of progressive humanity—a frontline sector in the fight for freedom for us all. It is because of the widespread recognition of this truth that—as in no other case in my experience—the call has risen across the land and been taken up by millions around the world: FREE ANGELA DAVIS NOW!

19

Statement
to the Court

As a preface to my brief remarks I now declare publicly before the court, before the people of this country that I am innocent of all charges which have been leveled against me by the State of California. I am innocent and therefore maintain that my presence in this courtroom today is unrelated to any criminal act.

I stand before this court as a target of a political frame-up which far from pointing to my culpability, implicates the State of California as an agent of political repression. Indeed the State reveals its own role by introducing as evidence against me my participation in the struggles of my people—Black people—against the many injustices of society. Specifically my involvement with the "Soledad Brothers Defense Committee." The American people have been led to believe that such involvement is constitutionally protected.

In order to insure that these political questions are not obscured, I feel compelled to play an active role in my own defense as the defendant, as a Black woman and as a Communist. It is my duty to assist all those directly involved in the proceedings as well as the people of this State and the American people in general to thoroughly comprehend the substantive issues at stake in my case. These have to do with my political beliefs, affiliations and my day to day efforts to fight all the conditions which have economically and politically paralyzed Black America.

No one can better represent my political beliefs and activities than I. A system of justice which virtually condemns to silence the one person who stands to lose most would seem to be self-defeating.

It is particularly crucial to Black people to combat this contradiction inherent in the judicial system, for we have accumulated a wealth of historical experience which confirms our belief that the scales of American justice are out of balance.

In order to enhance the possibility of being granted a fair trial, of which at present I am extremely doubtful, it is imperative that I be allowed to represent myself. I might add that my request is not without legal precedent.

If this court denies our motion to include me as co-counsel in this case it will be aligning itself with the forces of racism and reaction which threaten to push this country into the throes of fascism and the many people who have become increasingly disillusioned with the court system in this country will have a further reason to solidify their contention that it is no longer possible to get a fair trial in America.

MARIN COUNTY COURTHOUSE
January 5, 1971

20

Ruchell and Angela
Want to Represent Themselves
by Margaret Burnham*

Both Angela Davis and Ruchell Magee are demanding the right to represent and defend themselves against the State of California's bogus criminal charges of kidnap, conspiracy, and murder. In so doing, Ruchell and Angela join a growing number of Black prisoners who are dispensing with a lawyer-spokesman in the courtroom and insisting on their right to speak for themselves. The reasons why Black defendants are increasingly turning to self-representation spring from the nature of an inherently racist, repressive, and class-biased judicial system. Many poor Black defendants feel compelled to represent themselves because they know that no lawyer is available to them who will present their legal case with aggressiveness and sensitivity. At the same time, other Blacks, charged with crime for overtly political reasons are also turning to self-representation; these victims of legal repression try self-defense in their constant search to find new forms of forcefully and effectively defending themselves and their movement.

A court's decision to recognize or refuse an accused's demand to represent himself is a highly political one, made to advance the interests of a decaying but yet self-perpetuating bourgeois judicial system. The judicial concern overriding all others is the necessity to "move cases," to move the criminal process along. Often, a judge will deny the right to self-representation when the accused is by far his own best advocate because self-defense might, in such an instance, slow down the trial process, or result in the acquittal

---

* Miss Burnham is co-counsel for Miss Davis.

of a political foe of the regime, or in some other way prove counter-productive to a repressive system. Conversely, in some other cases, a defendant's desire to shoulder full counsel responsibility is hastily granted where an eager prosecutor senses that the accused will founder on the legal complexities of his case and the judge, either through negligence or to facilitate speedy disposition, makes no attempt to disabuse the defendant of his over confidence. What follows is an examination of the derivation of the right to self-defense, and of the related right to be represented by counsel, and of the utter perversion of these rights—for wholly political reasons—by judicial decision and judicially-related institutional policy.

I

The right to present one's own case in answer to a criminal prosecution is not a new one. Rather, it has its roots deep in Anglo-American law, and indeed was well-established long before the right to be represented by counsel developed. In England, prior to 1836, when a statute established the right to full representation by retained counsel in felony cases, persons accused of crime were not entitled to be defended in court by an attorney, or to be assisted by counsel during the proceedings, but were forced to handle all aspects of their case—legal and factual—alone. In short, self-representation was, in the beginning, the established practice, and only gradually did the law of the right to counsel develop so as to supplant the defendant-advocate completely with the attorney-advocate.

In the United States the framers of the federal constitution sought to protect against the evils of the early English system which forced an accused, unschooled in the law, to defend against a criminal prosecution without any legal assistance. They drafted the sixth amendment to the constitution, which guaranteed the right of assistance of counsel to every defendant. The sixth amendment right, however, was never intended to restrict or dilute a defendant's right to represent himself, but was conceived of as an *expansion* of the rights of the criminal defendant. It was designed to insure that those accused of crime who were uninitiated in the ways of courts and legal procedures would not be convicted simply because they lacked the legal expertise to present the best case in their defense, as had often happened in earlier times.

As with most provisions of the constitution, the intent of the sixth amendment—that the accused be represented by counsel in order that he might be able to put his best foot forward—has never been realized for Black and poor defendants. The race and class prejudice which has infected every other constitutionally-guaranteed "right," and permeated every other limb of the judicial order, has rendered the sixth amendment a meaningless guarantee for most criminal defendants. For until as recently as 1963, a man too poor to afford a lawyer who found himself charged with a crime—even one for which the state could imprison him until he perished— was forced to go to trial unrepresented. One rich enough to afford a lawyer could enjoy the sixth amendment "right" to counsel; the typically poor, Black defendant was without means to buy such a right. Often, desperate poverty led a defendant to activity which resulted in criminal charges; since the right to counsel depended entirely on one's wealth, of course such a person hadn't the money to hire an attorney. The accused, charged with crime because of poverty, unable to extricate himself because of poverty, was placed at the center of a vicious circle, and his constitutional "right" to have a lawyer offered him no means of escape.

Blacks suffered in other ways as well from the disparate dispensation of the right to counsel. As a direct consequence of racism, Blacks are frequently charged with crimes they did not commit. Purely by virtue of their race and residence, members of the Black community become the object of criminal suspicion. The police frame-up victim, the by-stander charged because he "looked like" the criminal, the individual convicted on the basis of a prior record, is most often a poor Black man. The sixth amendment provided no protection for the innocent Black defendant, who, burdened by his race and his poverty, needed legal assistance to establish his innocence and preserve his freedom in the face of an attack on it by the full force of white state power.

The 1963 court decision which changed all this held simply that poor defendants facing "serious charges" had to be provided with counsel by the state.[19] Thus the public defender, or the "P.D.," as he is known by his clients, arrived on the scene. But although the supreme court did say that all defendants, regardless of their ability to afford an attorney were entitled to representation, it said nothing about the quality of such counsel. States satisfied the constitutional mandate by setting up public defender offices as cheaply as they could. The lawyers whom the government employed as public defenders were generally poorly paid, poorly trained, and overburdened. The slipshod, superficial representation provided by the defender placed poor defendants in a complete bind—they could no longer complain about denial of their sixth amendment rights since they were considered "represented"; but there was no meaningful difference in their situation, as they were convicted and given stiff sentences with almost the same regularity as in pre-*Gideon* days.

Typically the public defender is an overworked, harassed cog in the wheels of the court apparatus. Usually a white male, he displays the indifferent, insensitive attitude characteristic of the petty bureaucrat caught up in and confined by the rigidity of a dysfunctional system. Indeed, insensitivity is a generous adjective to describe what, in most cases, amounts to a racist approach to cases and clients. To the public defender, Black defendants he represents are indistinguishable from one another; all of them have been "through it before"; and all are presumed guilty. The public defender is more interested in remaining on good terms with his peers, the judge and the prosecutor, than he is in his black client's welfare.

Another welfare worker, public hospital attendant, public school teacher, the public defender is white authority clothed in beneficence. He doles out his paltry services as if he were dispensing a charity and not a right. Despite the "right" bestowed by the sixth amendment, today, distribution of legal services still conforms to the capitalist formula for meeting needs. He who can pay for a good lawyer, gets one, he who cannot gets a lousy P.D.

The courts do not discourage ineffectual advocacy by the public

---

[19] *Gideon v. Wainwright*—372 US 335 1963.

defender. Rather, it suits all the purposes of a repressive system of criminal justice to have Black, poor people inadequately represented in court. Because the public defender lacks aggressiveness, and is unable or unwilling to push his clients' interests, the court is able to dispose of defendants represented by him with ease. The defender is grease in a judicial machine anxious to try, convict and incarcerate as quickly as possible. Frequently he will negotiate a deal with his crony, the prosecutor, "dealing" away his clients' freedom. A recent *Newsweek* article quotes one public defender's description of the affinity between P.D., judge, and prosecutor:

> You learn its folkways. "It's our court," Xinos [A Chicago public defender] says. "It's like a family. Me, the prosecutors, the judges, we're all friends. I drink with the prosecutors. I give the judge a Christmas present, he gives me a Christmas present." [20]

It is true that some public defenders are good lawyers and want to be effective advocates, but the institution is structured so as to discourage their efforts. It is unlikely that the public defender who wants to press a point on one occasion will risk the possibility of antagonizing a judge and prosecutor whom he must appear before day in and day out, and thus, he thinks, jeopardize other present and future clients that he has.

Appellate courts were quick to appreciate the virtues of the public defender system. With the defender by his side, trial courts could do anything to defendants, and no one could be heard to complain that the victim was unapprised of his legal rights. Blacks who were forced through the trial process at breakneck speed, and those who were given inhumane sentences after being importuned to plead guilty, appealed their convictions, but got no help from higher courts. Tactical blunders and gross injustices that might otherwise be subjects for appellate review were now sanctioned because they were done with "advice of counsel."

With good reason, Blacks have come to view the P.D. as a worse

[20] Peter Goldman and Don Holt, "Now Justice Works: The People v. Donald Payne," *Newsweek,* March 8, 1971, 20, 29.

enemy than the prosecutor. The image of the defender as a man, in cahoots with the prosecutor and judge, whose sole function is to pave the way for the conviction of the defendant and to mask the inequity and brutality of the criminal process, has become more and more commonplace. As the mistrust grows, more Blacks have begun to turn down the public defender's offer of "assistance" and become their own advocates.

Generally, demands for self-advocacy by defendants who would otherwise be public defender clients are met with resistance by the courts, because of the public defender's demonstrated ability to help the judge "move cases."

In order to discourage him from defending himself, courts have created a whole range of problems for the defendant who, although he has the "right" to representation by the public defender, chooses to go it alone. Perhaps the judicial rule which most inhibits would-be self-represented defendants is the one which forces them to elect between self-representation or complete reliance on counsel. In other words, a defendant who proceeds to represent himself is not entitled to have counsel to assist him on legal questions. He must go it alone. Nor will the trial judge assist such a defendant with technical problems. The courts expect that, faced with such a choice, a defendant unsure of his legal ability will opt for the public defender. This rule is designed for no other purpose than to punish a self-represented defendant for exercising his right.

In spite of these arduous problems many Blacks have nonetheless assumed the burden of defending themselves. Some brothers and sisters are able to handle the court-room scene with incredible skill, and often are correct in their judgment that they can present their own case better than the public defender.

But, as might be expected, many defendants who undertake to represent themselves, are unaccustomed to legal forms and therefore fail to make appropriate legal motions, or overlook defenses which are available to them, or in other ways contribute to their own conviction. Judges, usually unsolicitous toward self-represented defendants, are often apt to permit self-representation when they see that such an arrangement will, because of the defendant's ignorance of available time-consuming legal procedures, ensure a quick and easy trial. A prosecutor realizes that in many situations

the self-represented defendant is an easier target than one represented by the public defender, and a judge will often acquiesce
when he either appreciates the same point or realizes that per-
suading the defendant not to go it alone will simply cost more
precious judicial time.

James McClain's was such a case. In 1960, McClain was tried
for felonious assault. In that case, shabby representation by a public defender ended up costing the brother seven years in San Quentin. When he was arrested again in May of 1968 and charged with
attempted robbery and burglary, McClain chose to represent himself, and was permitted to do so by a judge who failed to make a
legally required inquiry into the extent of McClain's knowledge of
the law relative to his case. The evidence against him was
manifestly flimsy. Indeed, the prosecution offered no evidence at
all to prove an essential element of the crime. Any experienced
criminal lawyer could have obtained a dismissal of charges by
means of a motion demonstrating the crucial deficiency of the
state's case. But McClain had no legal assistance at all, and in fact,
was physically ill at the time of his trial. Thus, he failed to take the
necessary steps, and since neither he, the judge nor the prosecutor
saw fit to recognize what to them must have been an obvious legal
flaw, the self-represented McClain was convicted of a crime he
insisted he never committed, and sentenced to spend long years in
prison.

McClain was again arrested in August, 1968, and this time
charged with assault on a police officer. Again a review of the
facts indicates that McClain was an innocent victim of circumstances. And again, he sought to extricate himself from the web of
guilty inferences woven by police witnesses—without representation by the public defender. This time, however, McClain requested
that a defender be appointed merely to assist him in the legal
preparation of his case. This request the judge denied, saying:
"That's not possible. It places the public defender in an untenable
position, so you take your choice. He'll represent you in all respects and absolutely or none at all." McClain, self-defended a
second time, was convicted of the assault charge and sent to San
Quentin.

McClain had gained a not inconsiderable skill as a lawyer, however, as a result of his experiences in self-representation in the 1968 cases. While held captive in San Quentin, he was charged with assaulting a prison guard. The incident occurred on March 2, 1970, a few days after the tear-gas murder of another Black prisoner, Fred Billingslea, by San Quentin guards. The prisoners who initiated a campaign to protest the murder of Billingslea contend that McClain was innocent of the alleged assault, and that the charges against him stemmed from his political involvement in the Billingslea resistance movement. In any event, in June, 1970, on a charge of assault, McClain represented himself a third time, this time before an all white Marin County jury which could not agree on a verdict. Quite a remarkable victory—a hung jury for a self-represented state prisoner charged with assault on a guard—and a testimony to McClain's hard-learned skill as an advocate. For McClain, the practice of law was a matter of survival; through trial and error, he learned the ways of courts and law, and ultimately emerged an excellent advocate in behalf of his own right to live.

McClain was again brought to trial on the assault charge on August 5, 1970, and for a fourth time he represented himself. This time, however, the trial was interrupted, never to resume, by the events of August 7.

II

In addition to the treacherous incompetence of the public defender, James McClain felt compelled to represent himself in that Marin County courthouse for yet another reason: he viewed the assault charges against him as political in nature, and felt he could best counter them by means of a personal, frontal assault. As he could not rely on the public defender to present his best legal position in his earlier cases, he realized in the San Quentin case that only he could place the charges against him in their proper political context.

McClain was not the first Black defendant to assume his own defense to a political prosecution. The practice of self-representation in such cases extends as far back as Marcus Garvey, who defended himself in the mid twenties against government charges of mail fraud. In more recent times Blacks—and whites—charged with such political crimes as conspiracy, inciting to riot, subversive activity, have been forced to represent themselves because they could not obtain lawyers. Particularly during the McCarthy era, when government repression reached theretofore unparalleled heights, and "guilt by association" was the rule of the day, lawyers were hard to find. One Black Smith Act victim, James E. Jackson, recalling his experiences hunting for a lawyer in those days, described how the FBI would follow his footsteps, paying a visit to every lawyer he approached, warning each of them that they, too, could become victims of McCarthy terrorism. Few lawyers were courageous enough to withstand such threats, and more often than not, Black Smith Act defendants like James E. Jackson—as well as white victims—went to court unrepresented.

In a later day, Blacks in the South who faced criminal prosecution as one consequence of their involvement in the civil rights movement of the '60s were confronted with the same problem— they could find no one to represent them. White, racist lawyers would not risk loss of their white clientele to represent a Black defendant charged with violating a segregation ordinance, or illegally attempting to register Black voters, or some such "crime." Of the few Black lawyers who were available, many performed an indispensable role, providing round-the-clock free services to a beleaguered, arrest-prone civil rights movement. But they could not alone satisfy the need for legal counsel during this era of mass arrests, when constitutional liberties were indefinitely suspended, and virtually everyone who participated in a rally, march or sit-in was indiscriminately thrown in the county jail. During those days, many Black defendants handled their own cases, not by choice, but by force of circumstance.

Today, more and more Black political defendants are deliberately choosing to represent themselves, despite the availability of counsel, as James McClain did in the San Quentin assault case. Political prosecutions are as varied in form and purpose as are political defendants; thus, different reasons dictate the decision to defend oneself in different cases. However, the motive underlying all political prosecutions is to discredit the particular defendant as a political leader and his activity as a valid means of political expression. Because, fundamentally, such a prosecution is a challenge to an individual's political integrity, the target of such an attack—the person who best comprehends the specific political motives of the prosecution—is often the best person to defend his or her politics—better, even, than a lawyer. This rationale—that one's political views can best be explained and defended by oneself—is shared by virtually all self-represented political defendants.

More often than not, the conduct of the actual trial will bear out the reasons given in support of a defendant's pre-trial decision to represent him or herself. Certainly this occurred during the trial of the New York Panther 13, where defendant Afeni Shakur elected to represent herself. Sister Afeni, by her perceptive questioning of prospective jurors, was able to elicit unexpected responses which uncovered deep-seated prejudices and negative attitudes. Her antennae sharpened by her life experiences as a young Black woman and her unique political perspective, Afeni was in a better position to tune in to such attitudes than any lawyer in the case. Her cross-examination of a cop-prosecution witness was also particularly revealing because Afeni, as a principal party in the prosecution's fable, was singularly in a position to know all the true facts and circumstances concerning the incident about which the cop had testified.*

At the commencement of the trial Afeni characterized the case for the jury as follows:

> Evidence in this case will show that these thirteen human beings that are accused of attempted murder have been accused of these crimes but the accusers have not asked whether or not these crimes were, in fact, committed against us. . . . The evidence will show that our only intent was to protect ourselves against the very crimes that we are accused of, that we have

---

* The recent Seattle Seven conspiracy trial presents another instance of successful self-representation. In that case, the government's case toppled when Charles C. Marshall, who was defending himself, effectively destroyed a government witness-provocateur. Marshall forced the spy to admit that, on F.B.I. instructions, he had provided young activists with dynamite, guns, drugs, and other illegal items, and that he had tried to incite violent actions. The judge was forced to declare a mistrial shortly after the giving of this testimony. Clearly, the impact of this testimony had a great deal to do with the judge's action.

never advocated aggressive violence. It is counterproductive, it is counter to human life, but that we have always advocated adequate self-defense against police brutality and against police murder.

The prosecution had charged the defendants with plotting to bomb shopping centers and other public places during the Easter holidays. Many who knew the defendants as committed Black revolutionaries felt that the charges were patently absurd; in her opening statement Afeni explained to the jury one reason why they could not possibly be true:

> The evidence will show in this case that April 2nd, 1969, was indeed the Easter week-end and that there has never been a holiday in the calendar year that did not catch poor people unawares. There is no such thing as early shopping in our community. So that the holidays leading up into Easter, Christmas, and Thanksgiving find the department stores in the downtown area crowded with nobody but poor people. And to accuse any of us, any member of the Black community, of planning to annihilate those people, those people who we have sworn to protect, shows the craved fanatical mind of the state.

Not only was Afeni effective in framing a compelling political response to the state's charges, but her participation was important for yet another, related reason. The presence of Afeni, one of the defendants, as a live and vocal participant in the court-room drama forced jurors to deal with human personalities rather than voiceless, disinterested, accused men and women. Afeni, the person, the Black woman with human strength and frailty, the indignant accused, the fierce young revolutionary spirit, the victim—this was the defendant whom the jurors had to judge. In her final summation, Afeni appealed to the jurors to be fair with her life, as they had come to know it, and with the lives of the other defendants. Her statement—at once an impassioned appeal and a demand— was simple and clear, but it had a power of its own, a power that derived from the inescapable fact that this defendant was speaking of her own life, her political life and her actual life, a life which the jurors had come to know:

Why are we here? Why are any of us here? I don't know. But I would appreciate it if you would end this nightmare, because I'm tired of it and I can't justify it in my mind. There's no logical reason for us to have gone through the last two years as we have, to be threatened with imprisonment because somebody somewhere is watching and waiting to justify his being a spy. So you do what you have to do. But please don't forget what you saw and heard in this courtroom. Don't forget any of it . . . this extravaganza has already found its place among the Oscar winners. Let history record you as a jury who would not kneel to the outrageous bidding of the state. Justify our faith in you. . . . Show us that we were not wrong in assuming that you would judge us fairly. And remember that that's all we're asking of you. All we ask of you is that you judge us fairly. Please judge us according to the way that you want to be judged. That's all I have to say.

Afeni is part of a tradition of Black Panther leaders who have assumed a stance of struggle in the court-room. Perhaps most representative of this tradition is Bobby Seale, whose repeated demands to represent himself, made during the infamous 1969 Chicago Eight trial, earned him a four year prison sentence for sixteen specifications of contempt. Brother Bobby, forced to go to trial in Chicago without his lawyer, Charles Garry, insisted that if he could not be represented by the lawyer of his choice he would defend himself. Cognizant of the government's political objectives in prosecuting him and the other Chicago defendants, Bobby asserted his right to be represented by the lawyer whom he felt was most capable of pursuing a correct political defense strategy. He must have considered the development of a strong political line of defense of tremendous importance, for when his own lawyer could not be present to represent his political position, Bobby undertook his own defense. Hoffman, the judge, tried to force Bobby to accept two lawyers representing the other Chicago defendants as his counsel; however, Bobby's position, reiterated time and again, was "I don't want these lawyers because I can take up my own defense, and my lawyer is Charles Garry."

Bobby Seale fought hard for the right to conduct his own defense in Chicago, so hard, in fact, that the court, in a crude act of undisguised racism, resorted to binding and gagging in order to prevent him from speaking in his own behalf. One wonders what fear it was that prompted the judge to respond in this manner to Bobby's simple plea to defend himself. Surely the Daly-Hoffman-Mitchell matrix of political repression was not so fragile that the slightest deviation from the planned format—a single self-represented defendant—would threaten its balance.

Bobby never got an opportunity to develop his own defense, as his case was severed from that of the other Chicago defendants, midway in the proceedings. However, this episode is an important chapter in the story of the political defendant's struggle for self-representation, since it demonstrates the nature and depth of the fear of courts of the self-represented Black defendant. It was not enough to gag, bind and beat Bobby in open court and sever his case from the others. Bobby Seale's four year prison sentence for contempt was intended to serve as a lesson for all who would in the future attempt to personally present a political defense to political charges.

In movement circles, Reies Tijerina of the Alianza is perhaps the most well-known example of the self-represented political defendant. Back in 1968, at the height of the Alianza land grant movement, Tijerina was charged with kidnapping and other crimes for his role in the so-called Tierra Amarilla courthouse raid. Tijerina had several lawyers at his side when he went to court. However, none were Chicano, none had been involved in the Alianza movement, and none had Tijerina's personal dynamism and charisma. The defendant demanded to represent himself, and much to everyone's surprise, the judge consented. "O.K. You may represent yourself. You have thirty minutes to prepare your case," ruled the court. Tijerina later recalled that he was thus faced with the "biggest test of my life . . . testing myself and my courage. I wanted to break through that barrier of fear and terror that only a lawyer can speak for justice. I decided that even if I lost, I would give my people an example of courage."

In the half-hour allotted him, Tijerina made up his mind, dismissed all his lawyers, prepared his case and proceeded to trial. By himself, he selected a jury, made an opening statement, cross-examined the state's witnesses, and put on a defense. He proved to be a brilliant advocate, presenting a well-argued, well-reasoned legal defense while at the same time turning his case into a political statement in behalf of the Alianza movement. The jury, comprised of Chicanos, Anglos, and one Black, acquitted him of all charges!

So successful was he as his own lawyer that the next time the state prosecuted Tijerina the courts manufactured a reason to refuse to permit him to defend himself. No legal basis whatever existed for the state's position; Tijerina had already demonstrated his complete competence to successfully defend himself. The judges in the Tijerina cases established a new rule: a political activist who has shown he can defend himself shall not be permitted to do so.

III

It is against this back-drop that Ruchell Magee and Angela Davis make their demand to speak for themselves in proceedings at the Marin County Hall of Justice. Ever since his first court appearance on these charges, Ruchell has refused court-appointed counsel and insisted that he is his own attorney. In a recent hearing, Ruchell described, with an eloquence and clarity of expression which kept the court-room spell-bound, the reasons why he has consistently refused court-appointed counsel.*

His reasons for wanting to defend himself are very much like McClain's were; first, earlier bad experiences with court-appointed lawyers; second, lack of confidence in the ability of any court-appointed lawyer to place his defense in its political setting; and third, a reluctance to entrust the factual development of his defense to anyone other than himself—the person most intimately familiar with the facts at issue.

Counterposed to Ruchell's clearly articulated, well-documented argument in behalf of self-representation, the state, which, with this prosecution, demands a man's very life, posits two responsive arguments. Self-defense is "not in the interest of justice," prosecutors and judges have said, because Mr. Magee is "intellectually incompetent to represent himself" and because "Mr. Magee's

* See the transcript of Ruchell Magee's statement to the court which follows this article.

demeanor and conduct thus far lead us to believe that self-representation will be disruptive of court-room order."

In the court's view, the question of court-room discipline is inextricably related to the question of Ruchell's intellectual competence. A Black man who does not speak the language of the judge and prosecutor is deemed incompetent to defend his own life in their courtroom; an heroic effort to defend against white racism and capitalist, slavery-like oppression, is characterized as "disruptive behavior."

As to Ruchell's competence, one need only point to the transcript of proceedings in this case, for this document demonstrates beyond a shadow of a doubt that Mr. Magee is as knowledgeable —indeed, if not more so—as any other person as to both the law and the facts of his case. It is a paradox that defies solution that Judges McMurray and Lindsay—the very judges who were themselves forced out of this case because of Ruchell's legal maneuvers—nevertheless saw fit to disparage Ruchell's intellectual competence. What these judges and others are saying is that one must speak and act like a lawyer in order to be recognized as a lawyer; that one, who, by reason of his captivity, is self-taught in the law cannot utilize his skill and learning to express himself on the subject of his own life; that one who has been a prisoner of the law and who has, as a direct consequence of racism, been deprived of formal training in legal matters, cannot avail himself of the law to defend his life. It is a white man's law; white men shall apply and interpret it as it suits them; and Black men whose views of the law and whose legal language varies from the white norm, are thereby adjudged "incompetent" in the eyes of the law. Ruchell will never be competent in the law as long as competence is measured by a white man applying a white standard.

The judges' pronouncements on court-room order as it bears on Ruchell's right to defend himself are also premised on rudimentary racism. A little man with a delicately soft voice, one can hardly be expected to believe that the tone of his voice could upset the court-room arrangement devised by the state to take Ruchell's life. When Ruchell on occasion does raise his voice in protest, it is in defense of his right to speak for himself. If he interrupts a judge or prosecutor, it is not so much out of disrespect for order as it is to call attention to the order set out in the United States Constitution. The *idea* of a Black man persistently struggling for the right to defend himself is what disrupts the court, not an occasional loud remark or a shout from a spectator. But that kind of disruption— the disruptive image of a chained and captive man struggling for his rights—is not countenanced by the law.

This concern about order unveils the slight regard in which the court holds this defendant's right to defend his own life; that right is secondary in importance to the court's primary obligation to protect itself from dissonant noises. Ruchell's personal integrity and dignity count for nothing when measured against the court's interest in decorum. It would seem that, if constitutional due process has any meaning, it is a guarantee of individual autonomy; one element of the concept of personal autonomy must be the right of the individual to personally construct and present a defense of his life and his ideas. But the constitutional right to due process gives no protection to an embattled defendant like Ruchell whom the court seeks to keep silent.

"The defendant's below average intelligence, subnormal education, and indisposition towards courts of law do not adequately equip him to have his life," prosecutor Albert Harris has said. Even as the state seeks to snuff out this Black man's life it dictates the method of his defense, and orders him how to respond. With this statement, Albert Harris boldly proclaims Ruchell Magee a slave of the state. Arrested and convicted by the state, imprisoned for seven years for a ten dollar crime against the state, now the state seeks to direct his defense against a state claim for his very life. Surely it is a sign of impending fascism when pervasive state power dictates every aspect of a man's existence—including the method by which he may defend his only life.

Angela shares her co-defendant's aim to illuminate the genuine issues in their case, and thus she, too, is demanding the right to represent herself. In an early court appearance, Angela disclosed her intention to fight for self-representation, stating:

> As a Black woman and a Communist, it is my duty to assist those directly involved in the proceedings, as well as the people of the State and the American people in general, to thoroughly comprehend the substantive issues at stake in my case.

Functioning as her own advocate along with her regular attorneys, Angela seeks to play a vigorous and vocal role in all aspects of her defense, participating in the court-room activity as well as assisting in the development of legal strategy and tactics, and in the preparation of legal briefs. She does not intend to dismiss her attorneys. Rather, she will work in conjunction with them, the common goal being to fuse the legal defense with the political reality. In this respect, the self-defense arrangement which Angela claims as a constitutional right differs from that seen in the Tijerina, Shakur, and McClain cases discussed above. Although McClain asked for legal assistance in one of his cases, he and the other defendants conducted their trials in court entirely without a lawyer.

Angela, called upon to respond to a frame-up, is not prepared to carry the whole burden of her defense alone. By its very nature, a frame-up relies for its substantiation on the prosecutor's legal ingenuity. He must twist the law and construct complicated criminal charges in order to disguise a shallow factual case. He must resort to elusive legal doctrines like "conspiracy" and "aiding and abetting" to convert innocent activity into criminal deeds. The prosecutor's wicked legal machinations effectively compel Angela to defer to a skilled defense attorney who can guide her through the thicket of legal fictions and procedural traps created by the state.

At the same time, Angela can not rely solely on the skill of the legal tactician to formulate her defense. Fancy legal maneuvering is only half of the answer to a political prosecution. The essence, the design of such a prosecution—once laid bare by such legal manipulation as is necessary—can only be effectively attacked and destroyed by the defendant herself. Her lawyer's job is to separate out the false legal issues in the case from the critical political questions; Angela's participation in her defense is key to the proper delineation and exposition of those political issues. Neither approach can be underestimated in importance. The two lines of attack must be knit together to fashion a comprehensive legal-political defense to the state's frame-up accusations.

Put another way, Angela is saying that she will not forfeit her right to legal representation as the price of asserting her right to self-defense. She demands that the court give recognition to both rights by permitting her to act as "co-counsel" in her own defense. Her lawyers will speak for her, but Angela will also speak for herself. She will examine prospective jurors, cross-examine witnesses, perhaps make an opening or closing statement to the jury. The attorneys will assist her in her questioning and in addition will themselves conduct certain segments of the trial. In effect, Angela and her attorneys will contribute to the defense on an equal plane, complementing each other and together molding for the jury a concrete, well-integrated theory of defense.

Courts do not look with favor on schemes for joint representation such as Angela is proposing. In fact, California courts have almost uniformly taken the position that, despite the indisputably clear language of the state constitution, which provides that a defendant has the right to "appear and defend in person and with counsel," a criminal defendant must either be represented by counsel in all respects or in none at all. The defendant must decide between two rights; she is not entitled to the advantages of both in the same proceeding.

The articulated justifications for this court-invented policy, which flies in the face of the plain meaning of the language of the state constitution, are revealing. At its core, the policy is part and parcel of the judicial effort to erode the absolute right to self-representation. And close to the surface of the proffered rationale lie the strong self-protective instincts of the courts.

Most frequently, courts turn to the old shibboleth, "court-room order" to justify a denial of joint representation. The claim is made that a self-represented defendant who also has access to counsel will be more disruptive in court than one who does not. This analysis begs for elucidation; for what reason would such a defendant present more of a threat than the defendant who speaks completely for himself? If anything, common sense would lead one to believe that a defendant guided by counsel would be *less* likely, not more so, to speak out of turn, or disregard common court-room practice, than a novice defendant acting completely on his own.

In refusing to recognize joint representation, the California Supreme Court, quoting the attorney code of ethics, reasoned that defendants acting on their own behalf "do not appear to feel bound to maintain the respect due to the courts of justice and judicial officers . . ." or "to abstain from all offensive personality. . . ." This rationale—that self-represented defendants are less easily intimidated by judges and the mystique of the court-room than attorneys—should also be applied with equal force to the defendant without any lawyer. It represents no less than an attempt by the judge to gag the defendant in order to protect his own sensibilities. Whereas the courts feel compelled to accord some recognition to the long-established right to self-representation, they try to employ every means of destroying the right by refusing to give it substantive meaning. Thus, when a variation of the right is proposed, such as co-representation, the court, in refusing to grant the request, spells out its protest against self-representation per se.

Another concern expressed by courts in support of the policy is that joint representation would diminish the stature of attorneys. One judge put it this way: "The court should not appoint counsel and require of him in so doing that he surrender any of the substantial prerogatives traditionally or by statute attached to his office." The rule protects the attorney as well as the judge. An attorney who acts as co-counsel with his own client would, according to the courts, thereby be thrust into a "quasi-clerical" role; he might have to take some direction from the client in the conduct of the litigation; his professional judgment would be subject to scrutiny and criticism by the individual he represents. In other words, the lawyer's status position, presently maintained by his monopolistic control over legal knowledge, formalisms, and jargonism, might be threatened if he practiced in conjunction with his client.

Thus, the rule is designed to protect the status quo. Its purpose is to shelter the judge and his court-room from the outspoken, "disrespectful" defendant, and to perpetuate the status of the legal profession. The defendant's right to present his own defense is reduced to no right at all if its exercise might seek to threaten the stability of the judicial regime. The interests of lawyers and judges are paramount in this system; the roles which these men fill ensure the smooth operation of the machine, and no defendants' right will interfere with their execution.

Ideally, a court-room should be designed to provide the defendant with the forum most conducive to the presentation of a good defense. Instead, judges construct policies to insulate themselves and their institutions, rather than to protect the defendant. No matter that a defendant whose life is at stake may view co-representation as the best mechanism of court-room defense. The defendant's due process interests are inferior to the institutional interests of judges and lawyers, even though it is her life, not theirs at issue.

IV

Courts and prosecutors evince a limitless imagination when called upon to devise new forms of judicial repression. Laws are turned topsey-turvey; words lose their ordinary meaning; constitutional rights are converted into restrictive rules. Such has been the history of the right to self-representation.

Despite the right to counsel, innocent Black prisoners languished in jails for endless decades for no other reason than that poverty forced them to go to trial unrepresented. Others had to entrust their fate to the hands of incompetent, racist public defenders.

And when, in protest, Black defendants sought to assume control of their own defense, the courts invented obstacles to frustrate their efforts. They were denied the most rudimentary legal advice. Self-representation is made as difficult as possible for some; others are encouraged to risk it alone in court when their cases cry out for as much legal help as they can get.

Political defendants like Ruchell Magee are routinely being turned down in their demands to conduct their own defense. For when they have been allowed to speak for themselves, we have often seen victories. Witness Afeni Shakur, Reies Tijerina.

And yet, despite court-invented obstacles, I am confident that the people's movement will still find a way of expressing itself. The court may not permit Ruchell to represent himself, but his voice will be heard nonetheless. Angela may not be permitted to function as her own attorney, but her message will get out. Courts and prosecutors may be ingenious—after all, it *is* their law—but they cannot finesse away a revolution whose time has come.

21

Ruchell Magee:
Statement to the Court

On May 5, 1971 Ruchell Magee spoke on his own behalf in the Marin Court, addressing himself primarily to the issue of his right to act as his own attorney, and in particular the issue of his competency to do so. Presiding Judge Alan A. Lindsay had already appointed yet another attorney to represent Brother Ruchell, Ernest L. Graves, after two previously appointed attorneys withdrew from the case, at Brother Ruchell's request. During the session attorney Graves supported Brother Ruchell's right to self-representation. Brother Ruchell presented his arguments, seated behind the defense table in a chair bolted to the floor, without any notes, his hands chained to his waist, his feet shackled and his torso chained to the chair. Below is a portion of Brother Ruchell's statement to the Court.

Statement to the Court
On Self-Defense

BY RUCHELL MAGEE

. . . Your Honor, I would like to put something in the record that has not been in the record, nor in the press, concerning my competency, and reasons for my refusal of counsel. . . . It is not that I hate all attorneys, as a lot of peoples seem to think . . . I made several requests through court-appointed counsel in this case requesting [the] subpoena of records from—of the Los Angeles trial. That was in 1963 and 1965, and also records on appeal. I have made a request for these records [in order] to present evidence and show facts that upon appointment of—every California lawyer that I have [been] convicted through fraud . . .

. . . These records will show that for over seven years I have been forced to stay in slavery on fraudulent pleas of guilty, made by attorneys, court-appointed attorneys over my objection, over my plea of not guilty, and over my testimony of not guilty.

Upon attempting to appeal to the higher court to expose this, I was again appointed an attorney, an attorney who ignored the facts that the record was falsified. Thereafter he, the attorney, used those fraudulent records to have the case overturned, not in the interest of Mr. Magee, but for the sole purpose of having me taken back to court and declared insane.

Now, I have noticed also, "this moron and subhuman person," that the press has published constantly, indirect and direct, holding me up to public ridicule—this was based upon Mr. Harris's phony I.Q. test, and the inadequate hearing that was held over in San Quentin.

Now, we are back again with attorneys, and you tell me that, I need an attorney to represent me. Out of every attorney that this Court has appointed, that is, Marin County, the results [have] been the same; that is a lot of verbal talk, while evading confrontation with the true issues, that is, the issues that I seek to bring out and expose, which would be a part of my defense.

One of those main issues was removal [of the] petition[21] for removal, which has gone sour not only in court, but also [in the] press. The attorney now that the Court has appointed, states that he studied the records, and he concedes the statements made by Mr. Magee, where he had been denied due process; that is in reference to a hearing to determine his competency to represent himself. However, he makes no mention of the present petition for removal that is pending now in the Federal Court; he makes no mention that the Court at this particular time is acting in

[21] Magee refers to his petition to have his case removed from the State to Federal court, on grounds that the State of California was in violation of his constitutional and civil rights.

absence of jurisdiction, that is, based upon the fact that the removal is pending.

Now, I'm aware that Judge Conti, who has gotten personally involved in the case, a Federal judge, for the sole purpose of publicity and also to hold me up to public ridicule, stating that I filed many documents flooding the courts and abusing the processes of the Federal Court, but this order is being challenged at this time based upon the fact that Judge Conti's order is outdated, but this Court used that order, and continues to proceed in absence of jurisdiction; appoints attorneys, and drives over this issue, and brings to my attention what Judge Conti stated in his order, that is, "frivolous documents." Those documents that the Court refers to, and attorneys refer to, and Judge Conti refers to [are] documents containing facts; facts which I defy Mr. Harris or anyone else to disprove, and I have facts to support them, to support my argument.

Mr. Harris[22] conspired with Judge Conti to present that order, to give this Court an excuse to continuously drive over my rights; not only over my rights, but over the laws that was written by Congress itself . . . I have facts and evidence to support my argument, and if given a chance to be heard and present these evidence I would do so, but there is only one way I can do this, your Honor. This is through subpoena of evidence and witnesses, and when I say, "evidence," mainly it is records, the records which are at this time being concealed by members of Mr. Harris's—that is, Attorney General Harris's conspirators.

Mr. Harris in the Court's has brought about a charge of 4500.[23] 4500 means [a] mandatory death penalty for one who is serving a valid life sentence. Mr. Harris has [gone] to the Grand Jury and charged me with 4500. Mr. Harris ignores the facts that California law, that is, Penal Code Section 681, states that no person can be punished for a charge unless a conviction is a valid conviction—I do not have a valid conviction. Mr. Harris is aware of these facts; also the Attorney General Evelle J. Younger.

In [order] to have these facts—in [order] to silence me, they are appointing attorneys with excuses; that is, first they create the

[22] Mr. Harris is the prosecutor.
[23] Section 4500 of the California Penal Code.

false image, then they show the people that I need an attorney, and I say "conspiracy" because these are some of the same tactics that was used in Los Angeles in ordinary to yoke me with an attorney, and after yoking me with their attorney, it was trickery and fraud, which was used to convict me. When I file documents which were complaints requesting the Court to hold a hearing into this matter to prove fraud in the record, Judge Conti stated that the document was frivolous.

Then when I filed a document which was a complaint against Judge Conti, showing [that] he was only refusing to abide by law, they say I'm abusing the processes of the court, but while this is going on I'm being yoked with attorneys by the judges who have completely ignored the facts that you don't have jurisdiction in the case. This is in facts and in law, state and federal, Federal Title 28 U.S.C. Section 1446. 1446 states clearly that upon filing petition for removal, serving copy and notice of the petition upon the Court and the attorney, this stops all State court proceedings.

Now, what [were] the documents filed? What [were] the facts? What was the reason or the purpose for filing? The reason was because of the Court yoking me with an attorney, I requested removal from State court, because I am denied rights which are guaranteed me by the Constitution in the state court, [and I am] seeking to enforce that right in the federal court. The law has been well established that I have that right, but in trying to enforce this right I am held up to public ridicule, falsely accused of filing frivolous documents, falsely accused of having an I.Q. of 75 points. As the courts are aware, and also the records will show in prior proceedings, [I was] trying to prove that [the] I.Q. was fraudulent and known to be such, I requested a literacy test; I have also made several requests [to] the Court to allow me an opportunity to read law books, write paragraphs from these law books; that is, in [order] to show that the I.Q. test was a fraud, but all of this [came] about through force. And then, not wanting to continue the proceeding, I tried to stop it in [order] to prevent the federal court from stating at later date that I waived my rights to removal.

In protesting, I filed numerous of affidavits for disqualification of judges, because they ignored this law, have driven over—for example, you state that you appointed the attorney, that is, Mr. Graves here, for the protection of my rights. Well, in protecting my rights you also violated my rights when I challenged you. . . . You went to the press, and you answered that which Mr. Moore filed, which was a mere statement, and you quoted a law book; mine was one simple allegation, simple, and you refused to obey the law that has been handed down by Congress in refusing to stop state court proceedings after given notice and a copy of the petition for removal. You made no mention, you neither deny this, that after Judge Winslow Christian returned to this case [brought] this to his attention, and he ignores it; I file affidavits for disqualification of judge in [order] that he may not make [any] rulings, that is, concerning you in this issue, and he drives over that, too.

Now you come back to the case, and you go around, and you tell me, you know, about how you read the papers on this, and you read the papers on that, but if you read the law, that is, the Sixth Amendment, it guarantees the accused the right to counsel, but it doesn't say at [any] time that it can be granted [forced upon me] when it is properly waived, eloquently waived. I cannot eloquently waive the right, or properly waive it, because I haven't been given the opportunity or the chance to do so, and at this time, by trying to waive it, it would be waiving another right, which is guaranteed me by the Constitution, that is, the petition for removal right.

Removal requires that the State stop all proceedings pending that petition for removal. For me to request this Court at this time to appoint me counsel, or request this Court to allow me an opportunity to prove my competency to represent myself, then this would be forcing me to automatically remain in the state court while federal court controls jurisdiction.

I cannot accept an attorney, an attorney appointed by [a] state judge nor federal judge at this particular time due to the fact that I'm aware, and fully aware of a conspiracy that exists from President Nixon down to prison guards in this case, out to hide and conceal evidence in this case, evidence that will prove and show that the entire State of California, the American judicial system, prison system, is practicing slavery under the color of law, without legal power or authority. One would have to be very naive to be-lieve that any court could appoint one attorney to whip themselves, or expose themselves. This is the reason that I constantly refused attorneys, and I have explained this to them . . .

May 5, 1971

22

Angela Davis: Notes for Arguments in Court on the Issue of Self-Representation

On numerous occasions, my attorneys and I have expressed our profound apprehensions that my co-defendant and I may ultimately be denied the fundamental right to a fair trial. Far from allaying our fears, recent proceedings seem to have further confirmed them. In view of this, my motion requesting permission to actively participate in the conduct of my defense assumes an even greater significance and becomes all the more urgent.

As I will argue, the prospects of justice and fairness in this case are inseparably joined to the issue of my self-representation. I firmly believe that the possibility of my receiving a fair trial will be seriously undermined, perhaps even definitively foreclosed if I am prohibited from playing an active role in the defense, together and in consonance with my attorneys.

In granting defendants the right to act as co-counsel, the language of both the California Constitution and the California Penal Code is unequivocal. Article 1, §13 of the Constitution states that defendants in criminal trials have the right "to appear and defend in person *and* with counsel." Section 686 of the California Penal Code declares that defendants are entitled to "be allowed counsel as in civil actions or to appear and defend in person and with counsel." Section 686 of the California Penal Code declares that defendants are entitled to "be allowed counsel as in civil actions or to appear and defend in person and with counsel."

No special expertise is required in order to interpret this simple, clear and extremely plain language: The accused has the right to speak for himself and at the same time to be represented by counsel.

As a general rule, however, courts have held that despite the lucid language of the Constitution and the Penal Code, the defendant is not entitled to "have his case presented in court, both by himself and by counsel, acting at the same time." *People v. Mattson,* 51 C.2d 777.

There seems to be no rational explanation for the consistent refusal of the courts to affirm this constitutional and statutory right. The language of the decisions makes it evident, however, that courts have been overly concerned with decorum—and this at the expense of the defendant's rights. Most defendants, when confronted with this either/or situation, will inevitably elect to be defended by an attorney, for few non-lawyers are intimately acquainted with the complexities of the law. Brother Magee is obviously an exception. Parenthetically, I would raise the question as to why the law, allegedly designed to protect the rights of the people, is virtually incomprehensible to the people.

Moreover, courts are generally reluctant to concede defendants their constitutional right to defend themselves at all. Brother Magee has been consistently barred from presenting his case. Brother Bobby Seale in *U.S. v. Dellinger,* et al. was prohibited from presenting his defense. Is the judicial system so closed and self-contained and indeed so fragile that any ingression from the outside threatens its stability? Why must the defendant, whose rights the court has vowed to protect, remain a mute outsider to court proceedings?

If it were the case that defendants represented by attorneys were *a priori* prevented from speaking in court, grave questions about American justice would be raised even by the most ardent defenders of the status quo. Courts have not consequently held that defendants with counsel are incontrovertibly barred from speaking in their own behalf. A compromise solution has been worked out —courts have reserved the power to use their discretion in granting defendants what under these conditions becomes the privilege to act as co-counsel.

I contend that the right to act as co-counsel is unequivocal and that the court ought to grant my motion on this basis alone. In

this respect, it should be borne in mind that courts have on occasion relied on the wording of a statute, rather than authority in
order to properly interpret the statute. (*People v. Vogel* and *People
v. Hernandez*). In the event, however, that this court chooses to
construe the issue in the conventional, and in my opinion incorrect,
manner, I must ask the court to exercise its discretion in conform-
ity with the standards outlined in *People v. Mattson.*

It should be remembered that in the *Mattson* case, the issue
at stake was the right of an *indigent* defendant proceeding in
propria persona to a *court-appointed* lawyer as advisor. Much of
the court's decision, in denying the defendant the right to joint
representation, is based on his refusal to appoint a lawyer who
will be compelled to serve "merely as an assistant and an advisor
and not as a legal representative." (795.) The court held that it
would be in contradiction to the attorney's code of ethics to appoint a lawyer who would have to play an inferior role.

While in the *Mattson* case, it was held that joint representation
is not a right, it was nonetheless deemed proper where:

> ". . . *the court on a substantial showing* determines that in the
> circumstances of the case, *the cause of justice will thereby be
> served* and that the orderly and expeditious conduct of the court's
> business will not thereby be substantially hindered, hampered or
> delayed." (692.)

There is no doubt in my mind that the interests of justice will
be served if I am permitted to act as co-counsel and that no disruptions of courtroom proceedings will follow from the contributions I make. I am inclined to believe, in fact, that since it is I,
the accused, who is supposed to be the recipient of justice, it
should be left to the prosecutor to demonstrate definitively why the
cause of justice will not be served. But, as Black people have always discovered, we are never assured of justice without a fight.
For even the most basic human rights, we have been compelled to
struggle.

Once again, circumstances require me to assume the posture
of struggle. I will attempt to convince the court, indeed to make a
"substantial showing" that the interests of justice will be served

through my active participation in my defense and further that the court's business will not be disrupted.

1

I begin by directing the court's attention to the fact that as the accused in this case, I find myself at an enormous disadvantage. As a Black woman, I must view my own case in the historical framework of the fate which has usually been reserved for my people in America's halls of justice.

From the pre-Civil War slave codes and the equally pernicious Black codes of the post war period to the overt, codified racism of the South and the more subtle institutionalized racism of the country as a whole, Black people have consistently been the victims of what is supposed to be "justice." In a courtroom situation, the white prosecutor, white witnesses, especially white policemen are given far more credence by the jury—usually overwhelmingly white—than the Black defendant. In the event that the Black defendant has been previously convicted of a crime, his chances of acquittal are virtually nonexistent. He is therefore generally advised by his white court-appointed lawyer to enter a guilty plea even when he is manifestly innocent.[24] I think my co-defendant, Brother Magee, can attest to this fact. A leading Black lawyer, Mr. Haywood Burns, president of the National Conference of Black Lawyers, has concluded in an article appearing in the *New York Times* that the chances of a Black man or woman receiving a fair trial in this country are exceedingly slim. (July 12, 1970, New York Times Magazine.) Yale President Kingman Brewster has expressed the same doubts with respect to Black revolutionaries.

These comments are relevant because they indicate the nature of the institution in whose hands my life has been placed. They reveal the general circumstances and the prevailing atmosphere in American courtrooms whenever a Black man or woman is placed

[24] References: Leon Friedman, ed. *Southern Justice*, c.f. especially article by Charles Morgan; *President's Commission Report on The Administration of Justice* (material on court-appointed attorneys). *Kerner Commission Report.*

on trial. I repeat, as a Black woman, accused of three capital crimes, I am at an enormous disadvantage. The prosecutor, representative of forces which have continually upheld this institutional racism, has enormous advantages. The history of America is on his side. There can be no doubt that we are unequal adversaries.

This inequality expresses itself not only in broad, historical terms but is also quite tangible. No one can deny that the immeasurable resources available to the prosecutor, indeed the entire state apparatus of California cannot in any sense compare to the resources available to me. His financial resources are virtually limitless—the state did not for a moment hesitate to extradite me from New York by the unprecedented means of a special military guard. I, on the other hand, must rely on the donations of concerned citizens, many of whom have had to make tremendous sacrifices in order to contribute small sums.

On another level, the prosecutor's superior position has been buttressed by the widespread publicity in his favor. I place particular emphasis on Nixon's gratuitous and unwarranted remark when he congratulated J. Edgar Hoover for capturing "one who engages in terrorist acts."

It would seem that the overwhelming advantages enjoyed by the prosecutor would call into question the basic presumption of the innocence of the defendant. I contend that circumstances are *a priori* balanced in favor of the prosecutor. It would therefore be appropriate to suggest that the court exercise its authority in order to create, insofar as it is possible, a more equitable balance of forces. My contributions to the defense as co-counsel might constitute one step in the direction of combatting these inequalities.

It might be argued that I have ample legal assistance to adequately present my case. In this relationship it should be borne in mind that the prosecutor's superiority is not only quantitative, it is also qualitative, being bound up with the historical existence of racism. I believe that my role in the case will add a different and qualitative dimension to the defense. No matter how great the quantity of defense lawyers, they could never be considered a substitute for the qualitative contributions only I will be in a position to make towards my defense. The nature of these contributions will become clear during the course of my argument.

2

The political character of this case gives my request to represent myself all the more validity and force. The prosecutor evinces a total lack of understanding when he alleges that my claim regarding this political character is simply a fabrication designed to strengthen my argument for self-representation. It cannot be denied that I am a Black woman, member of the Communist Party, active in the Black Liberation struggle and in the larger revolutionary movement for socialism. This is directly relevant to the case against me, as indeed the prosecutor has affirmed. Reference was made to my political activities long before I had the occasion to appear in court. According to the indictment, one of the overt acts in the conspiracy with which I am charged consists in my advocacy of the liberation of the Soledad Brothers. My participation in the Black Liberation Movement is, in the eyes of the prosecutor, an element of the crime of which I am accused, namely the motive. Yet and still, he contends that I am determined to create a political event out of something which has no political implications.

The judge presiding over the proceedings of January 5 did not uncritically accept the prosecutor's claim that this case has no political elements. He contended that this question would have to be resolved in the future. If this is true, it must be conceded that the matter cannot be fairly resolved if I am prohibited from joining in its resolution—in a direct, active fashion. If this court denies my motion for self-representation, the prosecutor will have been allowed to obfuscate an extremely crucial aspect of my defense. This would be one more example of the court functioning as a mere appendage of the state, a tool of the prosecutor.

It seems to be a general rule that prosecutors attempt to obscure the political character of trials involving radicals and revolutionaries, only to later hypocritically reinject political content. I cite the case of *People v. Shakur,* et al. (Ind. No. 1848-1/2, pending in N.Y. Supreme Court)[25]—this is the case more commonly known as New York Panther 21. The prosecutor refused to concede that

[25] The defendants were acquitted on May 13, 1971.

the trial was political in nature, yet much of the evidence introduced against the defendants consisted of literature published by the Black Panther Party, the political party of which the defendants were members. I might add parenthetically that the court permitted two of the defendants to represent themselves.

I can anticipate that the prosecutor in this case will present evidence and call upon witnesses to give testimony pertaining to my political activities. A member of the Los Angeles Police Department has already testified before the Grand Jury regarding my activity around the defense of the Soledad Brothers. No one is as intimately acquainted with my politics as I am. Therefore, I alone can competently challenge evidence with political implications and cross-examine those witnesses whose testimony concerns my politics.

3

I am charged with three capital offenses—murder, kidnapping and conspiracy. My life is at stake in this case—not simply the life of a lone individual, but a life which has been given over to the struggles of my people, a life which belongs to Black people who are tired of poverty, and racism, of the unjust imprisonment of tens of thousands of our brothers and sisters.

It is this life, organically bound up with the lives of all the millions who struggle for freedom and justice—Ruchell Magee, George Jackson, John Clutchette, Fleeta Drumgo, Bobby Seale, Ericka Huggins, to name a few—it is this life which stands to be extinguished by the State of California. I alone can develop and explain its meaning. For these reasons, only in the stance of self-representation will I be able to properly and thoroughly confront my accusers.

I will be reminded that I already possess the right to testify in my own behalf and may be heard by the jury if I elect to take the stand during the course of our refutation of the prosecutor's case. This begs the question. The burden of proof as well as the burden of persuasion rests with the prosecutor. There is no obligation on the part of the defendant to establish innocence until the prosecutor has proved guilt.

4

The special circumstances of this case make it imperative for me to play an active role in the court proceedings. Out of a few disjointed facts which the prosecutor alleges, he has fabricated a complex series of events and a very serious set of charges. It may very well be the case that I alone can extricate myself from his allegations. Historically, this has been acknowledged as a valid reason for joint representation. In *Wilson v. State,* 50 Tenn. 232 (1871), it was noted that:

> "That provision [joint representation] was founded upon a profound knowledge of human nature, and a close and careful observation of human transactions. An innocent person is sometimes entangled in a web of suspicion by a curious combination of facts, which no one else can explain but himself . . ."

5

It should be fairly obvious that I consider my own participation decisive for my defense. One might argue that since I am determined to play an active role in the trial, I should fire my lawyers and assume the entire burden of the defense. This is to say, if I wish to exercise my constitutional right to defend myself, I must relinquish the right to counsel. This either/or situation in my opinion flies blatantly in the face of justice. Rigorously speaking, neither is a *right,* if one must be renounced in order to exercise the other.

Should I be penalized because I do not possess the legal knowledge, experience or expertise necessary to proceed entirely *pro se*? Alone, I would not be capable of carrying the total burden of my defense. An unfavorable decision would run counter to the interests of justice, for my limited knowledge of the law would be used as an excuse for denying me the opportunity to put on my best, most efficacious defense. In *People v. Bourland,* the defendant wanted to represent himself. Because the court decided he would not be able to develop the most effective defense, counsel was appointed to assist him. In this case, it was acknowledged that everything within the bounds of justice must be done in order to assure the defendant his rights: "Decisions in this state demonstrate the conviction that the state should keep to a necessary minimum its interference with the individual's desire to defend himself in whatever manner he deems best, using any legitimate means within his resources."

Black people have not forgotten that an American court decision once contained the words, "A Black man has no rights which a white man is bound to respect." *Dred Scott,* 19 Howard 393. Many a Black person has asked himself whether any fundamental changes have occurred in the 114 years which have elapsed since that decision. This country faces now, as it did when the Dred Scott case was decided, difficult and explosive times—times when challenges to the people's constitutional and democratic rights make the threat of fascism loom large. In view of the vexing and intractable problems which this nation now faces, I ask this court whether it can afford to provide one more example, to millions of people, especially Black People, of the general deterioration of democratic institutions. We hope this question will be answered in the negative and that in this minute, but critically important instance, the interests of justice will prevail.

There is one remaining issue to be discussed. According to the *Mattson* standard, a defendant may not be permitted to act as co-counsel if this is incongruous with the "orderly and expeditious conduct of the court's business." I realize that as co-counsel, I assume the selfsame responsibilities and am subject to the same restraints as any attorney who practices law as a profession. I can guarantee the court that insofar as I exercise a degree of control over the events which unfold in this courtroom, there will be no disorder. There will be no intentional provocations on my part. This is an extremely serious matter and I am anxious for my co-defendant and myself to be acquitted so that we may continue to work for the freedom of our people.

The court might maintain that disruption unprovoked by myself might occur as a direct consequence of my role in the case. The State cites a few "right ons," voiced by court spectators at my arraignment. But the Supreme Court has determined on numerous occasions that one does not forfeit basic rights because of the response of onlookers. *Terminiello v. Chicago,* 337 U.S. 1 (1949), and *Gregory v. Chicago,* 394 U.S. 111 (1969). Perceptive court dialogue may be disturbing, it may stir others to laugh or might even evoke a mild remark, but this is supposed to be the price of a democratic system as opposed to a repressive one.

It should be of interest to the court that some of the most serious courtroom disruptions of this period have proceeded from the failure of the court to permit defendants in political trials to represent themselves. This is to say, the disruptions were provoked in part by the presiding judges. My co-defendant sits here in chains like a slave—an exceedingly disruptive sight, especially to Black people. We already have enough reminders of our bondage. Brother Magee was chained as a direct consequence of the court's refusal to recognize him as his own attorney. The outrages which occurred during the Chicago 8 conspiracy trial—the chaining and gagging of Brother Bobby Seale—followed as a result of the court's denial of his right to defend himself.

I ask the court to consider the proposition that when formal considerations of order are placed above justice, it is usually disorder which prevails. On the other hand, out of a true and sincere respect for justice, order naturally flows.

VIII

The Campaign

23

The Political Campaign
by Fania Davis Jordan, Kendra Alexander, Franklin Alexander

On August 7, 1970 an heroic act of insurrection occurred in a Marin County, California courtroom. Jonathan Jackson, James McClain, William Christmas and Ruchell Magee were acting in the tradition of resistance with which Black people have withstood 400 years of the most brutal, oppressive conditions known to mankind. We must pose the question—what caused such bravery on the part of our brothers? We are persuaded it was their intense awareness of the inhuman, racist, fascist-like conditions in the prisons, the repressive nature of the judicial system and the use of both institutions as weapons to crush the rapidly developing political movement inside the prisons. Once the conditions of prison life, which these brothers were responding to on August 7th, are revealed and understood it will become clear that this resistance was not for foul or felonious purposes but to make an unequivocal and dramatic political statement.

The National United Committee to Free Angela Davis and All Political Prisoners, in defending Ruchell Magee, issued the following appeal:

> The sole survivor of the Marin Courthouse rebellion . . . is on trial for his life . . . He is being denied his right to act as his own attorney. The court instead [in February 1971] appointed counsel—Leonard Bjorkland—a rightwing office seeker. Magee charges that Bjorkland conspired to frame Angela Davis by offering him "freedom" and "immunity from prosecution" in return for false testimony. The threatened alternative—the gas chamber . . .

... After seven years of fighting fraud and perjury in courts rigged against any Black man without money, Ruchell Magee saw his chance to be free. When . . . Jonathan Jackson . . . entered the courtroom . . . Magee took the ultimate position on righting a wrong. Guns in hand, but injuring no one, they took hostages and tried to escape in a van.

The Sheriff of Marin County ordered that no attack be made on the van. The San Quentin Prison guards violated the order and emptied their guns. The result was the death of Jonathan Jackson, two prisoners and Judge Haley, followed by the conspiracy-murder trial of Ruchell Magee and Angela Davis—whom he had never met . . .

. . . Speak out now! The next political prisoner may be you. Demand that Ruchell Magee be allowed his right to defend himself with or without attorneys of his own choice . . . **Free Ruchell Magee!**

The arrest of Angela Davis on October 13, 1970 generated widespread spontaneous expressions of support throughout the United States and around the world. It was perfectly clear from the beginning that Angela is completely innocent of all the charges which have been levelled against her. After she had been placed on the FBI's Ten Most Wanted List people in the Black community in Los Angeles where Angela lived and worked rallied to her support. At a press conference conducted by Franklin Alexander, held in that community, prior to her arrest in New York, reporters asked what Franklin would say if Angela contacted him. He responded: "We love you, baby." Within days all the neighbors in the surrounding streets adorned the windows of their homes with bumper-stickers reading: "Angela, we love you, baby."

The morning of Angela's scheduled arraignment in New York City before a United States Commissioner, hundreds of Blacks and whites, representing every tendency of political and social thought in the United States, gathered on the streets adjoining the Women's House of Detention and demanded freedom for Angela. Their repeated demand—"Free Angela, Free All Political Prisoners"— has become the rallying slogan of the mass movement all across the country. Other gestures of support came by mail from concerned citizens in the US and from every continent.

We knew that the people's struggle to free Angela and all political prisoners needed an organized leadership to coordinate and direct its energies in order to raise that struggle to new levels of sustained and programmatic activity, to intensify political consciousness in order to score the ultimate victories. So at a mass meeting in a church in South Central Los Angeles in early November 1970, attended by 300 to 400 people, the National United Committee to Free Angela Davis (NUCFAD) was founded. Franklin Alexander, a member of the Che-Lumumba Club, an all-Black collective of the Communist Party of the United States, to which Angela Davis also belonged, and Fania Davis Jordan, Angela's sister, were elected to serve as the national co-coordinators of NUCFAD. 'The Committee,' as we call it, has been organized on the basis of a united movement and in a direct response to the national and international popular reaction to the arrest of Angela.

The Committee was able to organize more than 50 committees in every major city in the United States by the end of December 1970. We knew, however, that the people's struggle could not just be waged in the larger cities. To be truly and firmly rooted in the people's concern for Angela's freedom which arises out of the objective conditions of racial, national and class oppression and exploitation, which is the daily fare of America's Blacks, Chicanos, Puerto Ricans, Indians and white working class, we strained all our human, physical and financial resources to organize by the end of February an additional 150 committees in the smaller cities and towns. The result has been the organization of a nation-wide popular movement to free Angela and all political prisoners, based and deeply rooted in the Black community.

The local committees, with the support of the National Committee, carry on the organizing activity necessary to sustain a popular movement which stretches the breadth of a continent in the United States alone. Community activity has two prime purposes: to deepen people's understanding of the political implications of the case, and to attain the widest possible support. Each local committee organizes and carries out activities and programs based on the needs of its own community around the popular movement to free Angela and all political prisoners. Local committees conduct church meetings, neighborhood coffee klatches, leafletting, door-to-door raps, block meetings, distributing leaflets at factory gates, and organizing Free Angela committees in local unions. These efforts provide an opportunity for people to meet on a one-to-one basis and exchange information and ideas about the repression directed at Angela and other political prisoners. Support for both the national and the local community oriented campaign is mustered by the sale of literature and buttons at displays at shopping centers, boutiques, liquor stores, restaurants and other community service and recreation centers. The financial support for the Committee comes mainly from $1, $2 or $5 contributions from people in the community. Additional financial support is obtained from specific fund raising events and mass rallies.

The Committee has also worked closely with students. Franklin Alexander and Mrs. Sallye Davis, Angela's mother, addressed a rally at Sisters Chapel in the Atlanta University Center in Atlanta, Georgia in February 1971, which was attended by over 1500 Black students. The memorable thing about this particular student rally is that the students were literally hanging from the rafters and hundreds more were outside clamoring to get in so that they too, by their presence, could give visible support and manifest their solidarity with Angela. After that meeting the students in the Atlanta University Center organized a continuing student committee, Blacks for Angela Davis.

Similar committees have been and are being organized on other university and college campuses across the nation. The Committee has found such support and expressions of concern among high school students, in particular. In Chicago Black high school students went on a three week strike to demonstrate their solidarity with Angela, and other political prisoners.

At the national level, "The Committee" has sought and received financial help from a variety of Black professional, educational, religious and labor organizations. The National Bar Association, an all-Black lawyers association, has pledged both financial assistance and the free service of two of the most accomplished Black trial lawyers in the country, Orzo T. Wells of New York and James Montgomery of Chicago. The National Conference of Black Lawyers organized a committee of Black law school professors which has furnished invaluable legal research assistance to Angela's lawyers. The National Director of the National Conference of Black Lawyers, Haywood Burns, has spoken throughout the country on behalf of Angela. People from the entertainment world such as Aretha Franklin and Herbie Hancock have pledged their unstinting support. Mrs. Coretta Scott King and the Reverend Ralph Abernathy have been joined by an ever growing list of concerned Americans who have called for bail and a fair trial for Angela. It is the foremost work of the Committee to give direction and projection to this outpouring of support for Angela from so many and varied sources.

The writings which appear in this book were prepared under the auspices of the Committee in direct response to a life and death struggle—for the life and freedom of Angela Davis and all other political prisoners. This, however, represents a struggle of such magnitude and consequence that it goes beyond the limited perspective to free a single individual or even to free several central personages. When an answer is sought to the question as to what "terrible forces" drove a seventeen-year-old to take over a courtroom from armed deputy sheriffs and for three prisoners to join him, the broad social forces at play in the fight for the freedom of all political prisoners come immediately into focus. These writings are statements about those forces, their causes, their import upon individuals and upon society. This is a part of the history of the power of a people who have resisted so long that resistance is a way of life. This book—we hope—will become an organizing tool for those who are caught up in that resistance and who feel compelled to join it.

June 1971

24

Statements and Appeals

An avalanche of protest fell upon the government of the United States—the President and the FBI; and California State authorities and Marin County officials following the arrest of Angela Davis. The Black community especially closed ranks, and united around Angela's defense. It has led the movement for her freedom; and the defense has its firmest organizational roots in the Black community among the people. Leading figures such as Reverend Jesse Jackson, Congressman Ronald Dellums (Democrat, Calif.), Reverend Ralph Abernathy, Mrs. Coretta King have expressed their solidarity and support. Black academics in New York issued a Statement of Concern in March 1971 which read in part: ". . . as Black Scholars and teachers sharing the very concerns for freedom and justice for all humanity to which Professor Davis in this racist land has given so eloquent expression, we pledge that we will follow with vigilant attention and lively interest each and everything that will be done by those who now hold the person of our sister, Professor Angela Davis, in their power, to the end that in respect of our colleague, justice shall not merely appear to have been done, but that it shall indeed be done, and that she shall suffer no harm, physical, mental or otherwise in the process . . ." Aretha Franklin offered to post a quarter of a million dollars in bail for Angela, if it were necessary saying, "I have the money. I got it from Black people—they've made me financially able to have it, and I want to use it in ways that will help our people."

After Angela's extradition from New York to California in December (1970) the letters, cables and petitions poured into the Marin County jail, from all parts of the world. Rarely has a single individual evoked such displays of solidarity.

The mail alone reached such proportions that the authorities gave up entirely reading through it (and censoring it). Instead, the mail is packed into sacks, and the sacks are piled into a special office in the sheriff's department and turned over, unopened, to members of the Angela Davis defense committee. Weekly "mail parties" are held to sort through the letters. Since January (1971) it is estimated that Angela has received 500,000 letters.

Public statements of solidarity have come from intellectuals, trade unionists, teachers, writers, artists, women's organizations, student groups, liberation fighters, from every corner of the globe —Africa, Asia, Latin America and Europe. In all the Socialist countries—the Soviet Union, the German Democratic Republic, Cuba, the People's Republic of Korea, the Democratic Republic of Vietnam, especially, the support has been overwhelming. The Women's International Democratic Federation has circulated a petition calling for Angela's freedom and in a few short months they have gathered over 600,000 signatures. Women's organizations throughout the world issued special appeals for Angela's freedom on the occasion of International Women's Day—March 8, Dolores Ibarruri, heroine, a la Pasionara of the Spanish Revolution, issued an appeal to the women of Europe and America to free Angela Davis. Especially touching have been thousands of letters to Angela from children of all ages, and from all countries.

Political prisoners in the notorious Lecumbardi Prison in Mexico issued a statement of solidarity with Angela; and from Aegina Prison in Greece, Communist political prisoners sent a message of solidarity on Angela's birthday, smuggled out of the prison on a piece of toilet paper. The message ended this way: "We have the absolute certainty that victory will be ours. It will be a victory of all oppressed peoples and nations, of the whole of progressive humanity in our titanic common struggle against the powers of hatred, injustice, obscurantism and war."

An Appeal for Angela Davis demanding her immediate release is circulating in the Federal Republic of Germany. The appeal has been signed by more than 10,000 people (as of May 1971) including such well-known public figures as: Heinrich Albertz (former Mayor of West Berlin); K. H. Walkoff, member of the Bundestag; Professor Ernst Bloch; Pastor D. D. Martin Niemöller; and Jakob

Moneta. There is a similar appeal in France signed by over 400 intellectuals.

In the United States such diverse organizations as the Young Women's Christian Association, the National Association for the Advancement of Colored People, the American Philosophical Association, Eastern Division and many others have issued statements deploring the persecution of Angela Davis, and pledging their vigilance in seeing that she receives a fair trial. Ann Braden, Executive Director of the Southern Conference Education Fund, headquartered in Louisville, Kentucky, spoke of the need to organize, especially among white people in the United States, a massive defense movement: "We who are white are especially pointing out to white people that it has been the Black movement in the last 15 years that has pried open the doors to freedom for all of us. And that if we sit silent while the Black movement is even temporarily crippled by these attacks, there will be only two choices left open to us—either to be destroyed ourselves or to silently support more and more atrocities against humanity."

In the United States a petition is circulating—with the goal of securing one million signatures. It reads in part: "We who are of the people, sponsor freedom for Angela Davis. We are Black and Brown; we are Red and White; we are men and women workers; we are farm laborers, housewives and of the unemployed; we are students, artists and professionals. We are of all religious faiths and of none; we hold varied political beliefs; we are committed to no single political persuasion. We are, however, of one mind in regard to Angela Davis: We believe Angela Davis to be innocent of the charges of kidnapping and murder . . ." Thousands in the United States have already signed this petition.

To assemble all of these letters and petitions and proclamations would fill volumes. We have, then, selected only a few, from the United States and from various countries in the hope that they will convey the depth of feeling for Angela, and for the struggle to free all political prisoners in the United States, and the breadth of support Angela's struggle has already attained.

BETTINA APTHEKER

June, 1971

America's Most Wanted Criminal

BY HERBERT APTHEKER

Eras have their appropriate symbols: Nat Turner hung by terrified Virginia slaveowners; John Brown and his Black and white comrades executed by Bourbons deep in their counter-revolutionary plotting; Dr. Du Bois vilified, hounded, mugged and finger-printed by a McCarthyite ruling class; Henry Winston jailed and blinded by craven sadists.

But Turner and the Martyrs of Harper's Ferry and the incomparable Du Bois are immortal; and as Winston truly said in his unforgettable phrase, though his sight was taken from him, his vision endures. As for the executioners and jailers who, even now, remembers their names?

For the present U.S. ruling class and its chief cop—whose every corruption faithfully reflects his masters' filth—to plaster the nation with the photographs of Professor Angela Davis as one of the "ten most wanted criminals" is marvelously appropriate. If Nixon-Agnew are an appropriate Executive; if Eastland-Thurmond are appropriate Senators; if a J. Edgar Hoover is the accredited judge of "loyalty" and "patriotism," then, indeed, is our beautiful Comrade Angela a terribly dangerous "criminal."

Can one conceive of a higher honor for an American than to be placed high upon the list of "criminals" in the estimation of such monsters?

At the time of the U.S. war upon Mexico, Thoreau wrote: ". . . when a sixth of the population of a nation which has undertaken to be the refuge of liberty are slaves, and a whole country is unjustly overrun and conquered by a foreign army, and subjected to military law, I think that it is not too soon for honest men to rebel and revolutionize. What makes this duty the more urgent is the fact that the country so overrun is not our own, but ours is the invading army."

There has never been and there is not now anything remotely resembling justice for Black people in the United States; if a President of Yale can say, as he did recently, that no Black person can expect justice in a U.S. court surely this universally known fact needs no argument. Indeed, the record compels one to write of this positively, not negatively; there has always been and there is now systematic and institutionalized oppression, indignity and injustice for Black people in the United States.

The specific case that moved the young Black men to attempt to liberate their brothers from confinement is permeated with injustice, brutal treatment and political harassment; precisely what Angela Davis' connection therewith may or may not have been is not known, except—one may be sure—that what the putrid U.S. commercial press "reports" has only a coincidental connection with reality.

But those Black men and our Angela—as a Black woman, as a scholar, as a Communist—knew the truth about the U.S. ruling class and its racism. Oppression breeds rebellion; an oppressed people "have the right and the duty" (says the Declaration of Independence) to resist their oppression and this is the fundamental meaning of the Marin County liberation effort. No democrat—not to speak of a revolutionary—can be other than a partisan of the passion that moved those who made it.

A few words drawn from history will not be inappropriate. In September, 1851, a Black man named William Parker, living in Christiana, Pennsylvania, was claimed as a fugitive slave by one Edward Gorsuch. He, with slave catchers and a U.S. Marshal—all well armed—fell upon Parker's home with the purpose of carrying him into slavery. Parker defended himself with arms and to his defense came Black and white neighbors. In the battle two of the would-be slave-catchers, including Gorsuch, were killed and the U.S. Marshal was wounded. Parker fled and with the help of

Frederick Douglass reached Canada. Several of the defenders—
Black and white—were arrested and tried for treason—if you
please. They were defended by Thaddeus Stevens and they were
acquitted.

In September, 1858, three U.S. Marshals—fully armed—seized
a fugitive slave, John Price, near Oberlin, Ohio and proceeded to
return him to slavery. A rescue party of about forty white and
Black men from Lorain County, fell upon the Marshals and
forcibly liberated John Price. Two of the leaders of this effort—a
white man named Simeon M. Bushnell, and a Black man, the attorney, Charles H. Langston (of the family that produced Langston
Hughes)—were sent to jail and fined for their part in this effort.
Before being sentenced, Charles Langston told the Court:

"I know that the courts of this country, that the laws of this
country, that the governmental machinery of this country are so
constituted as to oppress and outrage colored men, men of my
complexion. . . . Being identified with that man by color, by race,
by manhood, by sympathies, such as God had implanted in us all,
I felt it my duty to go and do what I could toward liberating him."

Was Langston right—or the Court, the U.S. Marshals, the U.S.
laws? Langston was jailed, but was Langston a *criminal?*

Back in 1800, James Monroe as Governor of Virginia—and one-
time revolutionist—was faced with the task of meting out punishment to slaves who had been convicted of conspiring to rebel. He
asked the man just then elected President—the man who had
penned the Declaration of Independence—Monroe asked Jefferson
what should he do? Jefferson advised Monroe to display as much
mercy as his office permitted (it wasn't much) because, he wrote:
"The world knows who was right and who was wrong in this case."

So it is in the Marin County rescue attempt. Let the FBI put out
its "most wanted criminal" flyers; *the world knows who is right and
who is wrong as between Angela Davis and J. Edgar Hoover.*

September 1970

Angela Davis: Black Soldier

Miss Angela Davis was arrested by the FBI on October 13, 1970, on a charge of interstate flight to avoid arrest. The repressive forces of the state—Reagan, Hoover, Mitchell—would have us believe that Miss Davis was a fugitive from justice.

But in fact Angela Davis was a fugitive from injustice, from a vicious and systematic campaign to crush her spirit, her Blackness, her right to earn her living as a college teacher.

Angela Davis first became the target of this oppression over a year ago, in Fall 1969, as a professor of philosophy at UCLA, when she exercised her Constitutional rights of political advocacy and declared herself a Communist.

In flagrant violation of the Constitution, in cold contempt of human rights, Ronald Reagan and Max Rafferty demanded her dismissal, and in an action unprecedented in the University of California's history, the Regents overruled UCLA's recommendation and fired Miss Davis themselves in June 1970.

It became apparent that Miss Davis could expect no more justice from California courts than she could from the UC system —which was none. For in the racist words of Judge Taney's Dred Scott Decision, Blacks "had no rights which a white man was bound to respect." As long as this racist attitude obtains, then the reverse follows: "A white man has no laws a Black man need respect."

In first posting outrageous bail and then accelerating extradition, the New York Courts have cooperated fully in this conspiracy of injustice.

But what are the hard facts against Miss Davis? What crimes has she been convicted of? What is her criminal record, that would place a 26 year old Black college teacher on the FBI's "10 Most Wanted" list? None. There are no hard facts. She has been convicted of no crimes. She has no criminal record. She is accused of having purchased weapons that were later implicated in the Marin County shootout. Yet the complete gamut of racist charges has been hurled at her—kidnapping and murder—and they carry the death penalty.

Is this justice? Or is it legalistic lynching, with public hysteria, accusation, flimsy circumstantial evidence and red-baiting racism as the judge? The answer is obvious; and Angela Davis chose freedom as a fugitive, over prison as a slave.

Angela Davis is indeed a Black soldier.

Angela Davis' life is literally at stake. We of the Black community, and all men who believe in justice, must give her total support, in her struggle. The wintry forces of oppression have gathered for systematic attack against the Black liberation movement—against campus, community and vanguard—from the killing of students at Jackson State, to the killing of Black Panthers, to the armed occupation of Black communities. Angela Davis is campus, is community, is vanguard. When we support her, we support ourselves. Her struggle is our struggle, and her victory shall be our victory.

ROBERT CHRISMAN, Editor
November, 1970
The Black Scholar

The case of Angela Davis is a case of political prosecution: prosecution of a woman, a Black militant, a radical dissenter. She was fired by the Regents of the University of California on political grounds, in spite of her excellent record as a teacher and scholar —a record not even disputed by her enemies. Although the degree of her involvement (if any) in the killing and kidnapping at San Rafael has not been established, she was put on the FBI list of the Ten Most Wanted Persons, she was charged with murder and kidnapping on the ground of a California law the constitutionality of which is open to question. The media gave the case the widest publicity. The President of the United States went on national television in order to congratulate FBI chief J. Edgar Hoover on the capture of this dangerous person—thereby assuming her guilt. The case has served to intensify still further the hatred and hostility against radical dissent in this country.

Under these circumstances, can Angela Davis expect a fair trial?

She has devoted her life to the fight against oppression and injustice, to the fight for the Black people, to the fight for the wretched of the earth everywhere—she is now in one of the most terrifying prisons of the country. Her trial may take years. But regardless of whether or not she is found guilty, on trial will be the violent and unjust society which is responsible for Angela's present condition—a society which is now ready to destroy one of its most powerful accusers.

Angela Davis is fighting for her life.

Only a strong and sustained protest from all countries and all quarters, a protest that is heard everywhere and will not be silenced has a chance of saving her life.

HERBERT MARCUSE

October 31, 1970

The Black Panther Party Stands Behind Angela Davis

Recently it has become all too obvious that through their various means, the agents and agencies of the U. S. Empire's ruling circle have powerfully struck at the main artery of the heart of the struggle of Black people and other oppressed people. That is, they have struck at our unity, which is the core of our winning, of our survival, of our being free.

Divisiveness is the main tool the oppressor has to defeat the oppressed masses' struggle for liberation, revolution.

Every attempt has been made to separate our forces, the killing of our leaders, the jailing of those who openly oppose the fascist ruling circle, the extreme use of the mass propaganda media to determine how we think about each other, co-optation of our statements and revolutionary slogans. All of this.

The Black Panther party, however, has withstood verbal insult and attack, has withstood physical attack—jailings and assassinations, and has become stronger in our commitment to our people, to all the people to bring about the kind of unified mobilization of the people required for the pending revolution.

We have suffered attacks from the Super American Empire Structure because our programs, our ideology represent the true interests of the people.

And we have survived these attacks because our programs, our ideology represent the true interests of the people. And we know, as we always have, that because our aim is to serve the people, that we cannot be defeated.

The Black Panther party, per se, is not the important factor. It is the idea, the ideas set into motion. It is the programs, the survival programs, the programs to bring us all to a unified, organized and strong juncture, at which together we can begin to transform the society into what we choose, what we need, what we desire for the benefit of us all.

The important factor is that we not be waylaid, short-stopped by any devices or designs of these vicious men.

For time and history are on the side of the people in the long run. But if we can be divided now, at this period, in the short run, we, the people, may not survive to know or have our New World.

Then when we consider those who have been singled out for particular punishment by the Empire's forces for having said or done something in our interests, in our behalf, we must stand firm and not allow repetition—the wicked process of these pigs to nibble away before our very eyes those who are of our camp who speak and fight for our cause.

Angela Davis has certainly received a great deal of attention. But the Black Panther party has not made clear its our strong love and support of Sister Angela. And we know this leaves a gap in our camp, a schism in our forces, Black people's forces, oppressed people's forces.

Sister Angela is not unknown to us. She has been a part, a

strong force, in the revolutionary struggle of our people, of all the people.

And she has particularly, although no longer an official member of our party, devoted her work for the people to lending her support to those in our party who are, as she now is, held in the maximum security camps in the U. S. because of political ideas—that is, our political prisoners, prisoners of war.

Everywhere she spoke, she used the opportunity of her own case, surrounding her teaching at UCLA, to inform people about the case of Chairman Bobby Seale and Ericka Huggins. She came to see about Bobby, as Fred Hampton would say.

She was in fact the head of the Bobby Seale defense committee in Los Angeles, helping to raise support and funds for our incarcerated chairman. And she would use every opportunity to bring masses of people to the cry of "Free Bobby, Free Ericka."

For Angela knows and exemplifies that parties cannot, must not disrupt the maintenance of the solid support we must all, all of us in the revolutionary camp, have of each other.

That we must know that to divide us is the chief aim of the very oppressor we fight. And she made it clear that to cry, "Free Bobby," is to say free all political prisoners, free all the people. And personalities are not involved here.

However, the Black Panther party wants everyone to know that we appreciate our Sister, Angela Davis, for she is herself a unifying factor in the struggle of black people, of all oppressed people to survive, to live, to fight the racism, fascism, imperialism under which we all commonly suffer and to put an end to this forever and institute our new world.

And we want the people to know that the Black Panther party stands behind Angela.

For by everyone's making known his support for Angela, we can turn the power structure's trick into our gain.

Angela has been the example herself, in her action and practice, that to Free Angela is to free Ruchell, Bobby, Ericka, George, all political prisoners, the people!

ALL POWER TO THE PEOPLE!

March 13, 1971

"I bring an indictment against the American system"

BY REVEREND RALPH ABERNATHY

We meet in defense of Miss Angela Davis; therefore, let us ponder the question first, who is Angela Davis? Let us first recall this young Black woman who was born twenty-seven years ago today in Birmingham, Alabama, where the blood of her people flowed under a reign of official racism and terror.

She lived in a Black community which came to be known as "Dynamite Hill." As she grew up she learned of fifty bombings against Black people in her native Birmingham, all of them unsolved.

She knew four little Black girls, who were her friends, who were murdered in the bombing of the Sixteenth Street Baptist Church in Birmingham in Nineteen Sixty Three, but none of us knows the exact identity of the bombers today, because there were no arrests and the FBI did not possess the ability and the skill to find those bombers.

In the face of death every day of her life, Angela Davis began to learn the life of struggle—struggle for survival, struggle for her people, struggle for justice.

She participated in the battle against segregation in voter registration drives conducted by the Southern Christian Leadership Conference in Birmingham, Alabama.

Her courageous family made personal and financial sacrifices for the movement. Miss Davis pursued a brilliant academic career.

She found racism and oppression of poor everywhere she went. She knew the profound outrage of all Black people over the fact that the prisons and the jails of this country are filled with Black men and women while the college campuses and the offices of the American military-industrial government empire are filled with white men; and we don't like it.

Angela Davis is one intellectual who did not hide out in a library or behind a desk. She transformed her mental principles into an active commitment of struggle against injustice. She was not afraid to express her political beliefs; this ultimately cost Miss Davis her job, led to her imprisonment and presently threatens her with death. Let me repeat this point. A racist, oppressive criminal society is attempting to kill a militant, Black woman activist because of her political beliefs, and her commitment to those beliefs, and you and I will be just as guilty as the racist society if we permit it to happen.

Let me warn all of you this evening that today it is Angela, but if we sit silent and keep our peace, tomorrow it will be you and it will be me.

Angela Davis would be the first to remind us that she is not the only political prisoner in America. Ladies and gentlemen, brothers and sisters, there are thousands of political prisoners in America, and the only way to free them is to get out and struggle in a mass movement of the people. We need fund raising for Angela Davis, but we also need hell-raising for millions of others in this country.

Let us work to teach the people these things about the case of Angela Davis. Number one, in a democratic society, an accused person is supposed to be presumed innocent until proven guilty. And already in my estimation Angela Davis has been tried and found guilty in the news media.

Number two, an accused person has a right to a fair trial in which the accused is entitled to be judged by a jury of his or her peers, but I raise this question with you—how can Angela Davis get a fair trial in Ronald Reagan's California?

Number three, since the state itself has placed the political beliefs of Angela Davis in question, and since public officials and the mass media have unloosed a torrent of adverse publicity before Miss Davis has ever or even been brought to trial, this in fact is no ordinary criminal case, but a political case that raises overwhelming questions about the possibility of a fair trial. In fact I see it as a trial, not of Angela Davis, but a trial of America.

I see the American system charged with the kidnapping, the murder and the conspiracy. I charge the American system with the kidnap of Black people from Africa.

I bring charges this evening against the American system for the enslavement of Black people on this continent.

I charge the American system with the kidnap, with the imprisonment and the starvation of Black children on the plantations of Mississippi, in the ghettos of Chicago, and even right here in the ghettos of the North.

I charge the American system with the kidnap of young men and sending them to die in a criminal, racist, godless and unwinnable war in Southeast Asia ten thousand miles away.

I further charge America with being a liar and a hypocrite. For almost two hundred years ago the cry was heard in these streets of America, "There must not be taxation without representation," and yet today we are over-taxed and we are under-represented.

Almost two hundred years ago, Thomas Jefferson dipped his pen deep in the wells of ink and etched across the pages of history a document we call The Declaration of Independence. He said that, "We hold these truths to be self-evident, that all men are created equal, that they are endowed by their Creator with certain inalienable Rights, that among these are Life, Liberty and the pursuit of Happiness."

I want you to know today that we do not have those rights, we do not have that liberty but we are more determined than ever before that we are all going to have freedom in America or there will be no America to have freedom.

I further charge the American system, I bring an indictment against the American system. I charge the American system this evening with robbery of the Puerto Ricans, the Mexican-Americans.

I charge the American system of almost completely exterminating the Indians and then stealing the country from the few Indians that were left.

I charge America with hypocrisy. We have talked one thing and we have practiced another. We have falsely taught in our educational system; we taught our children that Columbus discovered America in Fourteen Ninety Two. But we have discovered that that's nothing but a lie. What did Columbus do? All he did was to sail across the Atlantic in some Spanish ships and once he got here in Fourteen Ninety Two he discovered that America had already been discovered.

But that's not the only charge that I bring against the American system this evening. There is a second charge I bring against the

American system this evening. The second charge is murder. I charge the American system with the murder of the Vietnamese people. I charge the American system with the murder of Malcolm X and my dearest friend, Martin Luther King, Jr. I charge the American system with the killing of Michael Schwerner, Andrew Goodman, James Chaney, Viola Liuzzo, Jimmy Lee Jackson, Medgar Evers and a host of others.

I charge the American system with murder in its genocidal tendencies which are clearly defined in the United Nations Charter. And the third charge I want to bring this evening. I'm the judge, I'm the jury and I bring the charge against America this evening.

The third charge I bring against America is conspiracy. I charge the American system with conspiracy to steal the resources of other countries. To cooperate and support not only a puppet regime in Vietnam, but a racist regime in South Africa. I charge the American system with a conspiracy to exploit peoples throughout the world, and to oppress millions of our people here in our own land. I charge the American system of spending billions of dollars to put man on the moon and spending countless of dollars to send Spiro T. Agnew around the world to pass out moon rocks when he ought to be passing out loaves of bread to hungry children.

I charge the American system with conspiracy to repress and violently subjugate those who resist. All you have to do is to look in any corner of this nation of ours, and you will see the conspiracy to repress the Black Panthers and to destroy this group of individuals under the disguise that they believe in violence.

Well what about the Ku Klux Klan? What about the Minutemen? What about the Birchites? What about all of these forces and groups in white America that have always believed in violence: CIA, Tricky Dick. We cannot sit idly by and let them repress and destroy the Black Panthers, for they are our brothers in this struggle.

So not only do I call for the freedom of Angela this evening, but I call for the freedom of Bobby as well as Ericka. I call for the freedom of the Berrigan brothers. Yes, they were in a conspiracy —to save lives, to feed the hungry, to stop the killing in the world. They were a part of a conspiracy, and I'm part of that same conspiracy.

You are a part of that conspiracy to save lives.

Jesus Christ of Nazareth was a part of that conspiracy, for he said that the "Spirit of the Lord is upon me, because he has annointed me to preach the Gospel to the poor, to free the captives, to set at liberty them that are bruised, and then to proclaim the acceptable year of the Lord."

We must stand up and cry out for the freedom of Brother Phil and Brother Dan Berrigan.

Now what is the penalty for these charges? The penalty for these charges is death. Either the death of kidnap and murder and conspiracy against the people or the virtual death of America.

Let us not only cry Free Angela Davis. Let it also be said "Free Twenty-five Million Black People in the United States of America."

Let the cry be heard, "Free Forty Million Poor People, Brown, White, Red and Yellow or Polka Dot in this wealthiest nation in the history of mankind."

Let the cry be heard "Free The Nation Of Racism, Free It of Poverty and Free It of War." And let the cry be heard from the highest mountain peak to the lowest valley, "Free the Nation of a Nixon-Agnew-Reagan Administration." "Free the Exploited and the Oppressed People Throughout the Society and Throughout the World. Free Men and Women Who Stand Up for Their "God-Given Rights." Free Men and Women so they can live in dignity. Free men and women so they can stand up and know that if a man has not discovered something that he is willing to die for, that that man is already dead.

Let us speak until the jailhouses fly wide open. Let us speak until Angela Davis is as free as a bird in these United States of America. Let us speak until we can roam the streets of America and there will be no policemen to beat our heads and we will not have to raise our sons to go off and be slaughtered somewhere in war.

Let the people speak. Power to the people. And may the people rise up as never before, and no longer be a part of the so-called silent majority, but let us rise up and get on the case and do our thing and sock it to America.

February 2, 1971

United States Labor

One of the strongest bases of support for Angela Davis is to be found among working people—young and old, men and women —and most especially among Black workers. Rank and file caucuses, local unions, individual trade union leaders and international unions have expressed their solidarity with Angela Davis. Thousands of individual workers have written personal letters to Angela; wired protests to government authorities; and joined Free Angela rallies in cities across the country.

Thomas Turner, President of the Detroit Metropolitan AFL-CIO Council said of the case against Angela Davis: "One of the things J. Edgar Hoover is trying for is to knock off or run out of the country many of these young Black revolutionaries, militants. He (Hoover) has done more to polarize race in this country, outside of his President, than anyone I know. I am concerned as a labor leader, that it could be Miss Davis today and me, Tom Turner, next time around if I don't speak out."

Likewise, Paul Schrade, Executive Board member of the United Automobile Workers Union issued this statement following Angela's arrest: "This society has centered at this period, everything on the name Angela Davis, to hide under cover of this massive witchhunt the needs of the poor people, the Blacks, workers, which she as an outstanding educator and Black woman leader had brought to light . . . I see in this a wide attack on a woman, on the Black people, on the academic rights of an individual. I supported her right to teach at U.C.L.A. and I supported her against Governor Reagan and will do what I can to help."

Meeting at its 19th Biennial Convention in Honolulu the International Longshoremen and Warehousemen's Union, resolved to defend Angela Davis. Their resolution read in part: ". . . There is a concentrated and relentless crusade to kill Angela Davis. Prejudice and frameup is now employed to crush Black militancy. The same device has always been used against labor when the powers of big business and government decide that organized workers are 'getting out of line' in their struggle for a better life . . . When President Nixon and Governor Reagan and the big money press incite the legal lynching of Angela Davis, experience and common sense tell us to beware. Those are our enemies, too, and it could well be us 'next time around,' or it could be you . . . Angela is also charged with conspiracy. An old gimmick used to repress the labor movement in this country from the time it was conceived. We defend ourselves by defending Angela Davis . . . The International Convention of the ILWU goes on record to support Angela Davis and to see that she receives a fair trial and is released on bail pending trial."

Similarly the California Federation of Teachers, meeting in convention in December 1970 passed a resolution expressing its concern that Angela Davis receive a fair trial; and noted that while Angela Davis was teaching at UCLA she was a member of CFT Local 1990. Many local teachers' unions across the country have passed very strong resolutions in Angela's defense, and some have called for her immediate freedom. The Executive Council of the Tamalpais Federation of Teachers in Marin County, for example, adopted a resolution in May 1971 which concluded that "Angela Davis has been persecuted because of her ideas and not because of any wrongdoing . . ." The Tamalpais Teachers then called for "the immediate release of Angela Davis and the dropping of all charges against her."

Garment workers, in New York City, members of the executive board of the Apparels local, sent a telegram to Governor Reagan and President Nixon, following Angela Davis' extradition to California:

"As Black, white and Spanish-speaking trade unionists we strongly protest the vicious campaign of harassment and persecution of Angela Davis.

"We are outraged that she has been tried by the press and FBI, subjected to a vicious manhunt, presumed guilty, denied bail, segregated from other prisoners, and not allowed to see the indictment against her—all in violation of her constitutional rights.

"As workers, we understand the necessity to struggle against racism—the main weapon of the bosses used to divide and weaken our ranks.

"As workers, we are familiar with the frame-up as a weapon of those who seek to intimidate opposition and suppress dissent.

"We therefore view the attack on Angela Davis as an attack on ourselves.

"We demand that this racist frameup be halted and that all charges against Angela Davis be dropped."

A Call to Black Women of Every Religious and Political Persuasion

"Something is wrong . . . Maybe the real criminals in this society are not the people who populate the prisons . . . but those who have stolen the wealth of the world from the people . . . and so every time a Black child dies . . . we should indict them for murder because they're the ones who killed that Black child."

ANGELA DAVIS

Black Children Are In Trouble: A poisonous snowstorm of heroin speeds many into the white-death habit. We buy caskets more often than any other U.S. citizens . . . our death rate is higher and earlier, and shrouds have now become common teenage wearing apparel. Our children, stoned away from school doors, are crowded into so-called all-Black public facilities where they receive white-supremacist "education" . . . which tends to breed a sense of inferiority, shame and hopelessness in our young.

Black Men Are In Trouble: Brave, good men struggling to build a better life are under-employed and condemned to an almost powerless position, not by their wives and mothers, but by white men who make the life and death power decisions which rule the country. Our sons and brothers are sent thousands of miles away to kill or be killed by other poor colored people without even having the right to vote for or against it.

Black Women Are In Trouble: We are constantly ridiculed and attacked by the evils of a corrupt, racist society. We live in fear of walking home alone . . . fearing that those we love and labor for . . . will hurt us. We must unite for the sake of our children and our men . . . they are subtly being separated and divided from us by the double-edged sword of a white myth called "Black Matriarchy."

We Are Tired of Being In Trouble: Today our youth, locked in battle-scarred communities, make important decisions; some seek to gain the approval and sympathy of their oppressors, others loudly condemn and expose the sins of all who deceive, mislead and slaughter the people. ANGELA DAVIS has openly placed herself in this latter group. ANGELA is a shining symbol of "the many thousands gone" who have been persecuted down through the centuries.

Black Women cannot afford to accept the senseless answer of more jails and more police repression . . . or to go on hiding behind triple-locked, barricaded doors. We cannot afford to idly watch the murder of innocents at home and on foreign battlefields. *We resolve to stand beside our children—remembering Sojourner Truth and Harriet Tubman, two Black women who would also be in jail if they were alive today!* Motherhood must mean more than giving birth to a child, and sisterhood more than being born into a relationship. We all share a common destiny and will no longer allow the destruction of our labor . . . the Black family. Let us come together and speak out loud and clear:

Angela Davis Must Be Free!

Harlem, New York
November, 1970

Statement by Coretta Scott King

Increasingly in recent years the basic American legal tradition that a person charged with crime is presumed innocent has come under diverse forms of attack, especially for Black people, and most frequently by courts and the high government officials. The injustice is sharply illustrated by the experience of the 12 Black Panthers acquitted in less than two hours by the jury, but for whom bail was set at an astronomical figure. Innocent people thus served a jail term of 2½ years; longer than very many convicted criminals.

The same question of discrimination and deprivation of the presumption of innocence arises anew in the case of Angela Davis. She has been denied bail, described as a terrorist though she has no criminal record and an exemplary record as a scholar. In transferring her to California drastic and dramatic methods of security were employed reminiscent of convicted Nazi war criminals. It is difficult to reject the conclusion that the conduct toward her is a consequence of triple bigotry. Angela Davis is Black, she is a woman militant and finally, an acknowledged Communist. For many, prejudice is a reflex in face of these facts, but our laws are intended to protect precisely against such prejudice.

It is easy to uphold civil liberties when the person charged is not controversial. It is not merely difficult, but perhaps dangerous, to support the rights of an unpopular defendant. Yet, it must be done or it may as well be acknowledged that due process is vanishing along with other basic American rights.

I have been impressed by the public statement of Dr. Herbert Marcuse, who was Angela Davis' teacher and friend for six years, that in his judgment she is one of the most non-violent persons he has ever known.

Dr. Marcuse, to my knowledge, is not himself an advocate of non-violence in political change so his remarks are of special interest. However, I do not presume to judge the case. I have clear differences politically with Miss Davis. But if her Blackness, her womanhood and her politics are being judged, and not the crime charged, then all Americans will lose some of their liberties along with her.

For these reasons I urge support to efforts to insure bail and a fair defense for Miss Davis whose situation has carried us a long way back to the agonizing inquisitions of the early fifties.

June 4, 1971

Appeal of Mrs. Shirley Graham DuBois

Cairo

We, Women far distant from the United States, yet well aware of the fate which threatens the brilliant and courageous young scholar, Angela Davis, would add our voices to the swelling chorus of freedom-loving peoples throughout the world, who demand the release of our persecuted Black Sister.

We have read with dismay of the charges made against her, of the brutal and unprecedented manner in which, like some wild beast, chained and manacled, she was conveyed from the Detention House in New York to the prison in California. We are shocked at the abrocation of fundamental human rights in her treatment at the hands of U.S. authorities. We are inspired by her steadfast and undaunted spirit.

A letter received in Cairo on April 5th tells us:

"She is kept in solitary confinement; one passes through three electronically operated steel doors to get to the steel door behind which lives Angela. But when you get in there one is with life and beauty. Her spirits are splendid and her thoughts are only of freedom—and the struggle.

"She asked us to remind you, as you rally support for her case, that you be sure to mention she is only one of the many political prisoners in the United States—remember the Soledad Brothers, Ruchell Magee, Ericka Huggins, Bobby Seale and the hundreds jailed for opposing the atrocious war in Indo-China."

Millions of Americans are sponsoring freedom for Angela Davis. They are White and Black, Brown and Red, men and women, young and old. We believe with them that Angela Davis is the victim of a racist frameup, which if allowed to succeed will result, not only in the blotting out of the beautiful Flaming Torch in the revolutionary movement of oppressed peoples throughout the world, but will surely diminish each and everyone of us. For all our sakes, Angela Davis must live! And no Woman is truly free while Angela Davis is incarcerated.

Freedom for Angela Davis is our demand!

Signed by: SHIRLEY GRAHAM DuBOIS and

CEZA NABARAOUY—Vice-President of the Women's International Democratic Federation

DR. HAKMAT ABOUZEID—Egypt's first woman Cabinet Member as Minister of Social Affairs

DR. AISHA RATIB—Jurist, Professor of International Law, Cairo University

AMINE EL SAID—Editor, *Haya* (a woman's magazine)

MAFIDA ABDEL RAHMAN, Member of Parliament, U.A.R.

BATHYNA WAHBA—in the Ministry of Information, U.A.R.

NAFISEL EL GHAMRAWY, Director of a Secondary Girls School, U.A.R.

AZIZA MEKY—President, Sudanese Women's Federation

DR. EGLAL ABUL ALA—surgeon

A'LMED HUSSIEN—journalist

and over two dozen other women in the United Arab Republic who are journalists, teachers, artists and members of various citizens' organizations and committees.

African National Congress, South Africa— Women's Secretariat

December 5, 1970

Miss Angela Davis
Professor of Philosophy
Women's House of Detention
10th Street, Greenwich Avenue
New York City

Dear Angela,

We have learnt through the publications of the Women's International Democratic Federation, with utter disgust the news of your arrest.

The oppressed and fighting women of South Africa, who have been, and still are victims of racial oppression perpetrated by a clique of white racists, have every thing in common with you and the just struggle of your people against racism and all the unjust deeds that go with it.

We admire your courage, self sacrifice and determination to free the lot of your oppressed and exploited population, faced with a ruthless enemy which claims to be the most developed militarily, economically, culturally and other wise, yet its own Afro Asian Citizens suffer from want of everything necessary for nature's human development. We are proud and inspired to have a young woman of your calibre.

We assure you and all peace fighters in your country, our full support for your demands, being aware that no peace can be achieved without freedom.

We demand from those responsible for your arrest, your immediate and unconditional release, together with all your colleagues languishing in prisons, for the same ideals.

Victory in your life time.

Your sisters in the struggle

FLORENCE MOPHOSHO
for A.N.C. Women's Secretariat

To Angela Davis
Occasion—March 8—International Women's Day
Send heartfelt greetings to our sister in struggle for freedom, justice, racial equality. Though U.S. warlike racist rulers jail you like other patriots in South Vietnam, they never can stop the advance of progressive people in U.S.A. and Indochina who firmly defend living rights, human dignity. We shall win. Militant greetings.

MME. NGUYON THI BINH
Provisional Revolutionary
Government of South
Vietnam representative
to the Paris peace talks.

1971

Georg Lukacs Appeal *

The signers of this appeal turn to the American public with the conviction that they express a deep apprehension, which is alive in thousands of European intellectuals, concerning the matter of Angela Davis. The Dreyfus Affair in Europe, the tragic fate of

---

* This appeal, written by the late Georg Lukacs, was signed by 59 leading European intellectuals and over 1,000 European students. The signers include such world renowned scholars as: Ernst Bloch, Iring Fetscher, Helmut Gollwitzer, Andras Hegedus, Rolf Hochhuth and Pjotr Leonidowitsch Kapiza.

Sacco and Vanzetti in America, have proven to every rational person that if prejudices against the accused are systematically and demagogically spread and encouraged it is possible to take a man's freedom and even to allow him to be murdered while formally obeying all the rules of judicial procedure.

Everything indicates that just such a psychological campaign is already being waged in preparation for Angela Davis' judicial murder. Two kinds of prejudice are being mobilized against her. The first and most important is racial hatred, which aims at terrorizing a group of people fighting for their freedom through the attack on a particular victim. The second kind of prejudice is directed against left-wing militants. One does not have to agree with the ideas of Angela Davis in order to respect her for living her cause and sacrificing herself for it, or to see through the nature and aims of a demagoguery that threatens her freedom. The signers of this appeal are united in their anxiety that an assault is being prepared, within the formal, irreproachable workings of the judicial system, against an innocent human being, and through her, a collective assault against millions of people.

We therefore turn to the representatives of the most diverse ideologies and views for whom, however, democracy and justice—in whatever way they may interpret these terms—are no empty phrases, so that through the force of opposing public opinion injustice, which is now being perpetrated, will be impeded and Angela Davis will again be given her freedom.

Dear Angela!

Your name has today become a symbol of tremendous willpower and courage for people of integrity throughout the world.

Everyone who has taken up your cause fully realizes that your arrest and the charges brought against you are a logical conclusion to a whole series of arbitrary acts whose aim was to force you to keep silent, because you are a Communist, because you are an active champion of the rights of the Black people, because you have a profound understanding of the racist, capitalist, exploiter nature of the system under which you live. You are being tried for your convictions, your beliefs, your world outlook, as a champion of justice, of equal rights for the national minorities of the USA, as a fighter against the sanguinary aggression of the USA in Southeastern Asia.

Moscow, March, 1971

Angela!

You are not alone. All those who are fighting for peace, for civil and political freedoms, for equality and against racist and social oppression are with you. Your "case" has called forth a movement of solidarity with the struggle of your people in many countries of the world.

And in our country, the Soviet Union, the campaigns for your liberation have become a nation-wide issue. Many-thousand-strong meetings "In Defence of Angela Davis" are being held in our enterprises and on construction sites, in collective farms and in educational establishments. Letters from Soviet people flow endlessly in to the Soviet Women's Committee, expressing profound concern for your fate. The general public of my country are indignant over the brutal reprisal which reactionary forces have organized against you.

"Our hearts are filled with anger. We demand freedom for Angela Davis, champion for the rights of America's Black people," is written in the resolution drawn up by the students and teachers of Technical School No. 42 in Moscow. "May our love for you, Angela, melt away your prison bars," write the pupils of a school in the city of Kuibyshev. From the banks of the Volga, from the Hero-City of Volgograd, the workers and employees of Volgograd Offset House send you, firm Communist and glorious daughter of the Black people, their passionate greetings. "From the bottom of our hearts we wish you to emerge the victor in your combat with the forces of reaction and obscurantism who have ventured on this disgraceful trial. We are sure that truth will triumph. May your firm staunchness win over evil! The whole of progressive mankind are with you, including us Volgogradites!"

Dear Friend, the hearts of millions of Soviet women are beating in unison with yours. We are with you in this difficult hour you are living through, and we will carry on our actions of protest against a vicious trial up to your final freedom.

With love and respect,

Valentina Nikolayeva-Tereshkova
Chairman, Soviet Women's Committee

A letter to Angela Davis from a matron at one of the institutions where she was imprisoned. . .

December 26, 1970

My dear Angela,

My thoughts and heart have been with you ever since that sorrowful night.

We miss you, gloom settled over the jail, because our light and inspiration have gone.

If you found us beautiful, it was because you made us that way. We related to you and your struggle in so many ways.

What little I could do to bring you a bit of comfort was nothing compared to what you gave us.

I miss you, and miss worrying and fussing at you about little things.

I listen and read everything about you and your struggle. Knowing you is the greatest pleasure any one person could derive. You're beautiful. You touched many of our hearts and lives.

When I feel cross or impatient with my brothers and sisters, I remember all the things you taught me and tears come to my eyes for the struggle you are going through.

Keep your head up and remember you're always in my thoughts and heart. All power to you Angela . . .

Love always,